MY FATHER HAD NO CHILDREN

A Memoir

Alana Lindberg Jolley

Copyright © 2024 Alana Lindberg Jolley
All rights reserved
First Edition

NEWMAN SPRINGS PUBLISHING
320 Broad Street
Red Bank, NJ 07701

First originally published by Newman Springs Publishing 2024

ISBN 979-8-89061-376-9 (Paperback)
ISBN 979-8-89061-378-3 (Hardcover)
ISBN 979-8-89061-377-6 (Digital)

Printed in the United States of America

For Walter, my dad

Foreword

There are not many books about the average man who died in World War II, outside of family accounts that might change over the years. *My Father Had No Children* is an excellent exception.

Based on accurate historical research from the records of the National Archives and elsewhere, Alana Lindberg-Jolley has brought the story of her father back to life. Her father was Flight Officer Walter B. Lindberg; he was killed in a non-battle glider crash at Tours, France, on February 22, 1945.

Born eight months before her father's death, Alana combed her family records to find out about his life prior to his time in the Army Air Corps. The result was a fascinating look at his life, both before and during his time in World War II. She has succeeded in making a man she never knew become real, both to herself and the reader.

Any reader who is interested in World War II or the ways that the loss of a loved one can affect a survivor's life will enjoy this book very much.

Bill Beigel
WWII researcher

Acknowledgments

My deepest gratitude is for the letters written to my dad overseas by family members during WWII. Along with his mother, there were aunts, uncles, and cousins who wrote from the United States and Mexico. Without those cherished letters, my and my dad's stories could not have been written.

I wish to thank William L. "Bill" Biegel at ww2research.com for his WWII research expertise. Without the official flight logs and other official government reports, which he acquired from the National Archives, for me, a major part of Walter's story would be missing.

My thanks and appreciation also to the dedicated researchers at the WWII Glider Pilots Association and their website (ww2gp.org) as well as the Silent Wings Museum in Lubbock, Texas. They both keep the records of the thousands of glider pilots who sacrificed so much for so many in WWII.

I am forever thankful to my husband, who has prodded me for many years to write my story. When the writing began, he was there to edit, make suggestions, and help me say important things that needed to be said—even though painful for me to write. I am deeply grateful for his love and support.

Introduction

*The two most important days in your life are the day
you are born and the day you find out why.*
—Mark Twain

If you don't know who you are, how do you know why you were born? My journey has revolved around learning who my father was, to find out who I am.

I wrote this book for my father, Walter Bert Lindberg, for my family, and for his posterity. I also wrote it for all children who feel lost and need to know where they came from and what life possibilities might be opened for them. Even in the sunset of our lives, we are still the children of those who have gone before us.

Who were my dad's parents? Who were his siblings? Where did he grow up? What was his education? What were his interests, his hobbies, his talents? Why did he volunteer to become a glider pilot in WWII? Who were his friends and associates, and what did they think of him?

The picture of him, so handsome in his military uniform, has been on my dresser forever. He died when I was eight months old. This book is my father's story, but within his fascinating story is also my story of discovery—as Mark Twain suggests—of *why* I was born.

Contents

1 My Father Had No Children 1
2 Questions—No Answers 8
3 Who Was Peach? 16
4 Walter 24
5 Walter's Youth—WWII Begins 33
6 Walter—Glider Pilot Training 41
7 Lil—My Mom 46
8 Romance Blooms 58
9 Laurinburg-Maxton, North Carolina 67
10 Prelude to Normandy 77
11 Home Front 83
12 D-Day Normandy 90
13 Operation Dragoon 102
14 Operation Market Garden—Holland 109
15 Bastogne, Belgium 119
16 Operation Varsity—Rhine River Crossing 130
17 Angels of Death 142
18 War Orphan's Tale 147
19 The Falls 160
20 Life in Las Vegas 172
21 Alana/Lee—Las Vegas High School 180
22 Uncle Johnny, My Father's Brother 192
23 Life and Letters 199
24 Familia—Mexico/Aunt Virginia's Book 207
25 The Glider Gang—More Letters 220
26 Lost in the Victory 229

27 What If? Walter's Legacy 239
28 Closure..249

Epilogue: My Father Came Back 263
To My Father 267
Appendix: Excerpts from GP Letters 271
Glossary 275
Annotated Bibliography 277

Now Ⓐ is for ALANA,
The Ⓛ could stand for love,
Another Ⓐ for Always.
For you both I'LL Always love.
The Ⓝ - could stand for Never,
To never ever part,
Another Ⓐ just answeres,
What is in my Heart.

My Father Had No Children

The day was penetratingly cold and dreary in February of 1967. It was exactly how I felt. My husband, Lee, and I were silent driving to the Social Security Administration office in Provo, Utah. I had a lot of apprehension about the meeting I was about to have with Mr. Bowcutt. He had insisted he needed to talk to me face-to-face and not over the phone. I was eight months pregnant with my first child, and the arduous task of finishing my degree at Brigham Young University was still before me.

I had been trying, for two years, to claim the Social Security benefits of my deceased-veteran father to finish my college education. I had two years of university studies behind me before I learned dependent children of deceased veterans could claim Social Security benefits for educational purposes. I had applied for those benefits over a year ago.

We turned the corner, and I saw an American flag waving on the building in front of us, which indicated we were in the right place. This was where the Social Security Administration conducted business, a federal building. Lee dropped me off in front, and I walked up the steps.

To say I was nervous would be an understatement. Why wouldn't Mr. Bowcutt give me the information I was seeking over the phone? I guessed it was just about government red tape and bureaucracy. Using the money for a dead veteran's child's education seemed appropriate to me since my father had made the ultimate sacrifice for his country.

The secretary at the front desk escorted me down a long, dingy hallway to Mr. Bowcutt's office. The file folder, chock-full of papers under his arm, was the first thing I noticed about him. As my apprehension increased, he put the file folder down while reaching across to shake my hand. He was tall and looked well built underneath his gray suit and perfectly placed tie. His hair, dark with streaks of gray, was parted and smoothed to flat perfection. He made eye contact with me through his black-rimmed glasses. We both sat down.

He began to speak in a low, deliberate voice, which conveyed to me an unwavering assurance on his part. I didn't know why, but my hands were sweaty, and suddenly I wasn't just nervous. I felt scared and uncomfortable. This meeting was the culmination of two years of what I assumed was government stall tactics. The reason for the endless numbers of forms I filled out, the phone calls nobody returned, and the meetings cancelled were all being methodically explained to me by Mr. Bowcutt. He fumbled with the papers, seeming perhaps a little nervous himself.

Much of what he said behind his oversized and over-cluttered desk made no sense to me. This meeting was about rules and regulations, time running out, and my age. I had made the request for college money two years ago. He said I was going on twenty-three and too old, or something to that effect.

I can still feel the coldness of that office with its piles of manila folders on top of steel-gray filing cabinets. The only decoration was the large picture of President Lyndon B. Johnson hanging on the wall behind the man who spoke to me. I thought he was going to tell me more about my father's service, et cetera, but somehow, I knew that was not going to be the case.

I did not know my father because I was eight months old when he died, but he was always my hero and a great influence on my important life decisions. I wanted him to be proud of me, as I was of him. I had imagined his bravery and distinguished service as a glider pilot in World War II. My mom had shown me some pictures of my dad in France and the planes he flew. That was the extent of my knowledge about what my father did overseas.

MY FATHER HAD NO CHILDREN

Though the war was won by the United States and its Allies, there were many children, like me, who were left without a father in that victory. Mr. Bowcutt kept on talking. Clearing his throat brought me back to the conversation, which I obviously wasn't paying attention to. He stated clearly, "You need to understand, Mrs. Jolley, that nothing we have uncovered in our exhaustive research, including conversations with your mother, can change the one element, which is the determining factor for whether you can receive your father's Social Security money for college."

"Well, I'm trying to understand what that one element might be," I said. He looked at me sternly and said in his ever deep, slow, and deliberate voice, "Walter Lindberg had no children. He *was* married but not to your mother. You are not eligible for his Social Security benefits under the rules of the Social Security Administration." I sat there, frozen in the moment, but it seemed like forever.

"Wait—what did you say? My father had no children?" As I processed his words slowly, in my mind, tears welled up in my eyes. I asked him, "How can you sit there so coldly and tell me such a thing when it isn't true?" I began scrounging through my purse. "I have something that proves I'm his daughter."

I pulled a faded and wrinkled light-blue envelope from my purse, producing a handwritten poem addressed to me, written by Walter Lindberg. "This is a Valentine poem my father composed for me. Look at this postmark! Here, see—February 1945. This letter is written to me, Alana Lindberg. I am his daughter! He wrote this less than a month before he died in a plane crash in Tours, France." I pushed the envelope across his desk onto the open file folder. "Who do you think sent me this Valentine from France?" I asked.

Valentine poem to Alana, February 1945

By this time, I was standing up and raising my voice through my tears. "I do not believe you, I do not believe you!" I plopped back down in my chair and buried my head in my hands. He pushed a box of Kleenex across his desk toward me.

"What does that mean, my father wasn't my father? How did my father have no children? I'm sitting right here in this chair! I don't believe your research! Your research is wrong! My mother kept that Valentine for me until I could read it myself. I've been carrying it in my purse for years because it was from my dad who never came home!" Mr. Bowcutt opened the tattered envelope, pulled out the contents, and carefully unfolded the letter.

He shook his head back and forth while silently reading the words. In that instant, I became sick to my stomach and not from being pregnant. I could have easily thrown up. I felt weak and shaky. My father's face—the face that had looked at me every morning from my dresser, so handsome in his uniform—was now distorted in my mind. The father I worshipped, and yes, I even prayed to him in times of childhood stress. How was all this possible, this person telling me I don't have a father?

I pulled my dad's uniform so many times out of a dull green footlocker in our basement. I used to put it on to pretend my father's arms were around me. I wanted Mr. Bowcutt to give me an answer!

"Why do I have his uniform if he isn't my dad?" I raised my voice again and told him very sternly, "Somehow you are wrong, I *know* you are wrong. You *must* be wrong!" I kept talking over Bowcutt's interrupting voice, "I just told you, I'm his daughter! He has a daughter! It's me, I'm sitting right here in front of you! Can you not see me?"

I also reminded him, "I have been going to school on Veteran's benefits. Peach, my father's mother—*my grandmother*—set up a trust fund for me after he died. I have received Veteran's benefits for every month I was a full-time student. I had to go to the VA office and sign for that money every single month!" His tart reply was, "Veteran's benefits are different from Social Security benefits. The Veteran's Administration has a different set of rules than we do here at the Social Security Administration. That's just the way it is, Mrs. Jolley."

"You can't be serious! Oh, the rules, it is about the rules? I have friends whose fathers died in the war, and they are getting their checks." I remembered the pile of papers in the VA office, from which I found my own form every month. There were so many of us, I was only one among those many. "Our fathers gave their lives," I told him. "Why shouldn't we receive money for our education?" Bowcutt shrugged his shoulders.

My father was dead, and I was alive. At that moment, I could not think; it was too painful. I hit the Kleenex box off the desk, sending it to the floor. Bowcutt stood up behind his desk. I stared straight through him. He kept talking, but I wasn't listening anymore. The painting of President Johnson was still hanging on the wall behind him. The room had not changed at all, but the gray metal filing cabinets closed in on me. I wanted to run out of there, but there was no energy left in my body. When I got up to leave, I could barely walk. Even if I had not been so pregnant, I could not have run.

I don't know how I made it down the long hallway, down the steps, and back to where Lee was waiting for me in the car. Somehow, I reached the glass door to leave the building and pushed it open. The cold air rushed in and was welcome on my hot and tearful face. It was nearly dark outside, and the streetlights magnified the falling snow flurries.

I was numb but not from the cold. "Walter Lindberg had no children?" "Really?" I whispered to myself, "Then who am I? Am I just nobody?" I did not have an identity crisis until that moment. I was twenty-two years old, married, and almost a mother, yet I did not know who I was. Where was I going to start to unravel that awful reality if it was, in fact, true?

I asked myself, "Did I not have a grandmother called Peach? Who was she?" I had the baby picture of me with my father's picture sitting next to me when I was four months old. In that picture, I am wearing a pink crocheted outfit my dad's mother, Peach, made for me. In the picture, I have on a silver bracelet made from glider pilot metal wings on my little wrist.

My father had that bracelet made from his glider wings, which identified glider pilots. He sent the bracelet to me from overseas. How could I not be Walter's daughter? And what about my Valentine poem? So many memories and thoughts pulsed through my now broken identity.

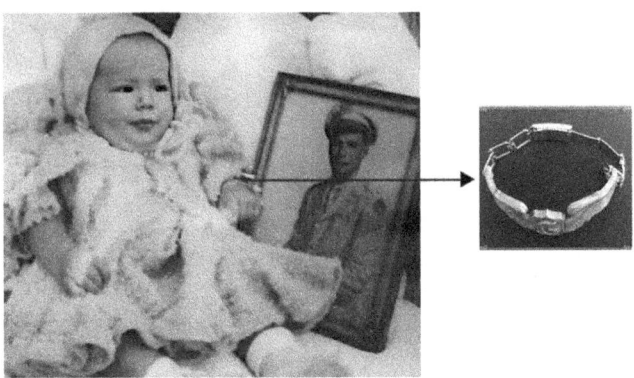

I had seen and held my birth certificate identifying Walter Lindberg as my father. His occupation, on the document is stated as "soldier."

I wondered how I was going to approach my mother about this. I went home that day with so many questions, which I was sure were going to need very long answers. On my slow walk to the car, I had a simple but frightening thought. I asked myself out loud, "If Walter

Lindberg is not my father, then who is?" In my heart, I was sure that he was no matter what I had just been told.

Lee had been patiently waiting for me in the car. The car had seemed miles away in my stunned state of mind. My whole life flashed before me while crossing the street. My chest was so tight I could hardly breathe. When I finally reached the car, I opened the door and I fell into the arms of my husband. I sobbed uncontrollably while relating to him what I had been told. He said, "Honey, don't cry, just talk to me. Why are you so upset?" In between my convulsive sobs, I replied, "You won't believe what I'm going to tell you! That man just told me, my father had no children!'"

Everything I was told in the previous half hour went against all I thought I knew about my father, my mother, and how I became Alana Jean Lindberg. Somehow, I was going to have to unravel all of this, but how? I had visited my uncle Johnny, my dad's brother, two years before in the summer of 1965, completely ignorant of this information. Should I approach him now about this? If so, how? I wanted to ask him, "Am I your niece or not?"

Those were some of the thoughts that crossed my mind. I wanted to ask my mother, "Is the child I am about to give birth to the grandchild of Walter Lindberg or not?" I had no idea where those thoughts were going to take me in the future. I didn't know if I would find the answers my heart would be looking for and hoping for. One thing I knew for sure was that I was going to find the truth.

2

Questions–No Answers

March 4, 1967, seemed like years from the day I spent at the Social Security Administration, but it was only three weeks. My daughter's birth arrived when I was still in the pain of seemingly losing my identity. In my arms I held a child, unlike myself, whose identity would never be in question. I loved holding, touching, watching, and smelling that new little person. Yet the happy emotions of motherhood were mixed up with the sad feelings of loss, unbelief, and frustration, which I had not been able to shake off since that awful day at the Social Security Administration.

That day, after my collapse in the car, we drove back to our house in complete silence. I did not tell Lee all that I found out. When we got home, I went straight to our bedroom. I grabbed my father's picture off the dresser and threw it face down into the top drawer, under my folded clothing. I couldn't cry anymore; I was plain mad! Why didn't my mother tell me all this? I could see why when I was a child, but then I wasn't a child anymore. As I look back, though, I'm not sure how she would, or could have, revealed her charade to me.

During the weeks of recovery from childbirth, I had many hours of contemplation tending my newborn. Lee was working two jobs and going to school, so my daughter and I were alone much of the time. I knew I wasn't going to finish my degree anytime soon, since the extra money was not forthcoming from my father's Social Security. At least that was put to rest. What about all the other questions I was still pondering? The following are the things I knew while growing up.

MY FATHER HAD NO CHILDREN

The only contact, over twenty-two-plus years, with any of my dad's family was with my grandma Peach when I was six years old and with Johnny, my father's brother in 1965, right before my twenty-first birthday. Did anybody else in my dad's family know that I existed? Walter Lindberg is named as my father on my birth certificate. How could that fact be wrong? Certainly, my mother would not lie about that, would she? But why did she keep me from my dad's family? I never saw Peach again after I turned six; I knew she lived in Los Angeles, but I didn't have an address or a phone number.

How was I able to receive Veteran's benefits but not my dad's Social Security? Why did Peach come to Louisville to see me and my mom when I was a baby shortly after Walter died? She drove across the United States from Los Angeles, California, by herself. There were no interstate highways, no GPS, and no cell phones. It took her several days to make the drive. I reasoned she would not have done that if I was not her granddaughter.

My mother kept a baby book for me with no more entries after I was eight months old, except the note about my father's death. My father's own handwriting in the book refers to Alana—that's me. The last picture in my baby book is of Peach holding me, my mother is sitting beside her, and my mother's overwhelming grief is obvious in the picture. I'm sitting on Peach's lap, and she has a little smile, but the blurry black-and-white photo has always made me sad to look at it.

Peach and Alana (March 1945) and Lillian (my mom)

The baby book has no other entries after Peach's visit. All the pages before have entries practically moment by moment of my baby life: when I first smiled, when I turned over and when I first sat up, and even when I had hiccups. All my measurements and my first teeth are recorded as well.

After I gave birth to my own daughter, I understood the excitement of having a newborn. I did the same thing exactly in my daughter's baby book, writing almost minute by minute her progress. My mother gave me my baby book so I could read what my dad wrote and what she wrote when he died. She wanted me to have it because it related to my dad, so I had something to show to my own children of my father, their grandfather.

Mother gave me the gold baby ring with my initial A on it, sent to me from France by my dad. She gave me my father's watch, his wallet, and the water-stained baby shoe that he carried with him in combat. I remember it because later it was mounted on a piece of decorative wood. His letter to my mom said, "The shoe got wet when I landed in a field, which the Germans flooded."

I had so much evidence, which I could have shown to Mr. Bowcutt if he had given me the opportunity. Besides my personal Valentine and the personal items belonging to my father, I have a compelling letter from my father's brother, Johnny. It was written to my mother on May 5, 1945, two months after Peach's visit to Louisville. "Somewhere in Germany" was the heading. It is typed, but the words seem to be sincere in their intentions to comfort my mother.

MY FATHER HAD NO CHILDREN

Following are excerpts from John Lindberg's letter. I don't know if showing it to Mr. Bowcutt would have made a difference, but it would have made me feel better if I had shown it to him. John wrote:

Dear Lil,

> The war is about over now—the war with Germany. No one will ever know the hearts that have been broken, the lives ruined, the destruction wrought, the lasting impressions this war has made on civilization as a whole. Our family has felt this war more than many others because in it we have lost so many fine young men.

The letter is long, and skipping over some parts, he continued.

> It is hard for me to realize that my only brother is gone, but I am thankful that he has a child because in his daughter, I know, flows the blood of one of the finest guys that ever lived. Try not to let this terrible thing ruin your outlook on life. Walt, above all, was never a quitter and could not understand defeatism. He wouldn't want this thing to ruin your life. You have his child, and yours, I know she is a real doll.
>
> For her you must carry on... He is gone, but his memory will never die. You must tell Alana about her father and how much he loved her... Someday, I hope to be able to hold your daughter in my arms because Walt and I were so close I feel that I have a few shares in Alana myself... Tell Alana that her uncle Johnny loves her with all his heart.
>
> Love,
> John

Johnny promised my mother, "I will come to Louisville to visit you as soon as I can. I really want to see Alana," but my mother said he never came. Why didn't I try to contact my uncle after I received the information from the Social Security office? I do not know the answer to that question. Should I have contacted him? Would he have been forthcoming with such information to me? He certainly had the chance to tell me everything in our short encounter two years before, but he didn't.

I have the wedding rings of my parents and letters from my dad written to my mother from overseas. My father sent pictures from France to my mother with explanations on the back of the pictures about what was happening. One picture has a large British Horsa glider in the background with Walter's handwritten words on the back: "Note the size of the Horsa. I flew one on D-Day, the invasion of France."

Those were some of the many thoughts that came to my mind over and over, which kept coming back when I relived that day in the Social Security office. The words have kept rebounding over and over in my head, "Walter Lindberg had no children. He was married but not to your mother." It still sometimes seems like a bad nightmare that never took place.

I went back to work at the dental office when my daughter was six weeks old. The girl next door was her babysitter. Working, parenting, and my volunteer work in the community kept me busy. Even so, the words of Mr. Bowcutt did not fade into oblivion. It was a wound that kept opening every time I thought about it. I had what I knew to be indisputable evidence that I was Walter Lindberg's daughter, but still there was a quiet little voice within causing me to think maybe I was wrong.

"These things happened during the war, you know, it's not unusual." Those words were so hurtful. Did Bowcutt think that explanation would make me feel better? It made me feel antagonistic toward him. He uttered them so matter-of-factly. Perhaps he was only doing his job!

Where exactly did I fit into this strange picture? No matter what I had been told, Walter Lindberg was my father. Wasn't he? All the tangible items, the wedding bands, the wallet with my baby pictures still in it, the glider pilot uniform, the dog tags, the letters he wrote were real. I could see and hold those items in my hands. Then there is the tattered telegram from Peach, which tells of my father's death in a plane crash. The telegram is addressed to "Mrs. W. B. Lindberg." Peach knew they were not married. Last, but certainly not the least, I can read the goodbye note in my baby book, promising, "I will come back to both of you somehow." It is signed, "Walter. Always remember I love you."

My mother was able to keep their secret until I was twenty-two years old. Had I not visited the Social Security Administration on that fateful day, the secret would have stayed intact. Her soldier was the glider pilot whom she was not married to and who did not return home from WWII. She told me, "I would have taken it to my grave." That's what she said when I confronted her with the information from the Social Security office.

The information given to me was truly astounding, disturbing, and so painful. All the words are still seared into my brain! I have remembered every detail explicitly. My mother did not have that experience in that office, and she did not feel my pain. She was only upset that I had been told the truth. I had prayed right there on the spot silently to wake up from that situation, but when I looked up, I saw Bowcutt's tight-lipped expression. He was convincing. I apparently was not convincing. None of what I told him or showed to him made any difference.

My father…my hero…was gone after that day. I hated the word *unusual*. Oh, sure, it didn't sound unusual to Bowcutt, but to me, Walter's daughter, it was a complete shock! Unusual that your father is not who you thought he was? Unusual that your father had no children, but you are here? Why were the rules different between the two government agencies? That made no sense to me. Why did Peach set up a trust fund for me if I wasn't her granddaughter? None of my own reasonings fit the narrative he gave me. I was so mad at both my parents!

So what if there was a war going on? Didn't they know their actions would affect me someday? No, they didn't. My father was sure he would come home to us. They must have believed in that nebulous hope. I wonder if they asked themselves how things would play out if he didn't survive the war. I'm sure they did.

In my adult life in the present, I feel empathy for their heart-wrenching and stressful circumstances that, quite frankly, were unsolvable at the time. It is hard to imagine being thousands of miles apart, my mother having pregnancy complications and contemplating a birth, and my dad in fearful combat situations and their communications only by mail with letters weeks apart. When I was sitting in the Social Security office, I was unable to feel that empathy for them or their grievous situation. I could only feel my own grief.

Twenty-two years had passed since World War II ended when I walked into the Social Security office that day. There were probably hundreds of college students in my same situation. War takes its toll in many other ways besides resulting casualties and deaths. So much sorrow and so much weeping keep going on.

At that time, the past years of my life evaporated into thin air. How can a few words and sentences change the world you thought you lived in? The crushing blow, which I absolutely could not fathom, was that the people I knew as my parents were not married—that my dad had a wife that was not my mom!

My mother told me, "We were together at Fort Bragg, North Carolina. We lived there until Walt left for England. I was five months pregnant when we said goodbye." Wedding rings were purchased, but my parents' plans for eventual marriage were never realized because my father did not return from the war. She never admitted it at first when I confronted her that there was a third person in the mix—that person being Walter's wife. At least Mr. Bowcutt assured me that Walter had no children with his wife! I didn't have to wonder if I had any other siblings.

My Valentine poem was written eight days before he died. Did that Valentine arrive at our home before or after his death? It would have been heartbreaking for my mother to receive it after the telegram message about his death. I wanted to have empathy for those tumultuous circumstances, but those circumstances were hard for me to imagine at the time.

Walter carried my picture and my baby shoe into battle. I often wondered, when my mother looked at me, did she see him? What kind of a person was he? What was his personality like? Those sought-after answers have been the quest of my life. I felt if I could find my father, I could find myself. I have been able to cope with the information I learned from Mr. Bowcutt because time heals wounds, but the void is still there to be revisited in dreams and periods of life's reflections. I read somewhere, "War never ends." It never does end when war takes a father or other loved one. Now, in my own life, I sometimes return to moments of tears and grief. Those moments are not planned, and they happen unexpectedly.

As I probed deeper, I wanted to find my dad's family and those who wrote to him and those who might still remember him. I have learned in some rather surprising ways more of my dad's story, resulting in my own story being altered. I knew little of my father while growing up, but I modeled myself after the person I pictured him to be. I wanted to please him and make him feel proud of me, as I was of him. As the years have gone by ever so quickly, he did fulfill the promise he made in my baby book.

"I don't know what else to say or how to say it, but I will come back to both of you somehow… Always remember, I love you. Walter."

Who Was Peach?

I sat on Peach's lap when I was eight months old. She came to visit my mom and me in 1945. Of course, I have no memory of that meeting, but I do have pictures. I received gifts from Peach at Christmas, on my birthdays, and on other occasions. I have a picture with Santa Claus when I was five years old, wearing a beautiful rabbit fur coat. When the coat and other things arrived by mail, I was told, "This is from your grandma Peach."

Christmas 1949

The gifts I received were the only things that reminded me I had a paternal grandmother, except for my sixth birthday when she came to visit me. That visit by Peach made me understand that she was someone special in my life. I never saw her again, but I kept getting packages from her and sometimes a short letter. She traveled to Europe and sent me gifts from there. She sent me a Bible with a carved wooden cover from Jerusalem and an embroidered red felt jacket from Spain. It was too big for me, and I don't know what happened to it. I had a special attachment to the Bible, though, so I still have it.

As I have learned more about Peach and as I write about her, I am overwhelmed at how much influence she has had on my own story and the trajectory of my path in life. Her valiant deeds on my behalf, which were unknown to me until I was an adult, have bound us together eternally through love as well as biology.

Peach was born Emma Carmen Cota on May 1, 1893, in the coastal city of Ensenada, Baja California, Mexico. She was the oldest of fourteen children and was baptized into the Catholic Church shortly after birth. Spanish was her native language, but she learned English while attending school in the United States. (Emma) Carmen Cota was better known by her family nickname, Camelina, because she and her mother shared the same name, Carmen.

It was during her teenage years that she became Peach. The story goes that she shocked her parents and siblings by dying her hair red. She told her sister, Virginia, "I don't want to be a Mexican girl anymore." The self-dying job did not come out exactly as planned. Her hair was more the color of a peach, so the name was first a joke, but it stuck. The word *peach* was so endearing that she became Peach to all those who loved her, including her son, Walter. That's what he called her his entire life as a child and as an adult.

Peach's family was a high-profile, socially well-established family in Ensenada since the 1870s. Jose de los Santos Cota, Peach's grandfather, brought his family of nine children, along with seven other families, north by wagon train from southern Baja California to the northern part of Baja. They were pioneers who traveled almost the entire length of the Baja peninsula, over seven hundred miles. They hailed from the southern towns of Todos Santos and San Antonio, traveling on unpaved roads to Ensenada. There were few resting places for such a large group of people, wagons, and livestock, so camping out was the norm.

Peach's father, Jose Fermin Cota, was born in the Spanish Mission town of Todos Santos, and Carmen Fernandez, his wife and Peach's mother, was born in the port city of La Paz, Baja California, Mexico. Though her parents, Fermin and Carmen, were both born on the peninsula, their heritage was deeply Spanish. They were known as Espanoles, meaning they were born in Mexico but had a long line of ancestors who came from Spain.

Fermin Cota held a prestigious job as a custom's officer in the Mexican government. They were a financially well-off family, so Peach's mother did not cook or do laundry or gardening. There was hired help for all the constant menial chores. The girls learned to sew and bake and were more interested in fashion than domestic chores. Besides raising so many children, Carmen was an exceptional seamstress and embroiderer. She created beautiful, embroidered blouses and dresses for her mother, her daughters, and other special women in her life. She taught her daughters well in those arts.

Ensenada, being less than a hundred miles south of San Diego, made it easy for wealthy Mexican families to send their children across the Mexican border to private schools in the United States. Peach's family lived in various small towns in Baja California, but she and her sister, Virginia, spent much of their childhood in Santa Barbara and Los Angeles with their maternal grandmother, Virginia Murillo-Fernandez.

Their wealthy grandmother took them to classical music concerts and plays at the Temple Theater in Los Angeles, which the girls loved. Virginia, named after her grandmother, explained, "We dressed up in beautiful dresses our mother made for us. Mama's embroidery on our dresses was exquisite, and we carried parasols when we attended such cultural events. It was our grandmother's Spanish customs and cultural upbringing to dress formally and beautifully when we went to the theater."

Fashion and clothing were very important to Peach's mother and her daughters. She ordered the best clothing from Europe and she ordered bolts of beautiful silks and linens, which came on large cargo ships from Italy, France, and Spain to the La Paz Harbor in Mexico. When Fermin, their father, was alive, he hired riders to go pick up the cargo when they were alerted that a ship had docked in the harbor. Their grandmother also delighted in providing her own daughter, Carmen, with expensive materials to make dresses for herself and the girls. The European tastes for fashion of the women in Peach's family were well entrenched.

In this three-generation photo, one can see the fashionable trends of the day: jackets worn with insertable dickeys and hats worn when ladies left the house. Such fashionable accessories were not just optional but signified not only the wealth of the wearer but also the social status.

(L–R) Carmen Fernandez, Virginia Murillo Fernandez, and Emma Carmen Cota (Peach)

Peach and her sisters were the "beauties" of Ensenada. They were the queens of special celebrations in Ensenada because they were well known, wealthy, and beautiful. Well-established merchants and soldiers of rank were their escorts and marriage potentials.

Peach's heritage, paternal and maternal, was predominantly Spanish, as the family surnames attest to. Their families were very proud of their Spanish ancestors who first settled in the Baja peninsula and in early Alta California. Peach's ancestors were among the first residents to establish the pueblos, which became the great cities of San Diego, Los Angeles, Santa Barbara, San Francisco, and others.

Peach's maternal grandfather was from Malaga, Spain, and established a great industry of pearl fishing when he came to La Paz. Other ancestors came from Toledo and Seville, Spain, during the three centuries the Spanish crown had cultural dominance over Mexico.

Peach grew up in both Baja California and Santa Barbara. She attended private elementary and secondary schools in the United States. Since her native language and culture were Spanish and Mexican, it must have been quite difficult for Peach *not* to be a Mexican girl, as she often expressed to her siblings! Her dyed hair mattered not. Life was busy, crossing back and forth between Mexico and the US, but stable until a major life event changed everything for Peach and her family when she was only sixteen years old.

In 1909, Peach's mother was thirty-three years old and pregnant with her fourteenth child. Peach was barely sixteen. Her father had recently resigned from his government job and gone into business for himself in the mining and freighting business. He traveled home at night by wagon, which was loaded with supplies and mining equipment. Heavy as it was, it was necessary for the wagon to be pulled by two horses.

Jose Fermin Cota and Carmen Fernandez, parents of Emma Carmen Cota (Peach)

One stormy evening, while enroute home, one of the horses became lame and could go no further, so Fermin slept under the wagon during the cold and rainy night. When it was daybreak, he continued home on horseback. He was slumped over in the saddle, shivering and wet. He had a fever, and the family noticed he was having difficulty breathing. Fermin died of pneumonia two days later, leaving Carmen, his pregnant wife, with their many children to care for on her own.

The sudden death of Peach's father left her, as the oldest child, to be responsible to help her mother. Peach and her next younger sister, Virginia, began working multiple jobs. They worked as seamstresses during the day and took second jobs in restaurants in the evening. After Carmen, Peach's mother, gave birth to her fourteenth child in El Rosario, the family moved north, back to Ensenada, where there were other extended family members to help Carmen care for the children.

Peach was growing up, and Ensenada was becoming a boom town. The Cota sisters were involved in a variety of social activities and gatherings. Peach and her sisters acted in plays, and Peach was a very good pianist, often playing impromptu. There was the legend passed down that Ensenada had the most beautiful girls in Mexico.

At one of the newly established restaurants for the outsiders coming in, a young man from Los Angeles learned that this legend was not a rumor but, indeed, was true. He came to work in the oil fields of Baja California. His name was Bert Richard Lindberg, who met a beautiful young girl called Peach. She was an assistant cook in the evenings at one of the popular restaurants. After meeting Bert, Peach soon found herself in an unexpected romance.

Peach and Bert made an unusual couple visually. Bert was tall and blond with blue eyes, and Peach was short with dark brown eyes and reddish hair. Neither spoke the other's native language, but they both spoke English well enough to make romance possible. Bert was a first-generation immigrant from Sweden and was only one of the many outsiders who came to work in Mexico in the 1900s. The residents of Ensenada welcomed such outsiders into their cultural landscapes. For Peach, her sisters, and all the young people looking for fun, it made ordinary life much more exciting. However, the proper chaperoning of young girls became much more a necessity and more intense.

Bert Richard Lindberg and Emma Carmen Cota (Peach) in 1912

The unexpected romance grew rapidly, and Peach's sisters all said, "Peach saw Bert as her ticket away from family responsibilities and a way to leave Mexico and go to the United States and become a citizen there." Undoubtedly that was true because nine days before Peach's twentieth birthday, she and Bert eloped to Los Angeles, where they were married on April 21, 1913.

Neither family of the couple was on board with such a hasty courtship and marriage. The newlyweds did not plan very well for their living circumstances either. They took up residence with Bert's mother and sister, who were both widows in Los Angeles. There was a lot of tension in the household due to the fact the widows spoke mostly Swedish to each other and to Bert. Peach was good at English but not Swedish! The older women expected Peach to take a big part in the domestic chores as well, which Peach wasn't mindful of since her family always had hired help to do all the menial things.

The first year of Bert and Peach's marriage was a whirlwind of taking advantage of all the new industry and entertainment adventures in Los Angeles. This was a thorn in the side of both widows, for they were homebound without many resources at their disposal. Often the young couple asked them to go with them to see live filming of movies for twenty-five cents, which included lunch, but they weren't interested.

Peach and Bert went to concerts by the Los Angeles Symphony Orchestra. Theater was an entertainment, which was important to Peach, because she and her sisters had gone to beautifully staged operas with their grandmother many times. Peach was indeed living her dream of not being a Mexican girl, for she was completely immersed in American culture. As much as she tried, though, she could not master the English language without a Spanish accent.

The only thing that slowed the young Lindbergs down was, after three months of marriage, Peach began to have morning sickness. They soon needed to find a place for their own little family to settle into. A few weeks before Peach was to deliver, they found a couple of rooms for rent in a two-story house in Downtown Los Angeles. Peach gave birth to their first child, Walter, five days after their one-year marriage anniversary.

Walter

Walter Bert Lindberg was born in Los Angeles, California, on April 26, 1914. Walt, as he became known, arrived under the Zodiac star sign of Taurus, which is an earth sign representing intelligence and dependability. Hard work, ambition, and mental tenacity are also Taurus characteristics. Such traits proved to be well integrated, according to family members, within my dad's character, personality, and lifeways as he grew up. Walter's namesakes were from his father, Bert, and his uncle, Walter.

In 1914, most children were born at home with the help of midwives. However, living in Los Angeles, Peach and Bert were financially able to take advantage of professional care at the nearby Clara Barton Hospital.

Peach recovered from childbirth in a private room for three dollars and twenty-five cents per day. When she went home, her mother was there to take care of her oldest daughter and her first grandchild. Mexican culture demanded such close bonding associations from the very beginning of a child's life. Though Peach was the oldest of Carmen's fourteen children, there was still much to learn from her mother's experience.

My father entered the world within a biracial family, which contributed to his overall good looks. His close friends also said he had an exceptional ability to get along with others. Walt's father, Bert Richard Lindberg (1884–1938), was Swedish, born of immigrants from Stockholm, Sweden. His mother, Carmen (Peach) (1893–1963), was born in Mexico.

 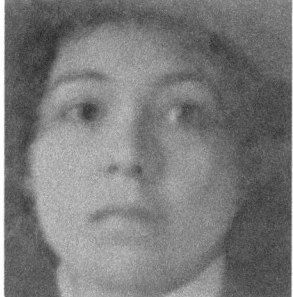

Bert Richard Lindberg and Emma Carmen Cota (Peach)

Walter had the opportunity to learn and speak three languages while growing up: Spanish from his mother and maternal relatives, Swedish from his father and paternal relatives, and English because he lived and attended school in the United States. Most of his Swedish and Mexican relatives were bilingual as well.

In December of 1918, all of Carmen's ten surviving children came to Ensenada to celebrate her forty-second birthday. Walter and his little brother, Johnny, who was two years younger, came with Peach for the party. The family photograph was taken at the family home on Gastelum Street. Walt's grandmother (Carmen) and mother (Peach) are seated in the picture. The others are Peach's nine living siblings.

A cute story about this family photograph was told to me by Walter's aunt Virginia. "Walter was a very precocious child and always wanted to be in the middle of every activity." In those days, a photographer was hired, and he brought in the necessary equipment, which was both heavy and cumbersome, and took a lot of time to set up. The individuals who were to be in a photograph had to be staged in certain positions, and they could not move, or the photo would not turn out right.

Every time the stage was set, Walter came running to his mother to be in the photograph. Carmen, his grandmother, wanted only her children in the picture—not Walter. He would not give up, and he was finally given a "swat" on his behind and made to go into the house, where his brother was napping. When the picture came back from the photographer, Walter was, after all, in the picture! He had gone into the house and pulled a chair up to the window overlooking where the family was posed. His little face shows clearly in the window above the family group! That was an early indication that Walter was a very determined child.

Carmen Fernandez-Cota and her ten children in 1918. (See four-year-old Walter's face at the window on the top left.)

In Walter and Johnny's early childhood, they also lived near their maternal great-grandmother in Santa Barbara. Peach lived with her grandmother there while attending Catholic private schools as a young girl. There were such close ties between Peach and her maternal grandmother that she often insisted Peach was more of a daughter to her than a granddaughter. Even so, Walter's life was greatly influenced by the many Spanish cultural attributes of Peach's grandmother, which she instilled in Peach through her love of the arts during Peach's early formative years.

Peach, Bert, and the boys making their home in Southern California allowed them to forge close extended family ties on both sides of the California-Mexican border. It was very easy then because the borders separating the United States from Mexico were porous in the early twentieth century. There were no United States Border Patrols asking for passports or IDs until 1924, when Walter was ten years old.

Families from both sides of the border had traveled freely back and forth. Passports and/or papers were mostly needed when traveling by ship. As a result, Walter spent much time with his grandmother, Carmen, in Ensenada, Mexico. Several aunts, uncles, and cousins lived nearby as well. Many extended Mexican family members lived in Tijuana, Mexicali, and Mexico City. Walt's Mexican family was well known for their great family reunions and celebrations south of the California border. Distance did not matter when there was a party or special occasion planned.

Walter's only sibling, John Louis, was born in August of 1916 in Ensenada, Mexico, not Los Angeles. The months prior to his birth were tense and turbulent for their biracial family. To understand why little Johnny was born in Mexico and not in the United States, a bit of local history is needed before we go on.

Johnny's birth came soon after the famous Mexican leader, Pancho Villa, and his guerillas attacked the small rural town of Columbus, New Mexico. Seventeen Americans died, and at least sixty-three Mexicans also died. New Mexico had only been a state since January 1912, a mere four years. The attack angered both the Americans and the Mexicans, almost to the point of war between the two.

Loyalties and patriotism for both American families and Mexican families became hotly disputed. Those conflicts for bi-ethnic families caused extreme stress on family ties. That was the reason Peach chose to birth Johnny in Ensenada, Mexico, where she felt safe and where her mother, Carmen, could attend to her needs. The family pictures below were taken in Ensenada, Baja California, Mexico.

(Left) Walter and his brother Johnny and (right)
Walter with his grandmother and aunts

Walter's aunts and uncles described him as "the more energetic and competitive of the two boys." They said, "Johnny was shy, and he did not like the family's loud and boisterous parties where we all spoke Spanish, and Johnny preferred English. Walt loved to speak Spanish and being around our family, and everyone treated him like the favorite that he was!" It was said by Walter's aunts that he spoke the sweetest Spanish. Language proficiency proved to be great cultural capital for Walter in his adult life whether in California, Mexico, or abroad.

Walter and Johnny in 1918

In trying to interpret Walter's immediate childhood circumstances and relationships, it is necessary to understand how he and his brother and their parents conducted their daily lives. Conditions of family life in that era depended on the breadwinner's occupation, which was most often the father's responsibility. Though Peach had worked before marriage, she opted to stay at home with her boys in their early years.

The pattern of Bert's employment was erratic with a lot of traveling to different states and/or wherever work was available. The Great Depression added to his employment difficulties, and that was another reason Peach and the boys spent so much time in Mexico. Bert was away for several months at a time during Walter's early years. Peach was not yet a citizen of the United States, and it was more difficult for her to find work in Long Beach than in Ensenada.

When Walter was going on four years old, the Great War (WWI) was almost over, but a terrible Spanish flu pandemic suddenly came upon California and the world. In 1918, sixteen days after Bert signed his draft card, officials in California began to quarantine seamen. There were complete lockdowns with closings of schools, theaters, saloons, shops, and other public places like pool halls, restaurants, and bars. Walter and Johnny were not in school yet, but masks were mandatory for all.

The newly developed film industry of Hollywood was greatly impacted by the mask-wearing and the shutdowns of filming. Before the Spanish flu pandemic, Bert and Peach took the boys to picture studios to watch live film shoots, but during the pandemic, those entertainments were not available. Walter loved the cowboy scenes from those days, and he was a fan of "shoot 'em up" films all the while he was growing up.

After living in the United States and then returning to Mexico often, Peach was aware of the differences in cultures and the better opportunities available for upward mobility in the United States. She wanted her sons to be educated in the United States, as she had been in her early years.

Peach did not allow her boys to work until they were in high school, and then she only allowed them to work part-time because they were involved in sports and other activities at school. Homework was a never-ending task, and the boys could not participate in extra-curricular activities until homework was finished.

Peach and Walter

At the time, it probably wasn't interpreted as historical, but the Hollywood sign, which is now a world-renowned symbol of California, and its motion picture industry, was constructed on top of Mount Lee in what is now known as Hollywood Hills. The boys marveled at the four thousand light bulbs that lit up the sign across the valley. That sign, over the many decades it has existed, is one of the most recognized images in America.

Walter at eight years old in a school uniform, 1922

Childhood for Walter was mostly play because he lived in Los Angeles and frequented the Los Angeles Athletic Club. Many people still lived and worked on farms or ranches in California; and children who lived in those rural areas were expected to help their parents with the hard work of raising crops or raising livestock. Some children, especially during the Depression, worked in factories to supplement the income of their parents.

Walter and Johnny played board games such as checkers and card games, which were popular with children. One activity Peach insisted on, especially during the summer vacations from school, was reading. She herself liked to go to libraries with the boys to help choose their books.

Peach had gone to both parochial and public schools in the United States, and she wanted her boys to have the same opportunities. It was much easier for Walter and Johnny because they did not have to leave home or go live with another relative to get their education.

Walter and Johnny were not classified as Latinos because they had a Swedish father. On their border-crossing papers, their race is listed as "White." By 1924, it became more difficult to cross the border for a Mexican national, like Peach. She wanted to get official status as an American citizen, especially since women were finally allowed to vote. She told her sisters, "I want to be a *real* citizen, not just married to one." It was many years before she accomplished her goal of citizenship.

The boys were growing up quickly, and their father's work opportunities were few, causing a lot of discontent and hardship in the family. There were health issues with Bert, as well as employment issues. By necessity, the boys spent more time with their aunts and uncles and their grandmother in Mexico.

Children sometimes lose interest in grandparents in their teens, but that was not the case with Walter. Both of his grandmothers were widows, and he was very attached to them. He loved visiting them no matter which side of the border they were on. With school and his athletics pursuits becoming more demanding, however, Walter's longer visits become less often.

Walter's Youth–WWII Begins

Shortly before Walt entered high school, the family of four moved to Long Beach from Los Angeles. In Long Beach, Walter was able to fish and go boating at the harbor, two activities he loved besides his physical activities at the YMCA (Young Men's Christian Association). He played all kinds of sports and took gymnastics lessons at the nearby athletics club. He loved fishing and horseback riding and was good in almost every sport.

There was no television for Walter and Johnny or any other kind of screen to keep them occupied. There were no Walt Disney characters like Mickey Mouse or Donald Duck in Walter's childhood. Yet Walter started very early to draw people and animals into cartoonlike characters. He did this for pleasure and as an outlet his entire life. His poems and/or letters home usually carried a signature cartoon somewhere within the script.

Walter's cartoonlike artwork

Walter at thirteen years old, boating at Long Beach Harbor

When Walter entered Long Beach Polytechnic High School, he tried out for the Gym Club and became an all-around gymnast. His gymnastic skills included routine floor work, the pommel horse, the vault, rings, parallel bars, and the high bar.

By the time he was a junior in high school in 1931, he was not just a teammate but also became the star on the gymnastics team and a letterman. His coach stated, "Walter Lindberg, an all-around star, will be back [next year] to bolster the squad." It was the Great Depression, and hardships were beginning to mount. High unemployment and thousands of misplaced peoples coming into California from the "dust bowls" would alter Walter's and his coach's plans for that next school year.

The anticipation of the 1932 Olympics to be held in Los Angeles gave the Polytech Boys' Gym Club the motivation to work harder. Excitement was so high; Walter's 1931 high school yearbook had this commentary:

> They will come not only as athletes but as ambassadors, chosen minions of a world drawn together in a spirit of friendship and athletic endeavor. It will be the pleasure of Polytechnic

High School to extend the hand of welcome…for 1932 that series of events of most consequence to all, the Tenth Olympic Games.

The Boys' Gym Club with Walter (sitting fourth from the right)

Walter's senior year in high school with him competing as a star gymnast never happened. He dropped out because he needed to work to help support his mother and brother while his father was away. Walter tried out, anyway, as a gymnast for the 1932 Olympics, and he made a good showing, but he did not make the final cut.

The Tenth Olympiad took place in Los Angeles on schedule, from July 30 through August 14, 1932, but Walt was unable to participate in the festivities with his high school Gym Club. Nor did he participate in the welcoming activities with his high school, as planned. This was a terrible blow and disappointment for him, the school, his coach, and his whole team. Instead, he was among the National Guardsmen whose duty it was to host the fencing team, as well as providing protection for the many athletes who were there to compete.

The 1932 games were the first to have an Olympic Village, and Walt and his fellow guardsmen provided security, where the athletes were housed up in the hills overlooking the "city of angels." It was not exactly how he wanted to be involved in the Olympic activities, but at least he was in a place to be somewhat of an observer of all the excitement and fun activities. It may have been Walter's first major disappointment, but future disappointments in his young life would make him forget this one.

The Roaring Twenties was said to be a decade of prosperity and fun, but the 1930s were just the opposite. They were roaring but not with fun or prosperity. Every day was filled with the brutal realities of unemployment, business failures, and depletion of important resources.

Walter at twenty years old

Shortly before the Olympics came to Los Angeles in June of 1932, Walter had enlisted in the California National Guard, which was part of the United States Army. He received a stipend from his Guard duties, as well as his other jobs. Little did Walter know that the training and discipline as a California National Guardsman was preparing him for another "great war," which was looming on the horizon.

California was the Golden State, but it was hard to keep up its reputation for opportunity, relaxing beaches, and great entertainment while in the middle of such economic collapses. By 1935 to 1936, Walt had two jobs and was going to night classes, but his days were usually filled with sunshine, and those coastal beaches, which he loved, were very near. Even if nothing else was good, the weather usually was.

In the case of great disappointments in life, it is hard to pick up and move on, but that is what Walter did. He finished high school by correspondence and eventually enrolled in some university courses, which were held at night. This allowed him to work full-time in the day and part-time at night. His National Guard duties were mostly on weekends.

Almost out of the blue, when he was twenty-four years old in 1938, Walter got married, hoping to have a family. His marriage, like his mom and dad's, was not viewed as a happy arrangement by either side of their families. Walter was brought up Catholic, though his father was Lutheran, and religion was important to him during his formative years. His German wife, however, upon learning that she had married into a very large Hispanic and Catholic family, informed him she would not have children. This was another disappointment he had not planned for.

The marriage deteriorated very quickly. His wife refused to go to the many family gatherings in Mexico. She didn't even particularly care for Walt's Swedish side of the family either. It was commonly known by his family that his wife had a drinking problem, and he was embarrassed by her many times in front of the family. In 1941, Walt's wife left him and went to Michigan to live with her parents. A divorce was imminent, but with a war in progress after the Pearl Harbor bombing, life became even more complicated.

Shortly after Walter married, his father suddenly died of pneumonia at the Los Angeles General Hospital. He had been working as a driller in the oil fields but was estranged from Carmen (Peach) and the boys at the time of his death. No family informant's name is on his death certificate, and exact circumstances are still a family mystery. Other disturbing things were happening in Los Angeles in 1938. It was a turbulent year for residents, along with the other hardships. There were other natural calamities happening independently in Los Angeles and Long Beach, where the family lived and worked.

According to a newspaper article during that time, "Intense rainstorms fell upon the city of Los Angeles and the surrounding areas in the late winter of 1938." Apparently, there was excess of thirty-two inches of rain within a short span of time. A catastrophic flood followed, which killed over one hundred people and destroyed some six thousand homes.

During the Depression, California became a place of refuge for hundreds of thousands of new migrants seeking work. The Okies, as they were called, competed for farmwork, taking over where Mexican labor had previously dominated. Peach, Johnny, and Walter were trying to survive among all the chaos without their dad, Bert Richard, as a provider in the household.

With disappointments piling up over several years, Walter was surely confused about what might lie ahead. He and his brother had hopes of starting a business together. They had both worked in plant nurseries during high school, and they both liked growing things. They dreamed of owning and operating a plant nursery or garden store as partners in Los Angeles.

If a long-term Great Depression with worldwide economic collapse and a devastating flood in California were not enough by September 1, 1939, Germany invaded Poland. In 1940, six more countries were occupied by Germany: Denmark, Norway, Belgium, the Netherlands, Luxembourg, and France. While most of the world had been "depressing," between 1936 and 1939, Germany had been fiercely building a war machine and training the youth of the country.

Hitler's nationalistic speeches convinced his young audiences that Germany needed to recover what had been lost in the Great War (WWI) two decades before. Walter and Johnny were both age-relevant for the draft if or when the United States entered any of the conflicts. Walter continued to register with his local draft board in Los Angeles, California, as all young men were required to do when they changed their address. He was pursuing university studies and working at the George Hall Company, which manufactured transport trailers.

Walter had tried hard to make his marriage work, and he and John helped with finances as much as they could. Walter and his wife moved in with Peach when his wife couldn't find work. Those days were obviously hard for so many, living in cramped circumstances altogether. Eventually Peach went to work for a Japanese businessman at a food processing plant in Los Angeles. That relationship eventually caused much stress for Peach in later years.

Early in 1941, Walter came home after night school to find that his wife had left him. Her clothes were gone, and she left a note that she was going to Michigan to live with her parents. In addition to all the other problems and hardships, a divorce was now on the horizon.

Two years after the occupation of Poland by Germany on December 7, 1941, every major radio station in the United States blasted this announcement, "We interrupt this program to bring you a special news bulletin. The Japanese have attacked Pearl Harbor, Hawaii, by air." When Japan bombed the United States Pacific Fleet at Pearl Harbor on that December day, Walter was twenty-seven years old. He had already been part of the military, so he well understood what might happen as he once again registered with the local draft board. Many people's dreams for their future, like Walter's, changed abruptly.

The United States of America was soon to be part of the war not only in Europe but also in North Africa, and after the Pearl Harbor attack, Japan was added to the fray. On December 8, 1941, the United States declared war on Japan, and on December 11, 1941, Germany declared war on the United States.

The George Hall Company, where Walter worked, was quickly converted to the building and manufacturing of airplane parts for the war effort. The long-term plans for millions of people worldwide were now put on hold. Walter's individual life was not going according to plan either. His hasty marriage to the German girl, whom he hardly knew, was ending. She had worked as a waitress, while Walt worked at a plant nursery in the day and at the airplane manufacturing plant at night.

His college classes were also at night, and he was forced to drop them in midsemester. Another issue was that Walter had always thought of himself as a father someday, but his wife wanted no "Mexican" children. His brother, Johnny, had already enlisted in the army, and Walt was contemplating doing the very same thing.

Since his wife had abruptly left him and gone to live with her parents, Walter had to make some important life decisions. He was working two jobs and sleeping alone in an empty apartment in Los Angeles, which was obviously pointless. His aunt Virginia, who took care of him most often in his childhood, told me, "Walter was very sad. He decided since he had no children and his wife was gone, he would enlist and become a pilot in the army."

Walter enlisted in the United States Army in Santa Ana, California, on June 3, 1942. He was immediately sent to Fort Morgan, Colorado, where he was assigned to the first Army Air Force Glider Training Detachment until July 4, 1942. He soon was assigned to the sixth AAF Glider Detachment in Twentynine Palms, California. After months of glider training, he was eventually assigned to Bowman Airfield in Louisville, Kentucky, where his life plans once again changed directions.

6

Walter–Glider Pilot Training

In 1938, Walter had no idea how the war in Europe would eventually have a transformative effect on his life in unimaginable ways. It wasn't yet a world war, but he had already served in the California National Guard for ten years since June 27, 1932, so he didn't have to wait to get drafted. There were no deferments from war allowed at that time, even if married, so he was obligated to serve.

Hitler continued to expand the war eastward toward Russia and into all parts of Europe. President Roosevelt was trying hard to keep the United States from entering the ever-expanding war by sending food, equipment, and other materials to England and other allied countries. The memories of WWI were still fresh on most everyone's mind. Therefore, politicians were not eager to officially declare war on any country.

The Great Depression was starting to wind down, and any chance of recovery was going to be slow. After such a shattering economic downturn during the previous decade, people were eager to get their lives back together. Walter's father, Bert Richard, did not serve in WWI, and his health deteriorated during the stress of irregular jobs and unemployment during the Great Depression. After his father died in 1938, Walter was then twenty-four years old. He took over responsibilities of his mother while also giving up his university studies.

He formally enlisted as a volunteer in the Army Air Force (AAF) on June 3, 1942, in Santa Ana, California. He wanted to fly, so he volunteered to be a glider pilot, as he was familiar with airplanes already. On July fourth, he was sent to Fort Morgan, Colorado, where he was assigned to the First Army Air Force (AAF) Glider Training Attachment. There he received elementary flight school training and education on how to fly beginning gliders.

Walter had not traveled very much within the United States, though he often crossed the border into Mexico because of family ties. From June of 1942 through September of 1943, he was transferred from state to state while learning and preparing for his pilot duties in the United States Army.

Over that period of flight training, Walter made stops in Colorado, Twentynine Palms, California, Kirtland Field, New Mexico, Lubbock, Texas, and back to California at the Victorville Flight Training School. He graduated from flight training and was honorably discharged on April 6, 1943, to accept an appointment as a flight officer. On April 7, 1943, he entered on extended active duty and was assigned to Bowman Field, Kentucky.

The 1943 glider pilot graduating class with
Walter standing on the far right

By the end of April 1943, Walter was on his way to Bowman Field in Louisville, Kentucky. There were thousands of military personnel stationed there during WWI and then in the years of WWII as well. The training was intense, brutal, and energy-depleting. Leaves for all personnel were in short supply, and even shorter for officers involved in the planning and staging of all the training exercises.

Walter arrived in Louisville, Kentucky, by train soon after his graduation and appointment as a flight officer. He and several of his buddies checked into the Seelbach Hotel in downtown Louisville, which was about seven miles from Bowman Field. They lived in the hotel for several days before their bunking arrangements were able to be confirmed at the airfield. There were so many military divisions coming in and leaving from Bowman Field during that time that hotel accommodations were usually necessary but never permanent. However, the Seelbach hotel was where the flight officers came to do swim training, as swimming was part of flight training. The Seelbach provided all the pool facilities necessary for the servicemen to train.

Ironically, the land that comprises the airfield at Bowman was originally owned by a German baron in 1920. It was the first commercial airport established in Louisville. Trans World Airlines and Continental Airlines flew commercial flights, bringing both passengers and mail in the 1930s and '40s. Charles Lindbergh (no relation to my father) landed the *Spirit of St. Louis* at Bowman airport in 1927. When World War II began, the airport was converted to a flight training center for glider pilots as well as military evacuation nurses and other personnel.

Bowman Field became part of the Ninth Airborne and Eighty-Second Airborne Division, 439th Troop Carrier Group (TCG), and the Ninety-Fourth Troop Carrier Squadron (TCS). Designated TCGs and TCSs did exactly that—they carried paratroopers and infantry into battlefields. Gliders were used to resupply battlefronts with medical personnel and supplies, food rations, and other necessities. They also rescued and transported wounded troops from combat zones.

Bowman Field was where hundreds of other glider pilots learned many glider flying techniques as well as learning battlefield survival tactics. Once the gliders landed behind enemy lines, the pilots were expected to enter combat with the ground infantry while making their way back for new assignments. Also, the complicated technique, including double tows and snatch takeoffs, were learned at Bowman as well. A snatch take-off was difficult because the glider sat motionless, fully loaded, and equipped on the ground, waiting for the C-47 towplane to come in and snatch the tow cable with a hook, which pulled the glider into flight.

During his training, Walter learned to fly the CG-4A Glider, which became one of the most important aircraft developed in World War II. The glider operations became the spear tip of every invasion, which took place in the European Theater from September 1943 through March 1945. The glider pilots were being trained to land the gliders behind enemy lines before an invasion began, often in the dark of night. Afterward, they flew to landing zones near the battlefields to resupply the fighting ground troops with more artillery, tanks, ammunition, and other small vehicles like jeeps.

The Waco CG-4A Glider was constructed of a metal tubing frame, wood flooring, and canvas skin. Its dimensions were forty-eight feet long with an eighty-foot wingspan. The CG4A payload was a maximum of 2,400 pounds, and it was large enough to carry a combination of twelve to fourteen infantry, along with ammunition, or a small jeep, as mentioned, with three to four infantry individuals. Due to its fabric skin, there was virtually no protection for individuals or equipment inside, and glider pilots rarely, if ever, wore parachutes during combat missions. Over twelve thousand CG-4A gliders were constructed for the war effort.

From Bowman Field, glider pilots were sent to Laurinburg–Maxton, Fort Bragg, and Camp Mackall in North Carolina. It was in North Carolina that more precise training for D-Day took place in the United States. After the training instruction in North Carolina, glider pilots headed to Boston Harbor, where they boarded ships for a thirteen-day trip across the Atlantic Ocean to deployment destinations in the European Theater of Operations.

During the same year and a half of Walter's training, the United States was building massive training bases in England and North

Africa for the arrival of the United States' military, which included paratroop task forces as well as the glider pilots. Both the paratroopers and the glider pilots were participants in the preparations of the major missions, which ultimately liberated Italy and France. Those missions were staged from Northern Africa but then went on to the western shores of Italy with additional amphibious invasions.

The British had been in hostilities in Africa since June 1940, even before Walter had checked in with his local draft board that year. However, the United States AAF did not arrive in Africa until later in the summer of 1942. Airborne operations began by flying British and American troops in nonstop flight patterns from England to Northern Africa in November of that same year.

Simultaneous to Walter's training preparations, a major secret mission was being planned for June 6, 1944, which was to take place almost two years later than the arrival of United States' troops to Northern Africa. Due to the enormity and complicated details of the invasion of Normandy, known as D-Day (code name Operation Overlord), it took two years to complete the planning details. Many people ask the question, "What was the United States doing for two and a half years before the D-Day invasion?" A precise answer would be: "It was preparation, preparation, and more preparations."

The Seelbach Hotel, several miles from Bowman Field, was a busy place from 6:00 a.m. to midnight, seven days a week. Military personnel swimmers used the Olympic-sized pool in the early mornings, and dancers claimed the beautiful dance floor at night, where various bands played continuously. Weeknights' entertainment stopped at midnight, but on the weekends, the music continued until 2:00 a.m. The Seelbach was a refuge, and a welcoming place before any rigorous training began.

A chance meeting of a young and beautiful hostess named Lillian after a vigorous morning swim at the hotel pool changed First Officer Lindberg's entire future in a way he could never have expected. There was indeed a war going on, but love can bloom anywhere at any time.

Lil–My Mom

A country bumpkin she never was, but Lillian Earl Cummings was born on May 24, 1921, in the small rural community of Rockvale, Breckinridge County, Kentucky. All her life, she was better known as Lil. Lil's ancestors were some of the first immigrants from England to settle in Virginia. On her maternal side, Lil's progenitors go back to William Bradford, who came on the Mayflower. Two centuries later, they settled in Daniel Boone territory in Kentucky. They were traditional farmers, as most early settlers were. Eventually, farming became a profession rather than a livelihood, and farmers, like Lil's dad, Silas Cummings, became tenant farmers. They grew crops for wealthy landowners on land they themselves could not afford to buy.

In Kentucky, after the Civil War, landowners sought laborers and low-income persons, like the Cummings family. They were called sharecroppers. That system in the early 1900s was widely used by career agriculturalists. It meant that a part of each crop the tenant farmer raised was given to the landowner for rent. It was a very hard life and financially stressful. If a natural disaster fell upon the crops, the rent on the farm property still had to be paid. Sharecroppers, like Lil's father, who were behind on their rent payments, became more like indentured servants. They had to produce more and more crops to pay their debt to the landowner. These were the hard circumstances that Lil was born into as the seventh and last child of Silas Cummings and Bessie Mamie Stone-Cummings.

I knew my mother for over many years. To my knowledge, she never returned to her roots—not even once was I ever with her at

Rockvale, Falls of Rough, or Short Creek, Kentucky, where she was born and raised. She never even returned there to bury her mother in 1962.

Lillian exhibited many characteristics of her birth order as the seventh and last child. The youngest child in a family, according to some psychologists, is thought to be highly social, very confident, creative, good at problem-solving, and extremely adept at getting others to do things for them. Youngest children are also sometimes described as "spoiled and coddled" and "unafraid to do risky things," and these characteristics fit Lil, except for not doing risky things.

Lil and her mother, Mamie Cummings, were unable to get along in her early childhood, and even less during her adolescence. Her mother was a pious woman and a firm disciplinarian. There was no room for disobedience of any kind in the household Mamie ruled. The duties of her children were set in stone, and all were held accountable if chores were not completed, whether inside or outside the house. There was great punishment to be had with "the feared razor strap" for misbehavior. Behind the woodshed was a real place in the Cummings' family life. Even the girls spent time there if they were found to have crossed their mother.

Farm labor required the help of all hands, whether it was milking, slopping the pigs, feeding chickens, collecting eggs, or carrying heavy buckets of water from the distant well. Besides the menial, everyday necessities, there were the seasonal workloads of weeding, hoeing beans and potatoes, and helping with the canning and preserving of foods for the winter months. There was little time for play or other distractions from the work that allowed survival. Even the youngest child had responsibilities.

Money was sparse, but there was always food on the table. During the days of the Great Depression, Silas Cummings did not have to worry about a job, unemployment lines, or food insecurity for his family, but he did have to worry about crop yields and the farm rent. My mom told me, "I never knew we were poor, but now that I look back on my family's circumstances, I can see that we were actually very poor, but so was everyone else. I guess that is why it wasn't noticeable."

I never attended church with my mother, nor did she ever attend church, not even at Christmas or Easter. However, church in her childhood was every Sunday, and the entire family was required to attend, rain or shine. My mother told me her family had no car. She said, "We all piled into our hay wagon in our Sunday-best clothes."

The Methodist Chapel was only a mile or two from their home, so it wasn't such a bad ordeal unless the weather was severe and made mud out of the dirt roads, or if the bridge over the falls on the Rough River was closed. Sunday was family time, but it was not always family-fun time.

When my mother talked about her father, she often became emotional. "I loved my daddy dearly, and he loved me more than all the others!" Lil said she rarely had disagreements with her father. Being the baby of seven children made her special in her father's eyes. She sat on his lap at breakfast time, "sharing my daddy's coffee with lots of milk until I was too big."

Little Lil rode with her father on the big tractor and the plow, and she followed him into his secret hiding place, where he made "moonshine." Her father did spoil her, and, yes, she was very coddled by him. She knew it and she loved him all the more for that reason. Even so, there was work for Lil, including learning the domestic skills she was expected to acquire like sewing, quilt making, and preparing food from garden to table. My mother told me, "I didn't mind sewing because I could sew for myself. Being the baby, I didn't have to sew for anyone else, my older sisters and my mother did that."

Silas Cummings was a hard worker, as he had to be, but he was also a hard drinker. In fact, Lil's father was what might be called a functioning alcoholic. He hid bottles of moonshine under the mattress in the barn and in the hen house. Each of my aunts and uncles admitted knowing this about their father. Lil told stories about how her mother confiscated the bottles and hid them somewhere else, or "if mother was really mad, she emptied the bottles!"

Lil's parents argued a lot, but she was always on her father's side whatever the situation. When her brothers sneaked into the moonshine shed, it obviously caused a lot of problems between her mom and dad besides all the other stresses of raising a large family, which they had to endure. Moonshine was important, however, for the extra money that could be acquired despite prohibition in the United States.

Silas Cummings never wanted to be a farmer, and my mother told me, "He loved music and he loved books, but he always said life directed his paths away from the things he loved." The Cummings family was always on the move during Lil's youth. They relocated from Rockvale to Falls of Rough to Short Creek to Leitchfield and back to Rockvale. Each move was an ordeal and was going to be the last one, but it never was. My mom said, "Where we lived depended on whose farmland daddy was going to be sharecropping on."

Nevertheless, even with the constant moving from place to place, the Cummings family had a piano. Lil never learned to read music, but she and her father played the piano very well by ear. Her father also had a fiddle, which he played by ear too. Lil became so adept at playing the piano without music that when she was in her early teens, she began to play hymns at church meetings. She told me, "I did not particularly like church, but I loved playing the piano there."

Practicing the hymns for her was an outlet and a relief from everyday life. Her mother allowed her to practice the hymns—so that was a good excuse when she was tired of the farm drudgery. Lil knew the words of the hymns by heart, so she sang while she played. That way she could hear where the notes sounded on the piano. She also listened to the radio, which her family was lucky to have. She learned to play contemporary music, which she heard on the radio at night.

Home, 1936

The poverty of the family's situation did not keep the children from going to school. Silas Cummings' love for books made it a necessity for his children to be educated. Many farm children dropped out of school if they were needed to help family finances, but none of the Cummings children were ever allowed to do that. Despite all the work to be done, the children had to go to school. All seven graduated from high school in an era where such wasn't the common. Lil's oldest sister, Lucille, also went to college and became a nurse. Her brothers also attended some years in college.

Lil's father insisted that his children should not only go to high school but also graduate. Lil graduated from Short Creek High School with honors. Only nine students were in her graduating class—three boys and six girls. In the picture below, Lil is the tallest girl, fourth from the left. She kept these pictures in her personal scrapbook, labeling and dating them. After I left home, my mother gave me a lot of her mementos, which she said was better for me to have in case something happened to her.

The senior class of Short Creek High School taken on April 6, 1939, the last day of school

Eighteen-year-old Lil was slender and tall at five feet and nine inches. She had very dark, nearly black hair and deep brown eyes. Her dream of marrying the perfect husband, who was a banker or lawyer or another type of successful businessman, seemed to be within her reach if only she could find a way to leave her rural life. She realized, soon after graduation, that none of her dreams were going to come true if she remained in Short Creek, Kentucky.

Lil could be funny and quite adventurous to a flaw sometimes, and her mother always told her during their disagreements, "You are so headstrong you will get into trouble someday." Lil might have been headstrong, as her mother said, but…surely she did not plan to get into trouble.

When Lil graduated from Short Creek High School, she was also determined to graduate from the lifestyle of her parents, grandparents, and great-grandparents. When she bid farewell at age nineteen to the friends she grew up with, they cried, but she didn't. Lil had bloomed into adulthood very quickly after graduation, and she was ready to begin a new chapter in her life.

She was not about to hold back her intentions to be a "city girl," which would make her an attractive catch for some young man who was also adventurous and willing to take a few risks. Lil was ready to make a new kind of life for herself. She left a heartbroken boyfriend behind in Short Creek because she was never going to be a farmer's wife!

Sharecropping, as a livelihood for many rural families mostly died out during the Great Depression, and by WWII, it was gone. The most common reason for sharecropping demise was the mechanization of farming. Small farmers, like Silas Cummings, could not afford the equipment needed to increase crop production. Many sharecroppers left the unstable farming system to seek better-paying industrial jobs in the cities. In addition, laws favored the landowners and made it difficult for the renters to sell their crops to anyone else other than the landowner, even if there was a surplus.

Mother told me, "Daddy had thoughts of going to the city, sometimes to find what he called "a real job." When there were discussions of such a move, however, she said, "Mother was fearful of another depression, and she would not even talk about leaving Short Creek." Mamie was adapted to farm life; what would she do in the city if something happened to her husband? Farm life was not for Lillian, just like city life was not for Mamie.

Unfortunately, the time for talking and/or contemplating such a big, life-changing step ended one early December afternoon. Silas Cummings suddenly had a massive heart attack and passed away on December 3, 1940. Nineteen-year-old Lillian mourned over her father's death more than any of her siblings, even more than her mother did. She played the piano at her father's funeral, and that was the last time she was ever to be in the country. She never even returned to Short Creek for her high school reunions or funerals of beloved relatives.

Silas Cummings was Mamie's second husband. She had married young, and she had a son, Edward, and her young husband fell ill and died suddenly. Her second marriage, with Silas, lasted thirty-six years and brought six more children into the world. At fifty-nine years old, there were no more husbands and no more children for Mamie. She began making and selling her handmade quilts for a living after she moved in with her daughter, Mae's family, at Falls of Rough. She made many "wedding ring quilts," which were her specialty, for newlyweds, and she sold them for $12 each. I remember well how Granny hand-quilted using very large round wooden quilting frames.

All of Lil's siblings had already left home, and since her mother was at her sister Mae's home at The Falls, there was no reason not to pack up her few belongings after her father's death and head to the city. She bought a one-way bus ticket to Louisville. The seventy-mile bus ride from Hardinsburg to Louisville must have filled Lil with excitement, not nostalgia.

It did not take Lil very long to figure out how to maneuver city transportation modes with the trolleys and taxis. She found that jobs were easy to get if one was willing to work hard. She moved in with her sister, Chrysteen, who taught Lil about paying bills and how to set up a bank account. She soon understood that the luxuries of an apartment with electricity and running water were not free.

When she and Chrysteen moved to 900 South Sixth Street in Downtown Louisville, it was a three-story, gray-brick apartment building on a busy corner. A Walgreen's drugstore was across the street. Lil adjusted quickly to her completely different life. The apartment building was not like any dwelling she had ever lived in. Living in a crowded apartment building must have seemed strange at first, but running water in the sink and not having to traipse to a stinky and spider-infested outhouse probably made any problems seem to Lil minuscule.

My mother told me how exciting it was for her and that "it was a big relief to not wake up at dawn for milking…and I did not miss the roosters crowing either." When we talked about it, I remember her disdain for all the things about living in such rural surroundings. She especially hated carrying heavy buckets of water from a pump during the winter. She said, "The snow was so deep, and there were no snowplows. When I was a child, the snow was above my waist. That was the only time I could miss school!"

One important thing, however, that rural life had taught Lil was a hard work ethic. In Louisville, she worked at all kinds of odd jobs at the post office, the drugstore, and even cleaning the landlady's apartment. My mom told me, "In 1943, things changed for me because I got a great job!" Chrys helped her to land a hostess job.

She also said, "I had no idea what a hostess did." Lil interviewed with the concierge of the hotel and somehow convinced him she could do the job. She quickly gained the skills needed, and she loved her job because the Seelbach Hotel was not just a famous and prestigious hotel, but many famous people came there for vacations.

My mother had never been to Europe, but the Seelbach's draw for guests was its European grandeur and luxury. Two Seelbach brothers from Germany built the hotel in 1905. They were wealthy immigrants and wanted the hotel to be unique in style and architecture, which it truly was. The main staircase was expansive and stunning with wide, red-carpeted steps, supported by marble stately columns imported Switzerland.

Seelbach Hotel in Louisville, Kentucky

The dining room, in which Lil was privileged to hostess, was the most exquisite of all three eating places in the hotel. The Rathskellar, as it was called, was simply breathtaking. It had Moorish-style arches and hand-painted tiles of many colors. My mom told me, "I thought fairy tales could happen there." Maybe she had hoped her own fairy tale might begin there.

There were so many unique little places in the hotel to explore with great artworks and very beautiful wallpapers. Each room was a work of art by itself. The furnishings were all imported from Europe and so much bigger and more ornate than any piece of furniture Lil had ever seen. Lil's hostess job allowed her to finally, and forever, make the break from country living. She must have imagined the charm, beauty, and experiences of a lifetime were hers to grasp and hold on to right there in the hotel.

Lil wrote to her oldest sister, Lucille, about her job at the hotel. Lucille had become a nurse and moved to New Hampshire before my mom graduated from high school. She married a prominent Jewish physician. Lil and Lucille had the same feelings about their rural past, and Lucille had encouraged her baby sister to go to Louisville to work. Lucille was interested in art, architecture, and history, so she wrote back to Lil how happy she was to learn about Lil's new job. She also encouraged Lil to go to college, but Lil was interested in more exciting things than school.

Lil was very positive about how her life was *not* going to end up. After all, the play she had been in, in high school, earned her a stage award for best actress. Perhaps, someday she might even go to Hollywood, which she had only read about. But in 1943, she was a hostess at a prestigious hotel, never to slosh through long dewy grass to milk a cow ever again! The Seelbach Hotel must have been an extraordinary place to chart a new path in her young life.

Lucille's return letters were full of information about the Seelbach and how it was famous because of F. Scott Fitzgerald's bestseller, *The Great Gatsby*, written in 1922. The book's setting took place during World War I, when the Seelbach was a hot spot for soldiers on leave. Such was also the case for hundreds of soldiers in 1942 to 1943 coming and going from Bowman Field in Louisville during WWII.

As soon as Lil got the first letter from Lucille about the Seelbach, she read the book, *The Great Gatsby*, where Fitzgerald described the hotel in all its splendor, as well as the city of Louisville. My mom said, "His descriptions were so accurate." The main characters in his book, Jay Gatsby and Daisy, supposedly fell in love at the hotel. The experiences of Jay and Daisy's fictionalized romance led many World War II couples to get married in Louisville and honeymoon at the famous Seelbach Hotel. Surely, Lil must have thought she might find romance there as well.

By 1943, there were thousands of servicemen stationed at Bowman Field before they were to be deployed to European and other foreign theaters. Many military personnel worked out in the over-sized pool at the Seelbach. Afterward, they ate breakfast in the Rathskellar dining room, where Lil was the hostess.

For most young people, when one door opens, it often leads to another door opening. Lil had no idea that the next door to open for her would change the entire trajectory of her life forever, altering in so many unexpected ways the Cinderella dream she had long imagined and planned for herself.

Lil's parents, Silas Cummings and Bessie Mamie Stone-Cummings

Mom and Lil

Lil at nine years old

Lil and her cousin Billie Louise, whom she was very close to. Billie Louise lived in Louisville, and Lil visited her sometimes when there was a school holiday. Visiting Billie Louise was Lil's first encounter with city life.

Chrysteen (left) and Lil (right) sitting on Chrysteen's first car, 1940

Romance Blooms

In 1942, it had been two years since Lil had left both her rural life in Short Creek, Kentucky, and her childhood sweetheart, Billy, behind. She and Billy had literally grown up together, and he was truly a wonderful person. All their young lives they had talked about when they would get married. It had been fun to imagine him as her husband until they graduated from Short Creek High School. It was then that my mom told me, "I realized Billy was going to be a farmer, just like his dad and my own father, but I never pictured myself as a farmer's wife."

That one sentence was just about all that my mom told me of her early romance, but my aunt Chrys told me more. She told me, "Billy was heartbroken when Lil decided to leave Short Creek. He couldn't believe she could just pack up her belongings and leave him and all their mutual friends behind." Aunt Chrys always thought it was her fault because she wanted my mom to move to Louisville to be with her. She also told me that my mother never saw or heard from anyone from Short Creek after she came to Louisville. "Telephones were few and far between at The Falls, so phone calls were not expected—and your mom was glad there was no communication. We didn't even have a phone for a long time."

Chrys talked about the pledge Lil made after leaving Billy behind. Even when Billy made a trip to the city, she wouldn't see him. "Lil was not going to get attached to any man, not just Billy, who might get in the way of her dreams. Lil knew her future did not include being married to a farmer." After their beloved father passed away, Aunt Chrys said, "Lil felt no necessity to return to the farm or the drudgery of farm life. She told me, 'I will marry a banker, a lawyer, or maybe a doctor, like Lucille.'" (Lucille is the older sister, living in New Hampshire, and married to a pediatrician.)

Lil usually walked to work every morning to the Seelbach Hotel unless it was bad weather, in which case she took a taxi. It was a short walk from Sixth Street where she lived. She had noticed as she cashiered each morning that a soldier named Walt always arrived with several of his buddies after their swimming workout in the hotel pool. He had caught her attention when she saw him with some other military personnel checking in at the hotel desk a couple of weeks before.

All the swimmers came to have breakfast together in the Rathskellar dining room where Lil worked as both cashier and waitress. She had learned the mystery soldier's name from the hotel desk clerk. None of the other girls seemed to know whom she was talking about. The unknown soldier was handsome, for sure, and his dark curly hair with one wet curl hanging on his forehead made him stand out from the others.

The Seelbach Hotel was a busy place from 6:00 a.m. to midnight, seven days a week. Military personnel swimmers used the Olympic-sized pool in the early mornings, and dancers claimed the beautiful dance floor at night, where various bands played continuously. Weeknights' entertainment stopped at midnight, but on the weekends, the music continued until 2:00 a.m.

Lil had dated several of the soldiers who came to the hotel, but none of them involved a serious relationship. Serious relationships were not the norm because most of the military guys soon left for deployment overseas. Lil had no plans to marry a soldier, anyway. Still, she wanted to meet the new guy who had recently arrived. The soldiers were all good-looking and well mannered, but most of them were wrapped up in their battle plans, and they didn't think about much else. Of course, she knew it was risky to get into a serious relationship with a soldier. Who knew what might happen to them with such a terrible war going on?

Lil didn't know much about what was going on overseas, but she listened to WGRC radio every morning before work. The station's news was painful to listen to, but it was important to be informed. She knew the soldiers at Bowman Field might soon be deployed to those far-off places she heard about on the radio, like North Africa, Italy, or the Philippines.

A mixture of all those things were probably on Lil's mind. However, there was one time of year when she always admitted she missed her previous rural surroundings. Whether at Short Creek or Falls of Rough, the early mornings and early evenings in the country were filled with mating displays and nesting calls of returning summer songbirds. Living in Louisville, so close to the Ohio River, she saw some of those same songbirds she recognized. She watched them flitting about from tree to tree, even in the city. The birds singing and nesting must have been a welcome distraction from all the chaos generated by the immense human struggle of a second World War, which was on everyone's mind.

When Lil's short walk to the hotel ended, the swimmers were already seated, and they were eating heartily. The soldier she hoped to see, the one with the wet curl on his forehead, was also there. When she scanned the table of eight, she immediately caught his gaze when his brown eyes looked up at her at the exact same moment. Their eyes met, and their smiles connected in that very instant. That was the story Lil told over and over about her first encounter with Walter Lindberg.

Walter Bert Lindberg wasn't an ordinary soldier but a glider pilot and flight officer. Many soldiers stayed at the hotel when they first arrived in town. It was a resting spot until their bunking arrangements were made at Bowman Field, where over two thousand soldiers were stationed in 1942 to 1943. That's the reason Lil had first seen Walt and one or two other soldiers checking in with their luggage.

The second time Walt's and Lil's eyes met on that same day was when he was paying for his breakfast at the cashier's stand. They struck up a conversation, and she learned Walt was from Los Angeles, California. She was so thankful he was a "city" boy. Walter, better known as Walt, had been going to college and training to be a horticulturist. He had dropped out of the University of California at Los Angeles (UCLA) after two years. He and his brother, John, were planning to go into business together after the war.

Such an idea as having a business of his own in a big city made Walt much more interesting than the farm-boy soldier from Nebraska who kept trying to get a date with Lil. The fact that Walt was a different kind of soldier, a glider pilot, was also appealing. He told her he had recently graduated from flying school in California before being assigned to Bowman Field. California was such a faraway place to Lil, almost like a foreign country, and it sounded more appealing than Short Creek, Kentucky.

While fighting was going on in Europe, the city of Louisville was providing entertainment for military personnel stationed at Bowman Field. The Seelbach and other hotels had beautiful ballrooms, where there was music and dancing every weekend. The ballrooms had flexible availability because the servicemen and women did not always have leave on the weekends. There were bands that played almost anytime they were asked to come to the Seelbach Hotel.

Another place for dancing was the Madrid Building, where there was an outdoor garden and a dance floor on the rooftop. Outdoor theaters and outdoor entertainment spaces were plentiful in the spring and summer in Louisville, as both temperatures and humidity could be stifling since there was no air-conditioning available.

After her first date with Walt, Lil received a vase of red roses and white carnations at the cashier's desk. A note was attached, which invited her to a night of dancing at the Seelbach. She accepted, even though she wasn't experienced at dancing with a live band. She confided hesitation about her lack of dancing skills to Walt, but he assured her he could teach her very quickly.

Since neither of them had their own car, they agreed to meet for dinner at the Seelbach before the dancing lessons began. They danced until midnight, and then Walt put her in a cab to go home. She hoped to see him again, but she couldn't be sure. She and her girlfriends knew that soldiers could be quite fickle in dating. That first date was on a weeknight, but on her next shift, she also found flowers from Walt, who was asking her, "Can we dance until 2:00 a.m. on Saturday night?" The bands played much longer on Saturday nights, as long as the dancers would stay and dance.

Bowman Field

Walt had been assigned to Bowman Field for combat readiness training, like thousands of other soldiers. Training for each category of military service usually lasted three months at Bowman but often much longer. Depending upon the training schedules, definite deployment dates were precarious. Glider pilots' daily training regiments were both grueling and long. They practiced single tows, combat scenarios, and search-and-rescue operations.

Bowman Field was the birthplace for Louisville aviation, and during World War II, it was "the busiest airport in the country," servicing both Navy and Air Force aircrafts as they regularly passed through. It was the temporary home for a variety of military personnel, including medics and flight nurses who all trained for their own specialties to ensure survival of the wounded in battlefield combat zones. Personal friendships with those various personnel could develop rather quickly in a very short time.

Such was the case with Walter Lindberg. One date with Walt led to another. Sometimes, when he came into town, he walked Lil home from work when her shift at the Seelbach ended. It gave them a chance to learn more about each other. Walter told her about growing up in Los Angeles and about his mother whom he called Peach. He told Lil, "Peach has always been my best girl." That gave Lil a good idea of how he felt about his mother and how he treated women in general. He told her he had not been very close to his dad "because he was always out of town when I was growing up." Walt joked about Lil's Southern drawl and how she and everyone else said "You all or y'all" before every sentence.

Lil told Walt about her rural beginnings, being born in the small rural town of Rockvale, Kentucky, and how she was so glad to be in the city. She told him, "Farm life is not for me." During those walking times, they were able to confide in each other and talk about things other than war concerns. Walt was seven years older than Lil, and he was more mature, and Aunt Chrys described him as "restless." He had a lot of energy that kept him going beyond being tired.

Neither Walt nor Lil had plans for a serious relationship. Walter told her, "I'm anxious to get to Europe and help to get this war over."

Other occasions took them to the famous Madrid Hotel known as "the best place to dance in Louisville." The admission for dancing at the Madrid was only a dollar per couple. Some of the best bands of the era played there, but one of the locals, Clyde McCoy of "Sugar Blues" fame, performed there with his resident orchestra. The beautiful dance floor was huge, and couples of all ages were seen there. With so many dancing dates with Walt, Chrys said, "Lil became quite the dancer after all."

Lil was not aware at first that those many fun hours were indeed bonding them together in ways more serious than learning to dance. She also would learn that Walt's restlessness had something to do with his past. That "something" was to impact greatly their relationship, especially any long-term plans they might think of making. Lil admittedly told Chrys one night after returning from dancing, "I'm afraid. I'm afraid I'm falling in love, I don't want to marry a soldier!"

Walter and Lil in Louisville, Kentucky, August 1943

The intense training at Bowman Field was a scary time for all military personnel sent there. The glider pilots' training was as dangerous as the combat missions they would eventually fly. Every few days there was an accident or some perilous event, which happened during training, often causing serious injuries and/or death. These events were reported in all the local newspapers in big headlines and on the radio as well.

In September 1943, five months after Walter arrived at Bowman field, two of his glider pilot buddies were killed in an aircraft training accident. Thirty aircraft were involved in a simulation of a glider mission, flying round robin from Bowman Field to Lexington, Kentucky. On the return trip, "two glider pilots collided during a left turn, doing major damage to both aircraft," as described by glider pilot Charles E. Skidmore Jr., who witnessed the accident. Both pilots died from "blunt force trauma on impact with the ground."

"Both Lil and Walter were traumatized by that event," my aunt told me. "It was a reminder to them of how perilous their relationship was." Shortly after that tragic event, Walter was assigned to the Thirty-Eighth TCG (Troop Carrier Group) and assigned to Fort Bragg, North Carolina. North Carolina is where he eventually would finish his stateside training before leaving for battlefields in Europe. That meant he would be leaving Bowman Airfield and Kentucky very soon.

About Fort Bragg

Prior to entering World War II, Fort Bragg added more barracks and a hospital, which could house up to sixty thousand soldiers. The fort was the largest post in the army at that time and became the home of the Ninth Airborne Division, which Walter was part of. Almost every aviator in WWII spent some time at Fort Bragg prior to going overseas.

Walter had not yet confided to Lil what he had never planned to tell her because they were not going to fall in love, but they did. Now that he was leaving to be stationed at Fort Bragg, it couldn't wait. One moonlit evening, he and Lil had dinner on the rooftop garden at the Madrid Hotel, where Lil was expecting another night of dancing. Walter was unusually quiet and rather subdued. On that night, he was a different person. Lil thought he was just apprehensive about his new assignment, but he was thinking about his past—a past he was about to reveal.

Lil thought maybe he wanted to discontinue their romantic notions because he was leaving soon. The scary thing to Lil was that now, she was not so sure anymore and that she did not want to marry *this* soldier sitting across from her with a serious look on his face. They had not talked about marriage, but Lil had begun to think about that possibility.

Looking across the candlelit table into Lil's smiling face, Walter's eyes began to tear up. Lil reached across the linen spread to hold his hand. Surely this was something she could help him with and make him feel better. He hesitated but then calmly and softly said, "Lil, I…I have to tell you something. I never wanted to hurt you…my feelings for you are genuine and real. I am truly in love with you but…I am married!" The shock to Lil was incomprehensible! Walt kept talking, "I have been trying to get a divorce for a long time—I'm leaving for North Carolina in a week. I will send for you as soon as I'm settled in there."

At the exact moment he dropped the bombshell news on her, he brought out a small blue jewelry box, which held two gold wedding bands. "These are for us to keep and wear until my divorce is final, and we can be married…if you are willing." Lil was almost twenty-two years old, and she had never faced such a serious dilemma. Suddenly, she had an extreme and harsh reminder that her romantic relationship with Walt had begun and flourished in deceit. How was this possible? What was she going to do now? Should she go to North Carolina to be with him, or should she break it off altogether? If she went to Fort Bragg, she would have to give up her job at the Seelbach Hotel. How was she going to tell Chrysteen about this new and awful development? A jolt like this one had not even occurred to Lil, even though her girlfriend and roommate, Dorothy, had had a similar circumstance.

Dorothy's soldier had left her high and dry. He didn't even tell her goodbye, and she was brokenhearted. Walt was not leaving Lil high and dry because there was at least some hope and promise for a distant future. Yet to say she was heartbroken and astounded at this unimaginable news was an understatement!

Lil had been taken by Walt's good looks and good manners. They had had deep and meaningful conversations. She felt she had known him for years, but this was such an unexpected happening. Her mother might indeed tell her, as she always did, that being headstrong, as she was, it had finally gotten her into trouble. She had exactly one week to make so many impossible decisions. One week, and Walt would be gone!

There had been a romance in high school, and she had dated several guys since she had come to Louisville, but none had stolen her heart like Walt. She had little control over the chemistry between them, which had immediately set them on a course they had not intended, from their very first glance at each other.

Even with the heavy burden she now had to carry with the information Walt had divulged; she knew she had to go to North Carolina. There was one train leaving daily from Louisville to Fayetteville, North Carolina. Lillian Earl Cummings was going to be on that train as soon as Walter sent for her. It wasn't something she had to think about, because not going was not an option. Of course, this was an emotional decision, and Lil had no idea where it was going to lead her.

The thought of Walt leaving to go overseas and the terrifying thought that he might not return made her decision to go a necessity. She wanted to spend every minute possible with Walter, and the impending important news she had to give him was another reason to get on that train.

Laurinburg-Maxton, North Carolina

Lil arrived in Fayetteville, North Carolina, in early October 1943. She had no idea how long she would be there. She had managed not to quit her job, but she took a leave of absence from the hotel. Walter had acquired a small apartment in Southern Pines for them to live in and be together once more. They became "married" per se, both wearing the purchased wedding rings, but there could be no official marriage license or documentation of marriage. Their time together was temporary and short because Walter had no idea of the exact date he would leave for England and the European Theater of Operations.

Flight Officer Walter B. Lindberg, North Carolina, 1943

Things were becoming more and more complicated on the domestic front with Walt and Lil. His mother was planning to come from Los Angeles to see him in North Carolina before he had to report overseas. His brother, John, and his wife were already in North Carolina. There was good news and bad news that Lil had not yet divulged to Walter. At the same time, the expanding war in Europe was beckoning more and more soldiers to more new battlefronts.

One night after dinner, they turned the radio on to hear part of a message from President Roosevelt. Thanksgiving was approaching, and he gave a Proclamation Speech to the world on November 11, 1943. Here are some of Roosevelt's words:

> God's help to us has been great in this year towards worldwide liberty. In brotherhood with warriors of other United Nations, our gallant men have won victories, have freed our homes from fear, have made tyranny tremble, and have laid the foundation for freedom of life in a world which will be free.
>
> Our forges and hearths and mills have wrought well, and our weapons have not failed. Our farmers, victory gardeners, and crop volunteers have gathered and stored a heavy harvest in the barns and bins and cellars. Our total food production for the year is the greatest in the annals of our country.
>
> For all these things we are devoutly thankful, knowing also that so great mercies exact from us the greatest measure of sacrifice and service.

The next week was a whirlwind of Walt in training and Lil not feeling well. One minute she was merely nauseous, and the next minute she had so much anxiety about Walt going overseas that she couldn't keep anything down. Finally, the week she was supposed to leave, Lil announced her good news-bad news, which she had been holding back. She told Walt, "I am pregnant." Walt was ecstatic he was going to be a father! Right away they had to go shopping. He wanted to get a baby book for Lil to record everything about the baby because he would not be around for the birth, and he was not sure when the war would be over or when he would be home.

The purchase of a baby book usually adds to the excitement of preparing for a first child. Walter and Lillian bought their baby's book in Laurinburg Maxton, North Carolina. Even though the times were so uncertain, they were happy they were going to be parents. There are places in a baby book to record the day-by-day story of the newborn. The beginning pages provide blanks for the baby's weight, length, and who the doctor was, and even a place for the name and location of the hospital where delivery might take place.

More excitement is compounded over the months of a pregnancy when both parents get to choose the crib, decorate the room, and buy baby clothes in neutral colors when the sex of the child is unknown. Lil and Walt had none of those fun and exciting choices available to them. They were not able to make any plans whatsoever. Lil would have to go back to the empty apartment in Louisville in the drab gray brick building. The apartment was so small there was no room for a formal nursery. Walter had no idea where he would be when the baby arrived. Since his time of enlistment and then active duty, he had been transferred from military base to military base in the United States and recently arrived in North Carolina to get ready to be shipped overseas to another base somewhere in England.

During such life-changing events as WWII, when Walt was about to leave for Europe, the baby book they purchased was the place where the future family-of-three memories would be recorded and put on hold in a tangible way.

Shortly after their excitement died down after Lil's announcement, Walter met his brother and wife at Camp Mackall. He wanted to tell them the latest news about himself and Lil becoming parents. Johnny's wife was a close friend of Walter's wife, and the four of them—Johnny and his wife and Walt and Lil—were going to be together for a couple of days.

Johnny and his wife knew of Walter's marriage troubles and the impending divorce, but they were not prepared for the news they received. They did not know Walter had already found a future wife or that they were expecting a child! It did not go over well for Walter with Johnny's wife, but their relationship had been tenuous at best. Tensions were high, but Walter and Johnny were close, and they needed to part on the best of terms.

Brothers John and Walter Lindberg in Camp Mackall, North Carolina, 1943

Johnny was at Camp Mackall for a couple of weeks training for MP (military police) and other duties. He was not an aviator and was not expected to be called into combat activities. There was not much time for explanations and no time at all for resolutions. Besides the incompatibility of Walt's family and his wife, Walt wanted to be a father. His wife was against having a family because of Walter's Hispanic roots. Also, Walt's wife still had family in Germany, and he was about to go to Europe to fight the Germans! These were such challenging issues with no possibility of any quick fixes.

Walter Lindberg in training at school in Southern Pines, North Carolina, 1943

Walter was here in front of the school in Southern Pines, where glider pilots were getting their maps and location training for a secret mission, which they were to participate in but which no one knew where or when it would take place. Walt liked his classes because they were like university courses. However, the grades in the US Army learning situations were not only crucial but mandatory to be high. Walt had no problem; he was an excellent student. Many lives would depend on what he was learning.

The time for Lil to leave North Carolina came quickly, and she left shortly before Thanksgiving. Though she was glad for the extra time to be with Walt, six months prior, she would never have dreamed of the predicament she was in. How was she going to explain all of this to her mother, who was at The Falls with her sister Mae? She would have to tell the details to Chrysteen when she returned to Louisville. She wasn't sure about telling her other siblings, especially her sister Lucille, who had such high hopes for Lil's education and future.

Lucille had recently written for Lil to come visit her in New Hampshire, or maybe she and her husband, Izzy, would come to the Seelbach Hotel for a vacation when the war was over. Lil knew explanations were not going to be received well by any of her family. Lil decided she would not reveal anything until she had to. Even then, when her pregnancy would become obvious, what other "details" should she tell?

When Lil returned to work and to her apartment, Walt was so completely wrapped up in training at Fort Bragg that phone calls were short, and there were long periods of time in between. The first letter he wrote was on November 26, the day after Thanksgiving. His letter was full of both sadness and hope. He tried to make Lil understand his unsolvable predicament with his wife. It was wearing on him, and he wrote:

> November 26, 1943
> Dearest Lil,
>
> Mother finally came to visit me here in NC yesterday. She was only here one day, but I was really glad to see her. I told her about you and I and about the (?) and I also let her know just how much we meant to each other. She is going to write to you and try to see you before she goes home about the fifth. She wants you and I to always keep loving each other and stay together for always.
>
> I think she can help us both—because, honey, I'm going to marry you and have you for my very own just as soon as I can get a divorce. No use talking about it anymore, I want you and

the baby, so payday I'm going to see about getting a divorce to HELL with everything and everybody, I'm going to start taking care of you and our baby. Above everything in the world, darling, I love you so much… I certainly don't want to lose you because if I did, well, I wouldn't want to live anymore—that's all—and I can't go on feeling that I might lose you because I don't keep my mind on my flying or anything—just muddles me up inside so I can't do anything right.

On payday, Walt did what he told Lil he was going to do. He went to Michigan, where his wife was staying with her family. He went there to have her sign the papers for a divorce, but she would have no part of it. After he told her he was going to be a father, she was even more hostile. Her parents encouraged her not to sign because they told her, "If Walt is killed in the war, you will get the death benefit, since you are the lawful wife." Walter was deeply devastated when he returned to Fort Bragg and the intense training for war. There was nothing more he could do. He immediately sent for Lil to return to North Carolina for the few remaining weeks or whatever time was left for them to be together.

One week before Christmas, Lil was again in Walter's arms. They were again "married" and in their Southern Pines apartment. They had already picked out names for their baby, depending upon whether a boy or a girl. Walt hoped for a boy and to name him Gary, after one of his best friends. But he wanted a special name, Alana, if it was a girl. In the South, where Lil grew up, everyone had to have a middle name, so it would be Alana Jean.

Christmas 1943 was a Christmas never to forget. Walt and Lil were snowed in for several days, which made it nice because there were no flying maneuvers in the snowstorms. They were together for three whole days without concerns for military schedules. Johnny and his wife were gone. The hope for a divorce before Walt was to leave was no longer on the table, and Lil had been in communication with Peach when she was in Louisville. She fully understood the extenuating circumstances Walt faced. Peach's phone call and a letter had given Lil hope that something positive might be on the horizon—if and when the war ended.

Lil was in North Carolina for a week or two before they learned of Walt's deployment schedule. They knew it was coming, but somehow the reality of Walt leaving and not knowing when they would be together again was an excruciating reminder that Walt was going to face combat and the possibility of serious injury or even death.

On January 25, 1944, Walt wrote a message to Lil and the baby in their baby book. It was exactly one month before he left from Boston Harbor by ship, the SS *George Washington*, for England.

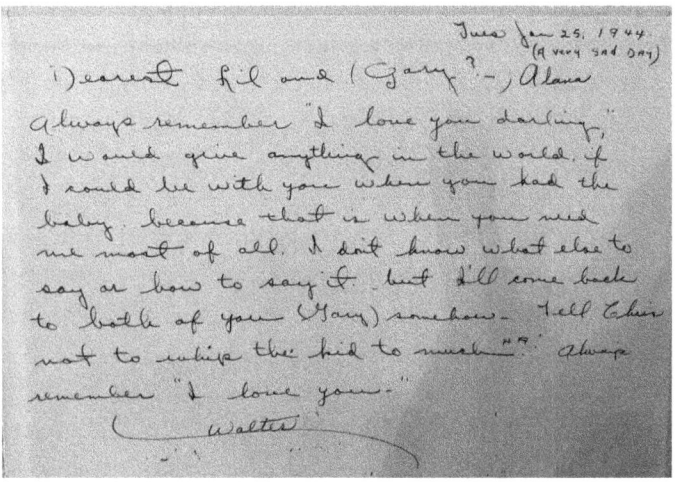

When Lil returned to Louisville again by train in February 1944, she was five months pregnant. She carried the baby book with her and she clutched it close to her heart. She and Walt had said their goodbyes with no set plans for their future as a family. It must have been that way for thousands of deployed soldiers everywhere. Such was the uncertainty of those perilous times.

Lil was now too far along in her pregnancy to continue working at the hotel. Her days were spent listening, almost every minute, to the radio for the news of the war in Europe. She had no idea where

Walt was or when she might receive a letter. He promised to write as often as possible but often was not possible, as she soon learned.

Her pregnancy began to take its toll as complications arose. Her doctor, Dr. Pearlstine, told her the outcome might not be positive. She needed to be prepared for every outcome, even if it was the worst. Every day she looked for letters from Walt. Every day she saw the Western Union vehicle in her neighborhood, praying it would not stop at her mailbox to deliver a telegram of grief. Lil's delivery and recovery date was scheduled for late June 1944. The continued drama and uncertainty for both herself, Walt, and the baby was the same day after day.

In Southern California, Los Angeles specifically, where Walter was born and grew up, June is often described as June Gloom. When the skies are dark gray and dreary due to regional ocean currents and strange weather patterns, the month of June brings hazy mornings and coastal drizzles, more often referred to as marine layer by those who live there.

June in Louisville, Kentucky, in 1944, where Lil awaited the birth of their first child, was in the state of June Bloom, not June Gloom. Temperatures in the balmy eighty to ninety degrees gave rise to multicolored roses, poppies, and pink orchids in gardens everywhere. The newscasts, however, were a distraction from the beauty and bounty of the summer's blooming landscapes.

Every newscast was about a victory or a defeat in faraway places Lil had never heard of. There was no location reporting, as there is now. Portable broadcasting and reporting equipment was not so portable, and neither was it digital or instantaneous. War correspondents were usually based in cities far from the front lines, and often they became "unwitting victims of misleading military briefings."

Broadcasting was not moment by moment, 24-7, as it is today. Interesting, also, were the behind-the-scene measures taken so nothing was leaked in advance about what was to happen. If only "the microphone could have been in the midst of the battle," one journalist wrote, but it was not possible during WWII. There was no eyewitness approach to journalistic broadcasting during combat activities.

Lil spent her time writing to Walt every day, but when she received a letter from him, there was never any continuity. Letters arrived weeks after they were written, and it was obvious on both ends that some letters were never received. For Lil, it was just about worrying—and waiting—and hoping and praying not just about Walt but also about the upcoming birth and confinement.

Prelude to Normandy

July 1943

One might ask the question, what was the United States doing in the two years after the bombing of Pearl Harbor on December 7, 1941? After all, the invasion of Normandy began some two and a half years later, on June 6, 1944.

The question can be answered: first, there was a two-year plan in the making for the invasion of Europe. Second, it took most of the next two years to build the enormous military complex. The manufacturing of thousands of different airplanes along with ground assault equipment such as, tanks, canons, mortars, rockets, bombs, guns, and ammunition were all needed. Not to mention the clothing needed for the hundreds of thousands of troops and other personnel. The people of the United States combined their efforts to help produce and manufacture the following equipment:

- 22 aircraft carriers
- 8 battleships
- 48 cruisers
- 349 destroyers
- 420 destroyer escorts
- 203 submarines
- 34 million tons of merchant ships
- 100,000 fighter aircraft
- 98,000 bombers

- 24,000 transport craft
- 58,000 training craft
- 93,000 tanks
- 257,000 artillery pieces
- 105,000 mortars
- 3,000,000 machine guns
- 2,500 military trucks

Along with all the other military hardware to be manufactured during the war period was also the construction of the United States version of their own combat glider.

The concept of the glider can be traced to the end of WWI. After the war was over, Germany was not allowed to have an air force. However, they were not prohibited from building gliders for recreational use, so glider clubs sprang up all over Germany. Learning to fly gliders was taught in high schools as part of the curriculum for those who wanted to learn to fly. When the Nazis came to power in 1933, those young glider students became the core of the newly formed German Air Force known as the Luftwaffe.

In the early part of WWII, Hitler was successful in perfecting the strategy of landing behind enemy lines in gliders in both daytime and nighttime invasions. When the United States began the task of constructing gliders, military contracts were issued to numerous US aircraft companies to build all the many different aircraft. The famous Waco CG-4A glider was designated as the design that would be implemented. The CG would stand for "Combat Glider." The conceptual design of the CG-4A originated with the Waco Aircraft company of Missouri, but numerous different contractors would participate in its construction. There were at least fifteen different aircraft companies that built the CG-4A, the largest constructor being the Ford Motor Company.

When the United States entered WWII, the goal was to build as many gliders as quickly and could be rapidly built. All total, over fourteen thousand CG-4A gliders were constructed between 1942 and 1945. Most often these gliders flew one-way missions and were not built to last beyond one crash landing as all were equipped with landing skids. During training and practice sessions, the CG-4A could also have landing wheels attached so that it could make landings on runways. The CG-4A was built to be expendable, as their landings in most cases would be a one-time-only semi-crash landing. One of the unique design ideas implemented in the CG-4A was that the nose and cockpit in one piece could be raised for loading in vehicles such as jeeps and artillery. These were the gliders that my dad and over four thousand other glider pilots flew into combat and landed behind enemy lines during the war.

Combat Glider CG-4A during the WWII

The Waco CG-4As were constructed of a metal tubing frame, wood flooring, and a canvas skin. It had an eighty-two-foot wingspan and was forty-eight feet long. The CG-4A payload carried a maximum of 4,100 pounds. It was large enough to carry a combination of twelve to fourteen paratroopers with ammunition or a small jeep and four to five troopers. The CG-4A received its baptism of fire on July 9, 1943, when a small number of gliders flew support missions for the British in the invasion of Sicily. However, the first great task for the pilots and their gliders would be eleven months later for the early morning invasion of Normandy, known as D-Day—June 6, 1944.

My father had previously been in the California National Guard but not as an aviator. Upon receiving his flight training during a two-year period, he was assigned to Bowman Field in Louisville, Kentucky. All of the glider pilots received flight training there in the CG-4A gliders.

Bowman Airfield was a critical training stop before shipping off to Fort Bragg and then overseas to England. In England, more training continued but not just training to fly the gliders. The training also included learning the logistics of constructing thousands of gliders, which were shipped from the United States to England in cargo boxes like model airplanes.

After his time in Louisville, my dad, along with other pilots of the 439 TCG, was sent to Laurinburg–Maxton Air Base and Fort Bragg in North Carolina where they waited for departure to England. Upon his leaving the United States in February of 1944 and travelling by ship to England, Walter was assigned to Upottery Field in the southwest of England with the 94 TC Squadron of the 439 TCG. That was his home base, but constant moving from base to base was typical for flight officers because of the curriculum and the specialty of flight activities being learned before going into battle.

During the winter months of 1943 to 1944, bases were being constructed all over England and North Africa for the arrival of the United States military, including the paratroop task forces, to initiate operations in preparing to liberate Italy. Those missions were staged from Northern Africa and were coordinated with other planned amphibious attacks in several other locations in Northern Africa, Sicily, and Italy, which started prior to 1944.

Though British and American troops were being flown from England to Northern Africa in November of 1942, Walter did not arrive in England until two years later in March of 1944. Prior to Walter's arrival, the 439 TCG pilots were flying from Upottery airfield in England to Algeria, North Africa, in support of the conflict between General Patton and Germany's Rommel.

In the late summer of 1943, while my father was completing his final training in Louisville and then Fort Bragg, the invasions of Sicily and Italy were underway. The two main landing points for amphibious landings in Italy were Salerno and Anzio. The objective was to drive the Germans northward out of Italy. Winter came early in 1943, and the task was made more difficult as ground troops encountered extreme cold and wet weather conditions as rain turned to snow during the fall and early winter.

One diary describes those conditions as follows:

> Thousands of men have not been in the dry for weeks. Other thousands lie at night in

the high mountains and the temperatures below freezing with the thin snow sifting over them. They dig into stones and sleep in little chasms behind rocks and half caves. They live like men of prehistoric times…

In the previous September of 1943, Walter's cousin Armando Cota from Baja, California, had already landed on the beachhead of Salerno, Italy, in preparation for advancing northward to Rome. Armando was fighting for the liberation of Italy that continued into the winter of early 1944.

Eventually, with Rome and Italy liberated, bases could be established in Italy preparatory for future missions into Southern Europe. The Germans had to be driven back to their homeland. Equally important airborne bases were established along the coastline of Italy for preparations for the invasion that would take place later in August 1944 in Southern France, known as Operation Dragoon, which my father and other pilots were practicing daily for.

At the same time in March 1944, during planning of these invasions, Walter was anticipating the arrival of his new son or daughter. In a letter from England, Walt sent a picture of the English Horsa glider and wrote on the back: "Getting ready for a mission, note the size of the British gliders." A select few of American glider pilots were also being trained to fly the British gliders because they were larger and could carry more equipment and more troops than the CG-4A American gliders.

British Horsa glider

From March until June, the thousands of men of the Army Air Forces (AAF) and infantry and paratroop divisions were engaged in other activities besides training. During the time of February through May, instruction classes were taught to include activities such as learning how to recognize German uniforms, enemy aircraft recognition, the tedious task of learning maps, including small towns and villages. The study of maps was critical in learning the coastlines of France, Belgium, and Holland. These maps showed potential landing areas as well as hazardous areas to avoid. Pop quizzes were given without notice for a pilot to recognize a small portion of the geography to ensure thorough memorization.

Learning escape and evasion techniques as well as avoiding booby traps were critical for survival. Learning how to recognize and transmit codes were helpful to avoid entrapment. Even classes on morality and manners were important to keep the trust of local civilians that surely would be encountered.

However, it was not all work and no play. Military command allowed the men to keep their competitive spirits alive by allowing them to participate in games, which involved competition between troop carrier groups to keep the morale high among the men. The competitions included one-hundred- and two-hundred-yard dashes, tugs-of-war, softball games, greased pig contests, and bike and sack races. These activities were sandwiched in between parachute-packing contests as well as their typical daily activities. It helped to pass the time as the men were waiting for the inevitable command that would come on the day before June 6, 1944. It was time for the invasion to begin.

Meanwhile, Lillian waited every day for the mail. She was looking for red, white, and blue envelopes with the return address "F/O W. B. Lindberg, T-1179, 94 TCS and 439 TC Group, APO #133 c/o Postmaster, New York, N.Y. USA," just as anxiously as she waited for each radio broadcast. She was also waiting for the baby to arrive. Rest and sleep, as the doctor had advised, did not come easily for Lil.

Home Front

While Walt was on the battlefront in Europe, Lil was on the home front, preparing for the upcoming birth. She was also helping in the war effort wherever she could. Walter was busy helping to build gliders, and he was also training for upcoming glider missions. Preparations in both the United States and England were in full force.

The *home front* is defined in the dictionary as "the civilian population and the activities of a nation whose armed forces are engaged in war abroad." The activities in the United States on the home front included activities at manufacturing plants, at hospitals, and especially at the many training places like North Carolina's Laurinburg–Maxton Air Base where Walt had spent the last few months before going overseas.

Laurinburg–Maxton in North Carolina and Bowman airfield in Kentucky were just two of the home-front installations, which were critical to war combat activities abroad. Laurinburg–Maxton had only been in existence since 1942, almost exactly one year after the Pearl Harbor attack and only one year before Walter arrived there. In that one year, it became the largest training base in the United States for aviators. North Carolina, like Kentucky, produced tobacco and textiles, but both states were known as giant hubs for "drawing people and money," which was so critical and necessary for liberating Europe and winning the war.

Every state was involved in some way—even if it was only the imperative activities having to do with rationing of goods and supplies for the purpose of preventing waste. Every person was issued a ration book with coupons. Even children were issued such books. No one could purchase rationed goods without their ration book or card.

There were lots of shortages on the home front but only in items critical to the war effort, like sugar, tires, gasoline, meat, coffee, canned goods—and yes, even shoes, which were on the rationed list! Fresh fruit and vegetables were not rationed, but there were shortages all over the United States, which was the biggest reason for encouraging everyone to have home-front gardens.

Rationing was hard on everyone on the home front no matter which state one lived in, whether in the cities or rural areas. People were encouraged to plant gardens on any spare plot of land available. In Lil's case, where she lived, people planted gardens on rooftops of garages and other buildings. The mantra of the day was, "Dig on for victory." Even children could work in the gardens on the home front to support the war effort.

It was later noted that people became healthier due to rationing. Eating patterns changed for the better. People ate more fruits and vegetables, and they ate less meat, fat, eggs, and sugar. No matter rich or poor, rationing affected everyone.

Rooftop Victory Garden, June 1941
Royal Hawaiian Hotel, Honolulu, Hawaii

Today we sometimes hear people talking about paying or giving "their fair share," and rationing was a guarantee that goods were distributed fairly on the home front. However, there were some things, like ice cream, not available on the home front. Yet ice cream was made available on the battle front and in hospitals for wounded soldiers.

Lil was in the last stages of her pregnancy, and the only thing she craved was ice cream—strawberry ice cream. Of course, there was no such thing available in Louisville! One of the first items to be banned on all the home fronts was ice cream. The brass in the army and Navy insisted soldiers should have three servings of ice cream a week. Some outposts even made their own ice cream to send into the battlefield!

Another major problem on the home front was that ration books and coupons could only be used by the persons whom they were issued to. It was difficult for others to pick up rationed items for those who couldn't go shopping for themselves.

Lil sometimes volunteered at the local rationing board, where rationing books were issued and where lost books were returned. There were other federal rules and regulations that Kentuckians had to deal with on the home front. The War Production Board (WPB) cut production of American automobiles so that jeeps and tanks could be made for the military.

Between the cut production edict, the gasoline shortages, and the rationing, there were fewer cars available for purchase. Another real problem, besides the unavailability of automobiles and not being able to have steak dinners for Kentuckians, was that gasoline and cigarettes became items that were sold on black markets at exorbitant prices.

The home-front occupations in Kentucky, which concerned Lil, were volunteer projects at the local Red Cross or the Salvation Army or other charity locations. The Red Cross was extremely important both at home and abroad. They provided emergency communications from family members, as well as collected blood and plasma for troops. Red Cross volunteers worked in hospitals and hospital ships. There were many activities locally that kept volunteers busy almost 24-7. Women were invaluable in all Red Cross services, whether nurses or volunteers, on the home front.

Red Cross volunteers at work
(Red Cross nurses pictures WWII website)

Both Lil and Chrysteen worked in packing plant facilities putting together C rations to send abroad. C rations were sent to New York first and then distributed to military bases everywhere. These were lifeline crucial activities, which supported all the soldiers in every battlefield location, as well as on home military bases.

There were home fronts for each of the belligerents—or war combatants, and whether on the winning or losing side, all countries had shortages, as well as black markets. Every country had their wounded and their dead to care for. Many home fronts had starving children and homes without heat, firewood, or food. Walter wrote to Lil about some of the home front horrors of war on his side of the world, which was much worse than Lil's problems in Kentucky.

There were blessings for Lil to count where she was; she did not have bombs whistling down on city streets; and Louisville was a bustling, thriving city on the move with war efforts. It was not a war-torn city in which people had to face smoldering piles of rubble and transportation at a complete standstill.

Another dilemma was that soldiers on foreign soil were paid in foreign currencies. Historians have written much about the wartime "currency control fiasco," which developed because of the dollar shortage in the foreign countries. Walter did not have money to send Lil very often, but when he did, it was either in pounds or francs.

The foreign currencies Lil did receive made it difficult for her to exchange. The exchange rates were always changing. Many banks were hard-pressed to exchange *any* foreign currencies because they were trying to maintain money controls to support the war effort both on the home front as well as abroad.

Even though Lil could not go to work, she still had to pay rent and get her rationed items. After all, she was eating and living for two rather than just herself. Walt tried to enclose money in his letters, as he promised to do. He wrote to her, "I volunteer for everything to get extra flying pay, and I take care of the brass' uniforms, which adds a little as well. Ha."

As Lil's delivery date drew closer and closer and complications began to arise with her pregnancy, volunteering and helping on the home front came to an end. She was confined to bed rest most of the time, with Chrysteen coming to bring her nourishment and to check on her well-being.

The war efforts in Kentucky, as well as all over the United States, were absolute *total* efforts. Many Americans purchased war bonds if they could. Women replaced men in so many venues, whether in sports leagues, orchestras, or in other all men workspaces. Women worked hard to create communities of volunteers that conducted scrap metal drives or clothing drives for the needy.

Women took over manufacturing jobs that once were held only by men. They became electricians, plumbers, welders, and riveters. Thus, some women became known as Rosie the Riveters while they worked in defense plants. Every effort and sacrifice was deemed imperative to build the armaments necessary for winning the war.

The WWII Home Front (US National Park Service)

Without the home front's full support of the government, many manufacturers turning out weaponry, citizens enduring the rationing of necessities, communities collecting scrap metal, and even women not wearing nylon stockings so parachutes could be made helped all those in the military who were fighting to win the war. Kentucky produced jeeps, cargo planes, machine guns, and components for atomic bombs, along with all the other dire necessities, for the total effort of winning the war.

The culmination of all the efforts and preparations both on the home fronts and the battlefields was to get ready for the largest amphibious invasion in history, which was unknown to all those individuals whose lives had been torn upside down for a war, not even in their own country.

Most people knew it was soon to be carried out somewhere in Europe, but no one knew where. The Allies on their own home fronts abroad were carrying on activities in various locations to divert the Germans from learning where the invasion was going to take place. They built fake tanks and artillery and other equipment and placed in locations to make the enemy think the invasion would take place far from where it was going to happen.

The Germans on their own home fronts continued their war efforts, but they had no idea that the beaches of Normandy were going to be where thousands of ships would land, bringing troops, tanks, and other armored vehicles and accessories for war into France.

D-Day Normandy

Soldiers, Sailors and Airmen of the Allied Expeditionary Force! You are about to embark upon the Great Crusade, toward which we have striven these many months. The eyes of the world are upon you. The hopes and prayers of liberty-loving people everywhere march with you. In company with our brave Allies and brothers-in-arms on other Fronts, you will bring about the destruction of the German war machine, the elimination of Nazi tyranny over the oppressed peoples of Europe, and security for ourselves in a free world. (https://www.eisenhowerlibrary.gov/sites/default/files/research/online-documents/d-day/order-of-the-day.pdf)

My father, along with hundreds of other glider pilots, were arriving each week in South Hampton, England, in March 1944. From there, they were transported to one of three different airfields in preparation for what would become known as D-Day (Invasion of Normandy, France). The new pilots were to spend the next few months continuing to practice flying and completing other duties, preparing them for the D-Day invasion, which was to be, "somewhere" in Northern Europe.

Among those men were two pilots, Eldon W. Mueller and J. Curtis Goldman. They both had recently completed their flight training in the United States at Laurinburg–Maxton airfield in North Carolina. They were about ninety days behind my father in their training and did not arrive in England until April 1944.

Eldon Mueller was assigned to the 439 TCG, 94 TCS the same as my father, and they became bunkmates. J. Curtis Goldman, Goldie to his friends, was assigned to the 441 TCG. The 439 TCS quarters were at Upottery Field, whereas the 441 TCG was assigned to Merryfield airfield about thirty miles away. When the flight officers were given leave, Mueller and Goldie met up as often as possible to have some fun.

A week before the planned invasion of Normandy, Goldie pulled a couple of flight "stunts" in an airshow that was held in front of some high-up military brass. Unbeknownst to Goldie, the brass among the audience was the Supreme Allied Commander, General Dwight D. Eisenhower, and the prime minister of England, Winston Churchill. Those on the ground watching were not impressed when they saw a glider pilot hanging out the window of his glider, showing off to all who were watching. Goldie's actions caused him to be reprimanded and cost him the opportunity to fly on D-Day, which was very disappointing to him. The 439 TCG, 94 TCS, including Eldon Mueller and my father, Walter Lindberg, participated in Operation Overlord without Goldie.

To the tens of thousands of Allied soldiers that participated, neither the date nor the invasion location was known ahead of time. It was a closely held secret only known to the Allied commanders. They gave it the name of Operation Overlord and unknown to the Germans, the beaches of Normandy would be the destination.

Operation Overlord was the name given to the entire planned invasion of Normandy. It was then broken down into specific missions and assigned other names, according to which branch of the military was assigned to carry out the mission. The assault area to be completed by the United States Eighty-Second Airborne behind the beaches of Normandy was called Operation Neptune. Those missions were further broken down according to the Troop Carrier Group (TCG) number. They were typically named after cities in the United States. In the case of my father's mission, the 439th TCG and the 441st TCG was named Hackensack after Hackensack, New Jersey. Other glider missions for D-Day were named Detroit, Elmira, and Galveston and included four other TCGs.

The glider pilots were trained to fly various types of gliders into Europe. One was the American-made CG-4A, typically called the Waco glider, and two giant British-made gliders, the Hamilcar and the Horsa. The CG-4A was a smaller glider with a wingspan of eighty-three feet. The Waco's length was forty-eight feet and height of fifteen feet. It had a carrying capacity of four thousand pounds.

The Waco carried approximately thirteen troopers with some light artillery, or it could carry a jeep and three or four infantry personnel. It was constructed of metal tubing, plywood, and an outer skin of canvas. By comparison, the giant Horsa glider was the second largest flying aircraft of WWII, next only to the Boeing B-29, which eventually came toward the latter part of the war and was the bomber that dropped the atomic bomb on Japan.

The Horsa had an eighty-eight-foot wingspan and was sixty-eight feet long. It could carry thirty infantry or paratroopers, more than double the Waco glider. The Horsa could carry as many as four jeeps or a combination of jeeps, other artillery, and infantry, even a tank. The United States purchased the larger gliders from Britain so that more cargo could be delivered. Some of the better American glider pilots were selected to learn to fly the large Horsas. Walter had demonstrated his unique flying skills and his steady and consistent decision-making process and was one of the most skilled pilots selected to fly the Horsa on D-Day+1. (June seventh), named Operation Hackensack.

Once settled in England, Walter's and other GP's duties, besides flying, were to assemble the gliders when they arrived in England. When the CG-4A gliders arrived by ship, they were unpacked from crates and assembled like giant model airplane kits. Walter had previous experience in his knowledge of aircraft building because he had worked at an aircraft facility in Long Beach, California, so it was a very familiar task for him and it came easily. These were typically the way days were spent until the middle of May when flight training began to intensify.

Finally, after almost four months of waiting, General Dwight D. Eisenhower, after much discussion with the others in high command, made the decision to proceed immediately to cross the English Channel and storm the northern beaches of France.

439 TCG glider pilot morning briefing before D-Day for Operation Overlord, with Walter sitting on the second row second from the left

The pilots and paratroopers were well prepared and ready to leave at a moment's notice. After much deliberation by all those in command positions, the Allied decision was made to start the invasion of the Normandy beaches—which were Utah, Omaha, Sword, Gold, and Juno—to commence on June 6, 1944. The following picture is of the Horsa and CG-4A gliders preparing for takeoff the morning before D-Day.

At 0647 (6:47 a.m.) on June sixth, a section of two beaches, each approximately eight miles in width, was previously designated as Utah and Omaha beaches. Splitting these two beaches was a rocky steep cliff area that divided Utah beach to the west and Omaha beach to the east. That high rocky point was known as Pointe du Hoc. This is where the American invading forces first came upon the Normandy shores.

On the morning of June 6, along those two beachfronts, the shoreline was quiet and serene. In the breaking light of the morning, the sky was overcast with a heavy marine layer that is typical for early morning hours at the beach. The tide was gradually receding from the shoreline, revealing over two hundred yards of smooth wet sand disappearing under shallow gentle waves that were quietly breaking on the sand. Small, feathered songsters were tweeting their tunes in the trees and bushes all along the beach that early calm morning. The birds had no idea that directly behind them were hundreds of German troops arising from their bunks in their sheltered concrete forts, still wondering if and when an invasion was going to take place. Neither the birds nor the Germans had any idea that hidden three to four miles offshore in the distance were thousands of Allied naval ships made up of battleships and other amphibious landing craft hidden in the early morning haze. The small creatures in the bushes and on the ground were sandwiched between the two most powerful military forces ever assembled. They were to be the witnesses of the largest amphibious land invasion in the history of mankind.

Suddenly, the silence was broken. In the distance out into the English Channel, huge balls of fire erupted from the muzzles of the large cannons of great battleships, followed by the enormous roar of the cannon fire, completely shattering the calmness of the morning. As the birds scattered from the trees, many fell from the sky from fright. The next eight hours brought the constant roar of German guns firing back on the attacking ships, along with machine gun fire aimed from the beach top hills directed at American troops as they were charging onto the beaches.

The American troops were attacking at Omaha and Utah beaches while the Army Rangers were scaling the cliffs of Point du Hoc to capture large German gunnery sites. Fifteen to twenty miles farther east were the British and Canadian forces attacking Juno, Sword, and Gold beaches. No one could have imagined the enormous armada of the combined forces of all the Allies attacking in unison.

Omaha Beach, June 6, 1944

The first airborne waves of the attack were those participating in Operation Neptune. The 101st Airborne was designated Force A and consisted mostly of C-47 aircraft dropping over thirteen thousand paratroopers behind enemy lines two to three miles behind Utah and Omaha beaches. The closest town to the center of the battle was Saint Mere Eglise, which is where a majority of the paratroopers landed, as well as gliders landing with artillery, medical supplies, and military vehicles.

The glider portion of Operation Neptune was referred to as Force B. On the British airfields, Upottery, Merrifield, and Exeter, over a hundred C-47 towplanes were assigned to tow the gliders. At the moment of takeoff, the massive movement of C-47s with 130 Horsa and 52 Waco gliders in tow lifted off and assembled into formation in the sky over southwest England.

The massive force of aviators then turned southeastward toward Normandy. The objective of their mission was to drop thousands of paratroopers directly behind the beaches. The gliders also carried infantry and supplies to various DZs (drop zones) inland from the beaches. The gliders then landed in one of four assigned LZs (landing zones). Each landing zone was given its own name. On June 6, the landing zones were Mission Detroit and Mission Elmira. On D-Day+1 (June seventh), the missions were Galveston and Hackensack.

The four designated landing areas for the gliders were referred to as the Coastal Sector. The objective of Force A was to drop paratroopers near and around German-occupied small villages. One such village, Sainte-Mère-Église, was two miles directly behind Utah Beach. During the assault in the early morning hours, unplanned wind gusts swept paratroopers beyond their drop zone area and put them directly into the German-occupied French village. It was the most catastrophic incident of the massive invasion. The paratroopers were shot in the sky while attempting to land. This was also the famous incident where one American paratrooper landed on top of the roof of the local cathedral and his parachute was caught, leaving him dangling high above the ground as a helpless target for the Germans below. To this day every year, as the villagers celebrate the annual liberation of Sainte-Mère-Église on June 7, 1944, there is a special commemoration for that American patriot.

Utah Beach saw the most ferocious and deadly fighting. In the surrounding fields and orchards of Sainte-Mère-Église, the glider pilots noticed Germans had flooded the agricultural fields from water of nearby estuaries, causing midflight changes during the landing approach at various landing zones. Numerous gliders landed in the flooded fields, making the extrication of men and equipment from the gliders almost impossible.

The Germans had installed four- to six-foot-high posts some twenty feet apart all throughout the fields so as the gliders approached their LZs, they would become deadly, colliding with the posts, which tore off the wings and punctured the bottoms of the gliders. Remember, the fuselage of a glider was only made of canvas, which was easily destroyed upon landing on those "kraut asparagus."

Glider landings at Sainte-Mère-Église during Operation Overlord, D-Day

Both British Horsa gliders and American CG-4A gliders landed in the flooded fields a quarter of a mile from Sainte-Mère-Église, France, as shown in the photo above. One can see only a small portion of the number of gliders that landed.

The Germans also trimmed tree branches form the trees so that the trees would be hard to see as the gliders made their landing approach. The trees were twenty to thirty feet high and could bring the gliders crashing to the ground full of equipment and troops. As surviving pilots and troops fled from the ruined gliders, they came under immediate machine gun fire from as close as one hundred yards away by German troops. Dozens of men perished by drowning amidst the gunfire, and almost 60 percent of the equipment was lost.

The next day, June seventh, called D+1, meaning one day after June sixth, the Eighty-Second Airborne, my father's 439th Troop Carrier Group (TCG), was joined by the 441st TCG and commenced their portion of Operation Neptune. It was part of Force B and was code-named Hackensack. The objective was to bring in more troops and artillery. The area was called Merderet Sector, named after the Merderet river, which was an area approximately five miles inland from Utah Beach and adjacent to Sainte-Mère-Église. The aircraft left their respective airfields at 0600 (6:00 a.m.) and repeated the same maneuver in the sky as the next wave of gliders headed toward Normandy. This serial of gliders included thirty British Horsas and twenty US CG-4As. My dad was flying one of those British Horsa gliders.

After an hour-and-fifteen-minute flight at 0900, the proposed LZ of Les Forges came into view. Over the next four hours, the gliders encountered many of the same treacherous landing conditions that had awaited the two missions the day before. The mission was deemed a success with all the men and supplies being delivered on both sides of the Merderet river, local bridges being destroyed, and German infantry in small French villages being captured.

With the success of the four TCGs that participated behind the beaches of Normandy, the glider pilots returned to the beachhead the next day to be transported by ship back to Southampton and then overland back to Upottery, Exiter, and Merryfield airfields, awaiting the next assignment for more critical ammunition and medical supplies to be delivered.

According to Walter's individual flight records, he flew missions from Upottery Field to France on the sixteenth, twentieth, and thirtieth of June, making a total of four flights in June. Of those dates, he flew the Horsa glider on the seventh, sixteenth, and thirtieth. He flew the CG-4A on the twentieth. Soon after the invasion of Normandy, the Horsa glider was retired because of its size and its unsafe flying record. There were many more casualties flying the Horsa gliders as compared to the CG-4A, most likely because of its size and difficulty landing in smaller LZs (landing zones).

However, twenty days after D-Day+1, the waiting was finally over. On June 27, 1944, Lil gave birth to a new little girl back in Louisville, Kentucky. Walter and Lil had decided if they had a daughter, they would name her Alana. Walter did not find out until a few days later about the new arrival of his baby daughter. Below is the telegram he received from Lil's sister announcing Alana's arrival.

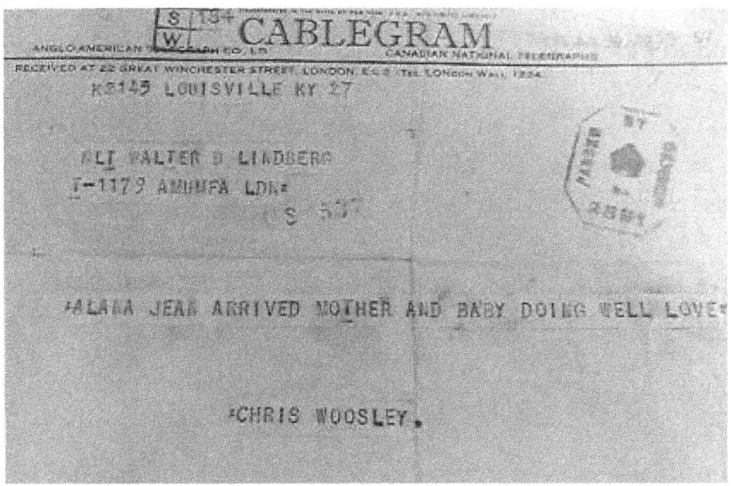

Another occurrence happened that day for Walter. He was awarded the Medal of Honor for his extraordinary bravery on his D-Day+1 mission. He wrote to Lil, "PS. Tell Alana her daddy received the Air Medal on June 27, 1944."

The toll of lost glider pilots for D+1 was, out of one hundred pilots, eighty-seven returned. The remaining thirteen had been either lost in battle or taken prisoner of war. By all measures, it was a huge success because the casualty rate for future missions ended up being much higher.

Already in the planning was the next mission that would come six weeks later. During that time, Walter flew additional fourteen flights to prepare for the next invasion. Having successfully completed Normandy in Northern France, the next invasion would now be directed at the coastline of Southern France and would be called Operation Dragoon.

Many decades later, my husband and I were able to visit that hallowed ground of Normandy beach. It was June 6, 2014, exactly seventy years later from that historic day. We were moved to tears as we observed the hundreds of rows of gravesites of our fallen American and allied heroes who died that day seventy years ago. There were the rows and rows of white crosses and Stars of David that marked the grave of each fallen patriot. There are over nine thousand graves of American patriots who shed their blood on the beaches of Normandy. We were equally moved at how the French population showed their appreciation. On one occasion, a young French teenage girl asked us, "Are you American?" My husband answered, "Yes, we are." In her French accent, she. Said, "Thank you for the sacrifice that you made for our fathers and grandfathers." We were moved that such a young person would declare their appreciation for us as Americans. In spite of what many say about how the French disparage Americans, we learned that day that in Northern France, they have not forgotten what America did for France.

The American flag waves proudly in the breezes over the beach on the hillside above Omaha Beach. It presides over that last resting place of those American heroes. My husband and I, as we were making our way down a pathway to Omaha Beach, noticed that due to its sacredness, the beaches were empty and only visitors paying respects may come down on to the beach. It is not a place for laughter and frivolity.

As we slowly walked back up the pathways from the beach, we reflected that we had stood on the sands of the beach where thousands had died. Along the pathways, there were still remnants of old German concrete barricades and concrete holes where machine guns had been mounted. Though our mood was solemn, our spirits were lifted as we heard chirping and tweeting of the songbirds singing once again in the trees and bushes that overlook that hallowed beach. They had resumed the singing that their ancestors had carried on before that morning of June 6, 1944. All was well once again on Omaha Beach.

Omaha Beach during the seventieth anniversary of
the Invasion of Normandy, June 6, 2014

Operation Dragoon

Invasion of Southern France
August 14, 1944

In early July of 1943, Allied troops were transported from bases in Northern Africa, initiating a large amphibious invasion taking place along the southern shores of Sicily on July 10, 1944, driving the enemy northward to the port city of Messina.

The invasion was so overwhelming that Italy surrendered within twenty days and Benito Mussolini was arrested on July 24, 1944. With Italy having surrendered and now out of the war, the Allied forces attacked Messina only to find out that over one hundred thousand German and Italian troops traversed the Strait of Messina crossed from Sicily and escaped into Italy. Accordingly, the Allied forces invaded Italy at the coastal port town of Salerno. Though the Italians had surrendered, the Nazi forces were still occupying the towns and cities of Central and Northern Italy. Thus, the Americans were engaged with the stubborn Germans for the next eight months in a fierce struggle through the winter and into the spring of 1944.

The Nazis knew the Allies would eventually be on the doorstep of Germany. The continued conflict in Italy had gone on longer than expected, making it impossible to establish bases from which to launch an attack on Southern France.

In December of 1943, while the Italian hostilities were in full swing, the Combined Allied Chiefs had decided on a plan to invade Northern and Southern France sometime in June of 1944 simultaneously. The two invasions would be called Operation Overlord (Normandy) and Operation Anvil (Southern France). Due to the demands of Overlord, Anvil was postponed from June to August, and it was later renamed Operation Dragoon.

Two weeks after the successful Overlord invasion of Normandy, a meeting was called in London to discuss strategies going forward among top Allied commanders for upcoming invasions. The British were highly in favor of pushing northward through Italy across Austria and into the Balkans as Churchill recommended. The desire was to keep the Balkans from being invaded by the Russians and falling into Communist hands. Certainly a worthy consideration because at the conclusion of the war, that concern became a reality.

However, the Supreme Allied Commander, General Dwight D. Eisenhower (Ike), decided that moving forward with the original plan of invading Southern France was a better plan, as it would weaken the German military on two fronts: France and Italy. The goal was to push the Nazis back eastward out of France and toward Germany while also pushing the Nazis farther north and out of Italy. Keeping the Germans fighting on two fronts would seriously weaken the Hitler war machine in France, thus expelling them and liberating France sooner.

The Combined Chiefs sided with Ike, and Operation Dragoon was back on. After a planning meeting on July 2, 1944, top-secret orders went out to Field Marshal Wilson with plans for the invasion. Ultimately, August 15, 1944, would be D-Day of Southern France, called Operation Dragoon.

As stated, the invasion of Southern France was originally scheduled to take place simultaneous with the Normandy invasion, Operation Overlord of June sixth. However, due to a shortage of men and equipment that would be needed for the execution of Operation Dragoon, it was decided to postpone the mission to a later date.

After the Normandy invasion, most of the Allied troops and pilots for Dragoon were transported from England and France to Morocco. My father was among the pilots to begin training in Marrakesh and Casablanca, Africa.

One day, while at lunch, Goldie (a glider pilot mentioned earlier) was with his friends when he was tapped on his shoulder by officers of the military police (MP). He thought to himself, *What have I done now?* He was instructed to immediately report to the airfield where he was flown directly to Casablanca, Algeria, Africa. He was reunited with his friend, Eldon Mueller and Walter Lindberg of the 439 TCG to, began training for Operation Dragoon.

After training in North Africa for six weeks, the pilots were transported to Italy where the invasion of Southern France was initiated. During the months of late June through August, the temperatures were the hottest of the year.

At the time, with the delays, Normandy was to receive priority. Certainly, in my father's case and as well as other glider pilots, he would not have been available for both missions. On D-Day June sixth, Normandy at this point was of much bigger consequence. August 15, 1944, and Southern France would be the most important priority after Normandy. To enhance the invasion forces for Operation Dragoon, the balance of the landing forces and gliders came from Merryfield and Upottery bases in England, which included Walter's 439th TCG.

Prior to my father leaving for training in early July, he continued to fly four more supply missions to Northern France, including the last mission according to his flight logs, on June thirtieth. He was then transported to North Africa in early July to begin training for the invasion of Southern France, Operation Dragoon. Lil had just left the hospital at the time Walter wrote a letter before his departure from England to Marrakesh, Africa. The letter was postmarked July fourteenth, the first letter since the birth of their baby daughter. Walter wrote:

> I'm duty officer tonight, so I am writing in my off moments. I can't tell you what I'm doing, but if I could, it would probably explain a lot of the things that are hard for you now… You told me Alana had a dimple. Is it in her chin? (Ha!) Do you need money? I have not received any let-

ters from you lately, but I know you will write when you can. I'm very anxious to hear all about the baby, so please don't wait too long.

With my dad going to Africa on what was a very confidential mission, it was quite some time before either he or Lil received any letters. This caused a great deal of anxiety for both. Lil was in a constant fear mode of seeing the dreaded boy delivering telegrams in her neighborhood, while at the same time, Walt was anxious to know how both mother and child were faring.

A letter received from George T. Hall, a glider pilot who knew my father, stated, "[H]e was among the first to volunteer for every mission," which included Operation Dragoon. According to others, it was common practice for Walt to be among the very first ones to volunteer for any ensuing missions that became available no matter the content.

Areas along the seacoast north of Rome became staging areas for the assembly of gliders and for amassing military equipment to be loaded on to ships. The stage was set for the 170-mile flight to Southern France for the invasion to take place in August of 1944, twelve weeks after the invasion of Normandy.

Walter, along with other members, including his roommate Eldon Mueller, of the 439th TCG, left from Upottery Field located in rural east Devon, England, to a destination over twelve hundred miles away in Marrakech, Morocco, in Northwest Africa. There they rendezvoused with the members of the 441st TCG who were close by in Casablanca. While there, Eldon Mueller once again reunited with his stateside training buddy, J. Curtis "Goldie" Goldman, who was with the 441st TCG.

Both the 439th and the 441st participated, along with other TCGs, in training for the eventual invasion of the French Riviera that was set for August 15, 1944. Temperatures in August were described as hot, with the thermostat sometimes showing over 120 degrees Fahrenheit.

The main objective of Operation Dragoon was to capture and hold the southern port city of Marseilles, France, thus giving the

Allies a major landing port to land equipment and supplies. It would also provide a southern platform to send troops northward to meet with other northern forces to squeeze the German army into an eastward retreat.

After training in Marrakech and Casablanca and with the Germans flushed out of Central Italy, the pilots were now able to be transported to Italy, which was in a closer proximity for an invasion of France. At the time, Allied assaults were taking place in Italy, driving the Germans up into Northern Italy and back over the Italian border. With the Germans cleared out of the region, the Allies then established bases in Italy, north of Rome where they could stage an assault on France. Walter and the 439th TCG were based at the airfield in Orbetello, Italy, about fifty miles northwest of Rome near the coastline of that portion of the Mediterranean Sea.

Coincidentally, Walter's cousin, Armando Cota, from Ensenada, Baja California, who had enlisted in US military service, arrived in the spring of 1944, some five months earlier, and was participating with the Fifth Army division that liberated Rome on June fourth. Armando had landed in Salerno and, over the next four months, helped in the ground offensive that drove the German occupation northward. (See Chapter 28)

The German army had been seriously weakened prior to June fourth by having to rush soldiers from the eastern front where they were also fighting with the Russians to reinforce the buildup of Nazi forces in France on the Western Front. German commanders knew there was going to be an Allied invasion. They just did not know exactly where or when it would happen. German military was seriously weakened from having to fight the Allied forces on so many fronts at one time.

The 170-mile flight to Southern France from Orbetello air base and other temporary bases nearby took place in two assaults. The British attacked at 0800 with thirty Horsa gliders and 40 CG-4A smaller gliders. The Americans attacked later in the day with 332 CG-4A gliders. Some 471 C-47 aircraft dropped in 5,700 paratroopers. Supporting the air effort were a thousand naval vessels carrying thousands of tons of ground equipment, ammunition, and other important supplies.

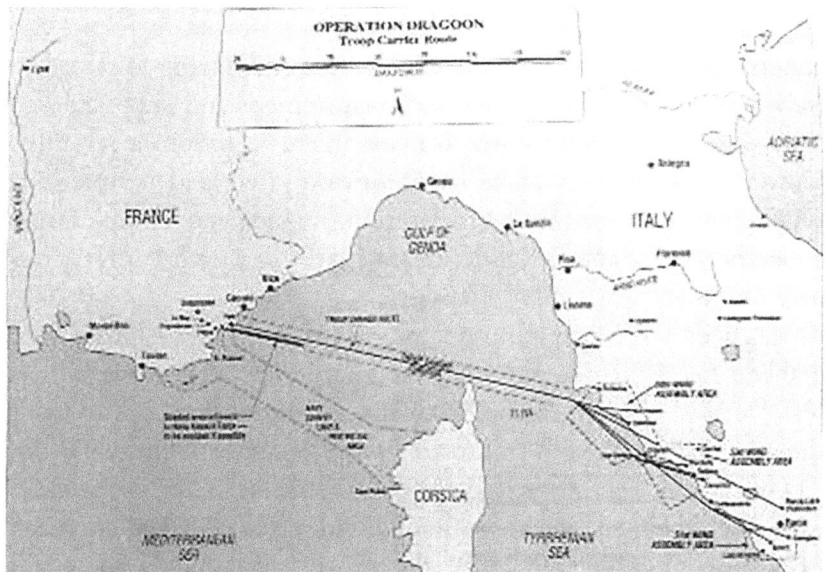

Glider flight patterns for Operation Dragoon

The airborne operation had its deadly challenges due to poor visibility with a low layer of fog. There were hundreds of aircraft, including gliders, in the air. There were also C-47s making paratroop drops. All were looking for drop zones for paratroopers, while the gliders were trying to find landing zones.

The gliders, upon release from their C-47 towplanes, were forced to remain in the air for longer periods of time than planned due to the poor weather conditions. This caused many gliders to land outside of their landing zones. Others made forced landings in unknown areas with heavy equipment. Some pilots were lost due to equipment sliding forward in the glider upon impact, causing serious injury. Eleven pilots lost their lives in attempting to land. As usual, the Nazis had planted their famous "asparagus poles" and deadly wiring apparatus from tree to tree across landing zones to cause further casualties to the landing gliders.

The main landing zones for the gliders were adjacent to the small village of Le Muy, France. Due to the low-hanging fog, there were a multitude of gliders soaring in the air above the landing zones waiting to land. The C-47 tow aircraft were forced to release the gliders earlier than planned due to low fuel and having to return to Italy to refuel and bring back more equipment and supplies. The skies were full of aircraft, which made midair collisions a certainty. However, due to the skill of the pilots, only two gliders were lost. One glider had a serious crash landing, missing the landing target altogether, while another glider disintegrated in the air with its crew over the sea.

Once on the ground, my father, along with other glider pilots, grabbed his Browning automatic standard-issue rifle, along with a pistol in his belt, and rushed into the small town of Le Muy with the other ground assault troops who were in combat with the Nazis. The Germans were no match for the Americans. The Nazi soldiers were overwhelmed, flushed out of buildings, and taken prisoner. According to military records, the mission was highly successful because the German army made a quick retreat. The actual battle only lasted one day, but the staging and landing of equipment lasted until the twenty-fourth of August.

The next combat mission for my dad was in Northern Europe with a target date sometime in September 1944.

Operation Market Garden–Holland

As they were planning for the invasion of Holland, September 17, 1944, began almost immediately after Operation Dragoon in Southern France. It became known as Operation Market Garden and was the third major glider mission my father participated in.

After D+1 Normandy on June 7, 1944, my father flew gliders into Southern France in late August. The two previous airborne assaults used almost all Allied Forces, in one way or another. The planned Holland attack was going to include paratroopers, as well as gliders carrying armed men, jeeps, motorcycles, and antitank guns. In total, it eventually became the largest airborne assault ever planned that no one knew anything about!

Unknown to the glider pilots at Upottery Field, there were generals and other officers one hundred miles away planning a large airborne assault mission to liberate Holland, which all available glider pilots eventually participated in. Had Walter known of the secret planning behind closed doors, he could not have written home about any of those plans. Letters were routinely read and edited by staff somewhere along the journey from the air base to the recipient.

The men doing the planning for the Holland assault decided that three British and three American divisions would be utilized to seize bridges crossing the Rhine River into Germany. British Horsa gliders were used, as well as American gliders from the Eighty-Second Airborne. Some Polish and Dutch forces were also included in the hasty planning. Altogether there were to be about twelve thousand troopers and infantry combined, not including the towplane pilots and medical personnel. American gliders carried the medics, as well as their life-saving equipment, such as the blood banks.

Walter, along with his glider buddies, were trained in air navigation, meteorology, aircraft recognition, as well as rifle skills because after their gliders landed, whether in Holland or anywhere else, according to the website www.military-history.org, they became part of the infantry force. Since the planning of the Holland mission lacked time and organization, it was perhaps destined to be an ill-fated mission by the army's airborne forces from the beginning to the end of the nine-day assault.

The main differences between the Holland mission and previous glider operations were, first, that the invasion would take place as the first major air assault during daylight rather than night or in the early dawn. Second, glider pilots of the Eighty-Second and 101st Airborne were to join the infantry once on the ground during the ground assault. The goal was to capture the Arnhem Bridge that crosses the lower Rhine River into the town of Ooesterbeek. Its location was a few miles from the German border.

The Arnhem bridge served as the most important supply route for the German military into Western Europe. Its protection was vital for future German missions into Holland and Belgium. Also, the Rhine River was the last great natural barrier of defense for Germany.

In mid-September 1944, the British and American troops had eventually closed in on the all-important bridge. The Allies' push continued eastward as the German troops now had their backs against the western border of Germany. Hitler knew if the Allies succeeded in crossing into Germany that Germany would be doomed. The German Army defended against Allied forces made up of British, Americans, French, and Dutch armies, with the British trying to take the bridge while the Germans fiercely defended it. Americans were providing the much-needed supplies of men and machines to support the British.

The invasion plan was the brainchild of Field Marshal Montgomery of the British Army. The brass who formulated the plan for Market Garden met in an eighteenth-century mansion, previously used as a jail for German officers. That mansion in Moor Park, Hertfordshire, England, was only one hundred miles from Upottery Field, where my father and other glider pilots were currently stationed, awaiting their instructions. However, my father was transferred to Balderton, England, on September first. Balderton is located about seventy-five miles north of London.

Flight Officer Lindberg and Lil in September of 1944 were parents of a baby daughter, nearly three months old. Lil was not back to work at the Seelbach Hotel because taking care of Alana Jean was a full-time job. Walter sent her money as often as possible, but letters were few and far between. It was agonizing to wait weeks for a letter from Walter.

The latest letter Lil had received from Walter was written on August fourth and postmarked August 8, 1944, but did not arrive until almost three weeks later. The timing of the letter was prior to the Market Garden invasion. As welcome as the letter was, Lil had no idea where Walter was or when she would hear from him again. In the letter written only one week after Alana's birth, Walter wrote:

> Darling Lil and Alana,
>
> It seems like years since I've heard from you… I'm very anxious to hear the latest gossip about the little flirt from Louisville called Alana. I'm awfully glad you're happy with the baby. You know how I feel about her—you and I and baby. What a perfect combination, right? I'm in such a position now where I can't write to you, this may be the last letter you'll get from me in a very long time, so please don't get worried if you don't hear from me. I'll write whenever I can, I promise. I can't tell you any more. I love you and miss you, and when you get to feeling blue, remember I'm

in the same mood over here… I love you both very, very much and miss you so.

> Always,
> Your husband Walter

This letter was not received until September first, two weeks after Dragoon and after Walter returned to England for Market Garden preparations.

Sending mail and other items was extremely difficult, as all correspondence was strictly censored to make sure troop movements and other information did not get into enemy hands. Letters posted in England went to New York and then were forwarded to loved ones from there. Walt was still stationed at Upottery Field in England, where he was allowed free time for sports, horseback riding, card playing, or cleaning and taking care of other officers' uniforms and shoes. He did the latter to earn extra money to send to Lil. His glider pilot friends all agreed, "Walt rarely takes leave." Lil did get one short note and a picture about horseback riding. The picture was of one of his buddies wearing a riding outfit that was much too small for him. Walter instructed Lil, "Keep this picture, this is a funny time to remember with a war going on. Ha."

The Market Garden plan was rushed, beginning on September 12, 1944, and the actual assault started just five days later, on September 17. It is said by some that had the plan been carried off successfully, it would have shortened the war by as much as six to eight months and saved hundreds of thousands of lives, if not millions.

Concurrently, there was another plan presented by General George W. Patton, who was commonly referred to as the Lion. The Lion's plan involved a corresponding invasion carried out by the American military. As expected, the British and American plans were totally different. In wars, generals often compete for the same glory, which would have been being the first to cross into Germany toward Berlin.

Ultimately, the Supreme Allied Commander, General Eisenhower, put forward a compromise that allowed Montgomery's plan to proceed before Patton's. General Patton, for a variety of reasons, was not happy with that decision. Of course, Walter and the other glider pilots stationed at Upottery Field, England, who were to take part in the invasion, had no knowledge of those competing generals who had their egos at stake.

Montgomery's plan required the airborne divisions "to lay a carpet of glider and parachute troops over a fifty-five-mile highway that stretched from Eindhoven to the Arnhem Bridge." Along that route are five major bridges, the last being Arnhem. Later, studies of the assault revealed exactly how and why the Arnhem bridge was, in reality, too far for the operation to be successful.

The object was to land as many troops as possible and then to seize control of the five bridges between Eindhoven and Arnhem. The capture of those important bridges, if successful, would allow the British tank divisions to proceed rapidly to Arnhem, outflank, and push back the Germans farther into their homeland. It seemed like a good plan, even though it was hastily conceived.

England's Lieutenant General Browning was then commanding the British First Airborne Corps. Even though he understood the task as outlined by Montgomery, Browning was concerned about the depth of the penetration of the airborne mission into Holland. While looking at a map and pointing to a bridge at Arnhem, Browning inquired, "How long will it take our tanks to reach us here?" while pointing to Arnhem. "Two days," replied Montgomery. Still staring at the map, Browning said, "We can hold it for four." Then as an afterthought, Browning said, "But I think, sir, we may be going to a bridge too far."

This quote from Browning about "a bridge too far" became the movie, *A Bridge Too Far*, after the book with the same title by Cornelius Ryan. General Eisenhower had appointed American General Lewis Hyde Brereton to oversee the army airborne procedures for Market Garden. At army airborne headquarters back in England, Browning met with Brereton to discuss the invasion plan. General Brereton made the decision to place General Browning in command of all the airborne troops taking part in the mission. He was to maintain that command until the airborne could establish a firm link with the ground forces. It all seemed like a good plan.

Browning was more than qualified as he had commanded the First Airborne Division from November of 1941 to May of 1943. His credentials were exceptional. Previously he had taken part in the airborne invasions of Sicily and Normandy. Browning was a qualified parachutist as well as an experienced glider pilot. Obviously, he surely understood the overall plans for the mission with a better insight than most of those putting together the logistics.

Brereton had planned to deliver approximately one-third of the airborne army aboard gliders in the assault into Holland. The remaining two-thirds of the divisions would land by parachute. However, Major General Paul Williams, commander of air operations associated with Market Garden, offered the discouraging news that there were not enough airplanes available to fly the needed airborne divisions into Holland. Williams was previously in charge of other air operations in Europe, prior to the planned Holland invasion.

Walter, my father, took part in the invasion as part of the Eighty-Second Airborne. During the final weeks of the Normandy invasion, then the Southern France operation in late August, and then September with the Holland invasion, Walter was unable to write as often as he wished. All the loved ones at home waiting to hear from their soldiers could only listen to the radio and hope for good news. The last letter Lil had received was on September first. With it being postmarked on August eighth, Lil and other family had no idea where Walter was or if he was even still alive.

As it turned out, the Dutch intelligence was poor, and the Germans were severely underestimated by Montgomery. My father, along with the other glider pilots, paratroopers, and infantry who successfully landed in Holland, survived in trenches, dodging snipers, until day 9, September 25, 1944, when General Urquhart sent orders to evacuate (a story of one glider pilot, Mike Hall, told by

Alan Jamieson, a WWII historian, on the seventy-fifth anniversary is found on the website www.military-history.org).

> During the night, in heavy rain, the survivors made their way to the Rhine. "We covered our boots with cloth to muffle our footsteps," says Mike. "Silently, in single file, following a white tape to mark the route, we left the Hartenstein [a bombed-out hotel in Holland] behind and saw small boats crossing the river towards us.
> "Engineers from British and Canadian companies were using storm boats as ferries—although they were no bigger than rowboats—to carry up to 12 men at a time across the fast-flowing Rhine. Some men attempted to swim, and many were drowned."

According to the website, www.military-history.org, 3,900 survivors escaped or were evacuated, 1,400 men were killed, and 6,500 wounded. Survivors were left behind to become prisoners of war. In the end, the plan was a setback for the Allied forces. Though Market Garden was less than a success, it was not considered a total failure in hindsight. However, the weary glider pilots, like my father, made it back to Upottery and Balderton fields to continue their training for what was hoped to be the last glider and airborne assault—the final crossing into Germany, which would be called Operation Varsity.

On November 6, 1944, soon after the Allied debacle in Holland, Walter and the other glider pilots at both Upottery and Balderton were packing their bags to move to France. The few salvaged gliders of Market Garden were being returned by truck to the Châteaudun Air Base in France. Châteaudun had been seized by Germany in the Battle of France. Before the Americans reclaimed the base, it was used by the Luftwaffe for raids on England.

The relocations of personnel and equipment were in preparation for future serials (supply missions), which were flown in the

Battle of the Bulge and Operation Varsity, the last glider mission, also known as the Rhine River Crossing.

From November on, the 439th serial missions were flown out of Châteaudun, France. Châteaudun was originally known as Dun, from the Celtic language. The Chateau Estate was also used as a Roman fortress during the time of Julius Caesar. The town has a romantic location overlooking the Loir River Valley, but it is doubtful that any of the glider pilots or soldiers of the USAAF found it romantic. Freezing cold, frostbite, and living in tents on frozen ground while conducting difficult and life-threatening training exercises doesn't sound too romantic.

Taken after a glider's safe landing. Notice how the cockpit lifts up to open, disembarking a jeep.
(https://taskandpurpose.com/history/d-day-laurinburg-maxton-air-base)

"The vast majority of the United States' glider pilots were trained there [Laurinburg–Maxton, North Carolina], including the forces who played an unsung role in the D-Day invasion."

Lil kept, almost daily, a record of Alana's growth and progress, writing notes in the baby book they had bought together while in North Carolina. It was a labor of love, which Lil hoped to share with Walt after the war so that he wouldn't miss anything. Lil took pictures of Alana (me) almost as often to send to my dad. He carried them in his wallet, along with my baby shoe for luck. When he was finally able to write, he could not disclose what his mission had been, but he wrote, "I carried Alana's baby shoe in my pocket for good luck on the mission. The Germans flooded our landing zones!" Later on, it was determined that the baby shoe had gotten wet during the landing and evacuation of Market Garden, not Southern France.

Alana's baby shoe that Walter carried to Holland

The following is noted from the website www.ww2gp.org/holland:

> In figures, approximately 1,820 U.S. gliders were dispatched to land in Holland. Approximately 1,570 did so. The other gliders landed scattered along the route from take-off point to the LZ. Thirty-eight glider pilots lost their lives in this operation. Approximately 80 C-47s were lost, claiming the lives of about 125 men.

At this point in 1944, no one could have predicted how or when the war might finally be over. Since the beginning in 1939, it had already lasted five years. There were still many loose ends, even after the great success of the D-Day invasion of Normandy and the complete liberation of France and Italy. Even if Germany had surrendered sooner, there was still Japan to deal with. Events soon to come would change dramatically the futures of Walter and Lil and their baby daughter.

When the stats were totaled for the Market Garden operation, it is amazing that Walt survived his third combat mission in the battle for the bridges over the Rhine River. Gliders always landed behind enemy lines, and the pilots were on their own to disembark the equipment from the glider. As soon as the equipment was unloaded from the front end of the crashed glider, the pilots became part of the fighting force.

The official casualties and losses for Market Garden of the ten thousand troops who made it to their designated locations are staggering. There were "7,000 killed, wounded, or taken prisoner. Allied casualties during the operation totaled more than 17,000, compared with around 8,000 on the German side."

Bastogne, Belgium

Battle of the Bulge 439 TCG

In November of 1943, winter had descended upon the western and eastern portions of Europe earlier and more harshly than usual. Hitler was fighting on the Eastern Front against the stubborn Russian army on the outskirts of Stalingrad. The casualties were mounting into the hundreds of thousands as both Russian and German troops were fighting in open battlefields for days on end, exposed to harsh subfreezing and snowy winter conditions.

Supplies were slow in reaching the German army due to trucks stuck in frozen mud, preventing munitions, food, clothing, and, most importantly, medical supplies for wounded and dying troops. Thousands of Nazi soldiers had already perished due to starvation. Hitler had thought his invasion of Russia would last a few days, but the Russians proved to be patriotic and fought for their country. Perhaps the failures of the Russian Revolution were still on their minds.

Hitler's army came to a grinding halt in those impossible conditions. The German war machine was beginning to be worn down as the Russians successfully defended themselves against Germany's Operation Barbarossa by amassing over five hundred thousand troops to the Germans' two hundred thousand men. It was a good time for the Allies to begin the invasions to liberate Europe on June 6, 1944. The Germans were thinly spread all over the continent, from the west coast of France to the western borders of Russia.

Over the next six months after D-Day, June 6, 1944, the Allied armies, led by the Americans, advanced across Western Europe, liberating France and western Belgium. They drove the German army eastward back to the German border. In mid-September 1944, the British and American troops had eventually closed in on the all-important bridge at Arnhem.

The Arnhem bridge was constructed over the lower Rhine River and was the main supply route from Germany into northern Belgium. The Allied push continued eastward as the German troops had their backs against the western border of Germany. Hitler knew if the Allies succeeded in crossing into Germany that Germany would be doomed.

The British and German armies fought a fierce battle, with the British trying to take the bridge and the Germans fiercely defending it. Americans provided the much-needed supplies of men and machines to support the British airborne and infantry troops.

By December of 1944, Lil had recovered completely from her ordeal of childbirth. Now that Alana was six months old, she went back to work at night at the Seelbach Hotel. The memories of her romance with Walt were all over the hotel. Chrysteen, always the positive sister, tried to keep things positive, even as the war dragged on. Since she lived next door, Chrys took care of the baby at night while Lil worked. The letters from Walt were far and few between, and one can see why with so much war going on. It was the radio news every day, all day, that kept Lil listening, but at night, work was a welcome distraction.

Gasoline was still rationed, but she had no car, anyway, so Lil rode the trolley to work and back each night. Even with the radio on constantly, it was hard to imagine what was happening so far away from the home front. There were so many campaigns going on simultaneously it was hard to keep track.

There was the European Theater of Operations, the Pacific Theater of Operations, the North African-Mediterranean, and even a China-Burma Theater of Operations, but Lil was only concerned with Europe because Walt was somewhere in England or France when he wrote to her. At the Seelbach dining room, there were still soldiers coming in swimming at the pool, even on the night shift. Lil talked to them to see if they had more information than what came over the radio, but they didn't talk about it.

Chrysteen was the only one with close encounters to Lil's emotional state during those stressful times. Two of their brothers, Clarence and Bill, were in the military, but they were not overseas. Lil's oldest sister, Lucille, was a nurse, and she and her husband, Dr. Isadore Zimmerman, lived in New Hampshire but were on call to nearby army hospitals in Massachusetts. Letters from her sister about the many casualties coming in from overseas, whom they treated, were very discouraging.

As my mother waited for letters and hoped for the best, that my dad was still okay, the eastward advance in Europe by the Allied forces continued. December was cold in Louisville but not nearly as cold as what the soldiers and glider pilots were enduring as the Americans continued their advance into central Belgium and occupied the small town of Bastogne.

Glider landing near Bastogne, December 1944 (Imperial War Museums)

Battle of the Bulge (Britannica)
Severe winter of WWII in 1944 in Bastogne, Belgium

The 101st Airborne was given the task by General Dwight D. Eisenhower to hold Bastogne at all costs. Though the military personnel of 88,000 men seemed adequate to hold the small town, the artillery and ammunition supply was woefully short of being able to hold off the German offensive, which came in full force, over 200,000 strong. Hitler was as determined as General Eisenhower was to hold onto the German-occupied town. Most everyone on both sides believed the Battle of Bastogne, which became known as the Battle of the Bulge, would be the turning point for one side or the other in the European Theater of Operations.

Hitler began relocating the troops from the Russian theater of operations and quickly brought 255,000 troops westward to go on the offensive in a big way into Belgium. The Germans amassed all 255,000 men in a seventy-five-mile-long line of military might on the eastern border in the Ardennes Forest of Belgium to push west toward the small town of Bastogne.

Bastogne had a population of fifteen thousand souls. Included in the German Army's attempt to drive out the Americans were numerous divisions of the much-feared German Panzer and Tiger tanks, which numbered about six hundred tanks. The largest German Army assembly and the ensuing battle was given the name of the Battle of the Bulge, peculiarly because of its geographic location and the way the men were strategically placed. It became one of the most famous battles in WWII history.

Lil served dinner nightly to soldiers and other military personnel in December 1944. There were still dances at the Seelbach Hotel, which brought back tearful memories of the nights she and Walt had danced until 2:00 a.m. Lil went home exhausted every night but always woke up early to the radio announcing a new battle or the result of an ongoing battle somewhere in Europe or the Philippines.

Hitler's army was encircling Bastogne, and thousands of German soldiers were heading to the port of Antwerp in northwest Belgium. The port was important because it was where Americans were unloading critical supplies for their continued eastward push toward Germany. The goal: cut off the American supplies, making it impossible to continue the advance to Germany. Ironically enough, the mission was given the name: Operation Repulse.

On December sixteenth, all hell broke loose as the German infantry continued their advance to Bastogne. By December twenty-third, Bastogne was surrounded by 255,000 Germans. The town was being defended by a mere 88,000 Americans with only 358 Sherman tanks. But worse than being outnumbered was the short supply of ammunition, medical supplies, and especially needed medical personnel.

Bastogne and Nurse Augusta

The purpose of Augusta's story here is to highlight the horrendous conditions that became part of the history of the Battle of the Bulge.

In Bastogne lived a Belgian doctor, Dr. Chiwy, who twenty years earlier had lived in Rwanda, Africa, serving as doctor among the people there. While serving there, he had a child out of wedlock with an African woman. The little girl was named Augusta. (See Bibliography)

When the time arrived for Dr. Chiwy to return to Belgium, an important decision was made concerning the child's future. He pondered whether to leave the child in Africa or bring her home to Belgium. With the girl being biracial, he wasn't sure how the local population in Bastogne would accept her. Dr. Chiwy decided his little daughter, Augusta, should accompany him to his hometown of Bastogne. He knew there would be challenges for his biracial daughter, but he wanted her to get an education and be productive in her life.

Dr. Chiwy settled back home in Bastogne where young Augusta adapted to going to school with children not exactly like her. She had some difficulty in mastering some academic subjects, but she did well in learning French and English. As she grew older, she wanted to follow her father's profession. With his financial help and emotional support, she became a nurse. She loved nursing and found no task too difficult.

Augusta was in her twenties when WWII arrived on her doorstep on December 24, 1943. Bastogne, Belgium, was caught in the crosshairs of that huge assembly of German forces, which surrounded it. Augusta did not know that the town and the battle would go down in history as one of the most critical struggles of WWII. Hundreds of the civilians living there had fled, taking few belongings with them. They had no idea if they would see their small homes, cottages, and beautiful farms ever again.

In early November, American Army troops had entered Bastogne to liberate the people from the German takeover. They had come there to protect the population from further ravages of the Nazi war machine. The Gestapo, upon entering the town, had gone from home to home, searching for residents who may have assisted the Americans in any way. Many were taken out and executed in front of their friends and members of their family.

From December 16 through 23, the fighting intensified, and the casualties began to mount. The shortage of medical supplies was beyond critical. In early December, a small group of American doctors volunteered to be flown in from France to Noville, Belgium, a few miles north of Bastogne. They were transported by truck into Bastogne before the German Army closed the noose around the perimeter of the town. One of those doctors was an American volunteer doctor, Dr. Jack Prior.

When Dr. Prior arrived to attend to the wounded, he discovered two different locations in home basements where there were groups of at least eight hundred wounded soldiers. Even worse was the fact he had almost no medicine and operating tools with which to work. Medically trained personnel and nurses were practically nonexistent in Bastogne because they were captured by the Nazis. The captured medical personnel were forced to tend to the wounded German soldiers.

Prior desperately needed an assistant to help him with surgical procedures. He needed any professional help he could find to bind up and bandage the wounded and injured from the Allied side. At the same time he was treating the wounded, German mortar shells were landing indiscriminately on and around the town, causing more and more injured to need medical help.

Dr. Prior was told there was still a young nurse living in the town who might be able to give him assistance. He was directed to the home of Augusta Chiwy, and he asked her, "Are you available to help me?" She accepted even though the task of communicating was going to be difficult. Augusta spoke French, but her English was not that good. Dr. Prior spoke English but not French.

At the time, Bastogne was populated mostly with stranded civilians who had not been able to escape the city before German occupation. The rest of the population consisted of American and Allied injured troops who had survived the German Panzer and Tiger tank assaults.

The weather conditions were so severe—cloudy and foggy—that the Americans had no idea of the number of the enemy that surrounded them. Due to the weather conditions and the inability to supply the much-needed weaponry, only one-third of the Americans had adequate weapons with which to fight. According to Warfare

History Network, even civilians were gathering up guns and ammunitions to give to the Americans.

Dr. Prior took Augusta to a three-story building next to a small tavern in the middle of town that had been converted to a hospital. The basement below had thirty wounded patients, all American military members, many with serious wounds. Dr. Prior and Augusta hurriedly attended to the wounded. They were prioritized according to the seriousness of the injuries as they worked tirelessly. It soon became apparent that it was going to be difficult to help or even save lives because of no medical tools and scarce medicine.

In one case, a young American soldier had a serious foot wound that was infected with gangrene. The only possible remedy was amputation. Augusta poured cognac down the throat of the soldier and held the young man down as Dr. Prior proceeded to "saw" off the foot with a serrated army knife.

It was December twenty-fourth, Christmas Eve, and the wounded had all been attended to. Dr. Prior and Augusta went next door to have a somber Christmas Eve celebration with some refreshment, leaving others behind to attend to the treated patients. After a subdued celebration, Dr. Prior and Augusta were exhausted from the previous day's activities and were beginning to rest when suddenly Dr. Prior was awoken by bright flares that had fallen into the street from the sky. The street was brighter than daylight. Suddenly, he recognized the high whistling from a falling bomb dropped from an aircraft above. As the whistling became more like a scream, it was apparent that the bomb was going to fall very near where he and Augusta were resting. Suddenly, a massive explosion blew the walls in next to where they were located. The three-story building next to them took a direct hit from a five-hundred-pound German bomb, killing all the personnel and all the patients they had cared for that day.

On Christmas morning, saddened and discouraged from the previous night's disaster, Dr. Prior and Nurse Augusta were taken to the basement of another building in the town. There lay over six hundred wounded soldiers for them to attend to. The task was daunting and seemed impossible, especially with no medical supplies.

On December twenty-sixth, the Ninety-First, Ninety-Second, Ninety-Third, and Ninety-Fourth Glider Squadrons of the 439th TCG assembled on the runway at Châteaudun, France, in preparation for delivering medical supplies and the voluntary medical personnel to Bastogne, which were needed to complete Operation Repulse.

My father, along with his close friend, Pershing Carlson, and other members of the Ninety-Fourth Troop Carrier Squadron volunteered to fly the much-needed personnel and supplies into Bastogne. Due to the weather conditions and the town being surrounded by more than a quarter million German soldiers, it was impossible to deliver any supplies via the road system. The only course of action that could be taken was to drop the supplies by air, which meant using gliders and C47s. There were no airstrips, so supplies were either dropped from the C47s or brought in by the gliders.

The next three days included hundreds of flights by C-47s air-dropping ammunition while 50 CG-4A gliders made landings in the snow and ice right in the middle of the war zone near the town. While the propeller-driven C-47s dropped artillery, the CG-4A gliders delivered medical personnel and medical supplies the only way that could be done. It was accomplished by the gliders flying over the enemy through the cloudy and snowy weather and landing directly in the middle of the battlefield and successfully delivering the precious cargo of doctors and nurses, who were not able to parachute in. Since the perimeter of Bastogne was completely surrounded by the enemy, the only way doctors and nurses could reach the war zone is by directly landing them into the snowy fields close to the town. Since doctors and nurses are not paratroopers, they could not be dropped from the C-47s but had to be landed safely on the ground by the only method available—the gliders.

There were no runways to land any type of aircraft. The CG-4A glider was the only aircraft that could land in the uncertain terrain. The gliders were the only method that could silently penetrate the stranglehold of the Germans by flying over the adversary and safely landing the personnel in the snowy fields near Bastogne. My father participated in this heroic mission by flying a glider and safely landing. Many of Walter's glider pilot comrades were captured by the Germans and were POWs the remainder months of the war.

Unfortunately, there were many who did not have the same outcome. While about 70 percent of the medical supplies needed were delivered, the remaining 30 percent did not make it. It required the supreme sacrifice of the glider pilots and other voluntary medical doctors and nurses who did not survive the landings.

As the gliders landed, Dr. Jack Prior and Augusta Chiwy immediately ran from their cover out into the frozen snow to retrieve the medicine, personnel, and surgical tools from the gliders. Such supplies were critical for medical help to get into the operating areas. Hundreds of American soldiers and countless civilian lives were saved due to their tireless efforts. Both worked tirelessly for the next week operating and bandaging up the wounded and frostbitten soldiers.

As suddenly as Dr. Jack Prior had arrived in Bastogne, he was called away. Augusta Chiwy was deeply saddened as she and Dr. Prior parted. They had served almost two weeks saving the lives of soldiers and civilians alike and had developed a bond that can only be described as special—an American volunteer doctor and a biracial Belgian nurse who were thrown together in the middle of the most ferocious battle of WWII.

Not only were there heroes on the ground saving lives but there were also heroes from the sky, which made it possible for those on the ground to save lives. In one of the most heroic and dangerous landing missions of the war, eighteen C-47 crew members lost their lives from being shot down by enemy fire while delivering ammunition and clothing, with another twenty-one becoming prisoners of war.

Among the glider pilots that delivered doctors, nurses, and medicine, there were three glider pilots killed with fourteen captured becoming prisoners of war. Among those was one of my father's best friends, Pershing Carlson. After his towplane was shot down, he landed his glider short of the landing zone, amidst the enemy. His glider was full of munitions and was on fire. He hastily exited and headed for the forest. As soon as he reached cover, his plane exploded.

He then dug a trench and remained there four days, eating only the fruitcake his wife had sent him for Christmas. He remained a POW until Germany surrendered. He wrote in a letter to me:

> Your dad was one of my best friends. As you may know, our squadron suffered extremely high casualties during the war, losing 87% of our original cadre. Your father was a kind and generous person. He was a good pilot and good officer... I am really sorry that you had to grow up without him... I was a POW when he was killed... I'm sure his last thoughts were of you.

Mr. and Mrs. Pershing Carlson

16

Operation Varsity Rhine River Crossing

For at least twenty centuries, the Rhine River has provided a natural border between eastern Gaul (France and Belgium) and western Germany. It still provides a natural boundary for those living west of the Rhine River. For centuries, that same boundary has kept out invasive tribes from the east.

One cannot help but marvel after two thousand years how the same strategy for procuring the freedom of the peoples of France and Belgium still involves crossing the Rhine River. Historically, the Rhine River seems to be always a main military objective when the goal was defeating Germany. It seems, for sure, that history does repeat itself!

In 60 BC, Julius Caesar spent ten years on a Roman conquest to defeat the Gallic tribes of Gaul. He went to Gaul with four legions (over fifty thousand men). At the same time, Caesar was also policing the eastern border of Gaul to prevent further hostilities of Germanic tribes crossing over the Rhine to invade his newly conquered territory. After uniting the newly defeated Celtic tribes of Gaul, Caesar enlisted their help to fight against the barbaric tribes of Germany, who were a natural enemy to both Rome and Gaul. By the end of the Gallic war, Caesar had amassed eleven legions.

Finally, in 55 BC, Caesar instructed his legions to construct bridges across the Rhine so he could take his army "in a display of force intended to deter any other German tribes from invading Gaul."

The Gallic tribes, in loyalty to Caesar, offered vessels to cross the Rhine River. This might have sounded familiar in 1944, when the Allies miscalculated the war strategy at the Arnhem bridge in Holland. Caesar believed the option of boats provided only a temporary solution and was too risky. What advice would he have given to the Allied troops, fleeing in the small storm boats, across the Rhine in 1944?

Romans took great pride in their engineering prowess, especially in building bridges. At Caesar's command, a bridge was constructed within ten days, providing a permanent structure to cross over the Rhine River into Germany. Both ends of the bridge were heavily garrisoned for protection.

The location of Caesar's bridge today puts it in proximity between modern Coblenz and Andernach, Holland. It is about one hundred miles downstream from the Arnhem bridge, which the Allies were trying to capture. Not long after the grueling and freezing Battle of the Bulge in Bastogne, Belgium, the next military effort, much like Caesar's, was to contemplate crossing the Rhine River to invade Germany.

One might wonder if Caesar would have used gliders (if he could have), or would he have thought they were too risky as well? Caesar's bridge is gone, but the "bridge too far" still stands today as one of the most iconic places on the Liberation Route, as stated in the website: https://www.holland.com/global/tourism/holland-stories/liberation-route/operation-market-garden-a-bridge-too-far.htm.

The biggest strategic difference between the mission to cross the Rhine River and the other missions of Operation Overlord, Operation Dragoon, Market Garden, and the Battle of the Bulge was that those other missions involved paratroopers and gliders flying over and landing quietly behind enemy lines into German-occupied territory, most of the time in the dark.

The Germans, up to early 1945, occupied the territories of Poland, Hungary, France, Belgium, and Holland. They had a military force of almost eight million by that time. The occupied countries, and their populations were friendly to Americans and their Allies. They provided aid, food, protection, and information about the enemy, along with smuggling Allied troops back to the home front, preventing them from becoming captured. Operation Varsity was to be much different. The mission's goal was not about landing behind the enemy in an occupied territory, but it was confronting the enemy face-to-face in and on their own homeland. There were no friendly citizens to protect the Allied forces in Germany. Those preparing to enter Germany were told, "Everyone is your enemy."

There was promise and real hope that Operation Varsity would be the last glider mission of the war. By 1945, the United States had at least sixteen million men and women in uniform, nearly twice the number of Germans and Russians. Within that large force, there was the promise of hundreds of new "virgin" glider pilots, who had yet to fly an actual mission. There was still much training to be done with the many new arrivals coming from Bowman Field in Louisville, Kentucky. The competition was fierce among pilots; they were eager to participate in the last glider campaign of the war.

In the month of February, after the Belgium serials, the various Troop Carrier Groups made their way back to France and were quartered in scattered locations approximately forty miles west of Paris. One of those locations mentioned before was Châteaudun, where my father and many other glider pilots were bunked. Some pilots were housed in the old, bombed-out French military academy, which had previously been occupied by the Germans. Other pilots and new infantry arrivals were set up in tents in the freezing weather with only makeshift stoves that burned wood gathered from the nearby countryside. Sometimes, the local residents brought in coal, if it was available.

From these different locations, the pilots traveled to Tours for more training exercises. Tours, France, was near at least three other Troop Carrier Groups of the Eighty-Second Airborne: the 439th, 440th, and 441st. Tours became the main practice hub for the three units mentioned, and hundreds of practice missions were flown daily in preparation for the crossing of the Rhine River. These practices were flown at a new airfield the Allies had constructed, named A-39B, in Tours.

A short explanation of the gliders' practicing maneuvers is necessary to understand their complex formations. The common method of practice was single tows of CG-4A gliders behind a single

C-47 twin-engine aircraft. The gliders were towed behind a towplane with a 250-foot nylon tow rope. The tow rope also contained a separate communication phone line intertwined within so the glider pilot could communicate with the pilot of the C-47.

The practice for the Rhine River crossing was slightly different because many more gliders were needed for that last mission. The typical pattern for the Operation Varsity mission was to be two gliders with one flying in echelon (staggered) to the right of the towplane. Thus, the glider on the left was on a slightly shorter towline than the one on the right.

C47 towing two gliders—double tow

On February 22, 1945, roll call was made for all the pilots who would practice double tows on that day. With the names called out in alphabetical order, after Walter Lindberg's name was the name of his roommate, Clifford Mueller. After Clifford Mueller's name was read, there was a silence. Clifford Mueller was, for some reason, late for the roll call that day. The next name was Eldon Mueller, in alphabetical order. Eldon Mueller, instead of Clifford Mueller, stepped forward as pilot for the day, Walter being the copilot.

Eldon Mueller had just returned from leave from the small town of Dreux, France, twenty miles away. He had been there to visit his close friend J. Curtis Goldman (Goldie), mentioned earlier. They had celebrated their mutual birthdays together on February 13, 1945. After a fond farewell between the two, Flight Officer Mueller returned to Châteaudun, at Tours, to resume training for Operation Varsity on Airfield A-39B.

Mueller had participated in four previous missions: Normandy, Southern France, Holland, and Belgium (serials). He was well experienced, like my father, who had also participated in those same missions. They were both exceptionally experienced veteran pilots, flying together that day in correct formation with the other double-tow gliders.

The planes and the gliders were lined up on the runway, arranged in groups of four C-47s in line with two gliders behind each towplane. They each taxied and took off in this arrangement. They were to rendezvous in the sky one thousand feet above the ground before dropping to eight hundred feet with the four towplanes flying in echelon to the right with two gliders in tow in echelon to the right as well (see diagram). The gliders were numbered by pairs. The first C-47 towed gliders number 1 and 2, the second C-47 towed gliders number 3 and 4, and so on with eight gliders.

Mueller and Lindberg were in glider number 6, meaning that glider number 5 was slightly in front and to the left of their glider. As each pair of gliders released, the gliders banked off to the left in pairs, circling down, proceeding into a 360-degree flight pattern, taking them on the proper landing course back to the airfield. Dozens of gliders successfully completed this procedure throughout the practice session that day. It was not the case for Mueller and Lindberg's glider.

It is not known exactly what happened, but when my father's glider, number 6, released, it continued in a straight pattern momentarily instead of peeling off to the left. The ill-fated glider was late in starting into its turn, making it also late in starting the descent. Directly behind them, by less than six hundred feet, was the last C-47, which was towing gliders number 7 and 8. By the time this group was ready to release, they had approached Mueller's and my father's glider at a distance described as less than one hundred feet.

When gliders number 7 and number 8 released their tow ropes, the ropes swung straight down. By this time, my father's glider had started its turn. It was at a near right angle, about forty-five feet below the trailing number 7 and number 8 gliders. Mueller's and Lindberg's glider was not clear of the swinging towline. Cy Shaffer who watched helplessly on the ground described what he saw in a letter many years later to me:

> [M]y worst fears came true as the tow rope swung down—it wrapped itself around the tail section of your father's glider, ripping the tail section completely off.

At an elevation of about six hundred feet, the glider plunged straight down and, within a few seconds, hit the frozen ground, burying the nose section six feet into the earth. Both my father and Mueller died instantly upon impact.

One glider pilot wrote: "When we talked about death, we always said we hoped it would be quick. Your dad's death was very quick."

The following two diagrams illustrate the complexity of the glider flying formations. The second diagram shows how the accident happened. It was a windy day, and no one knows exactly what went wrong.

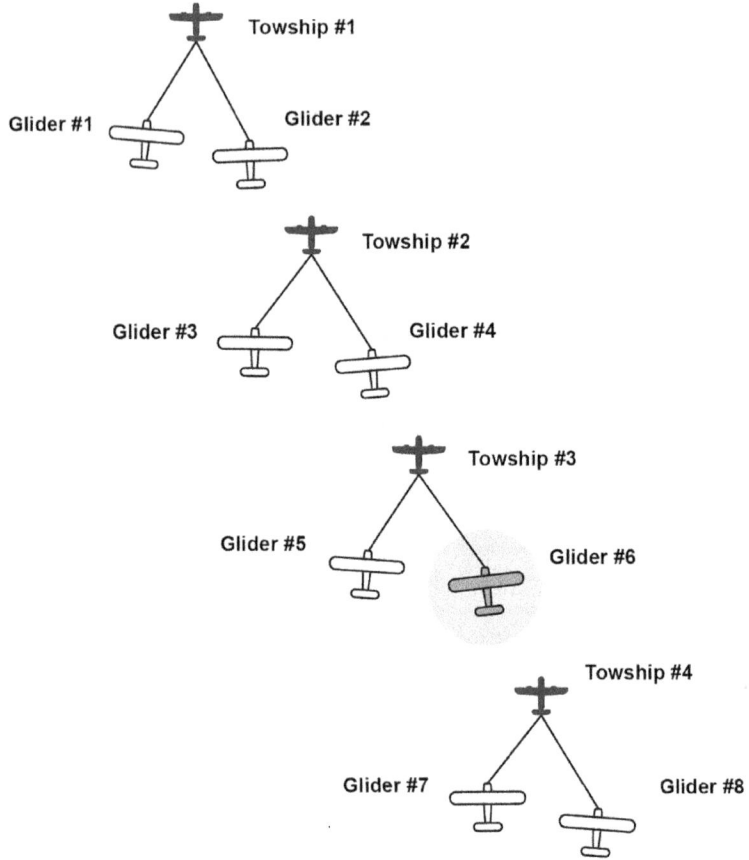

Flight Officers Walter Lindberg and Eldon Mueller in Glider #6

MY FATHER HAD NO CHILDREN

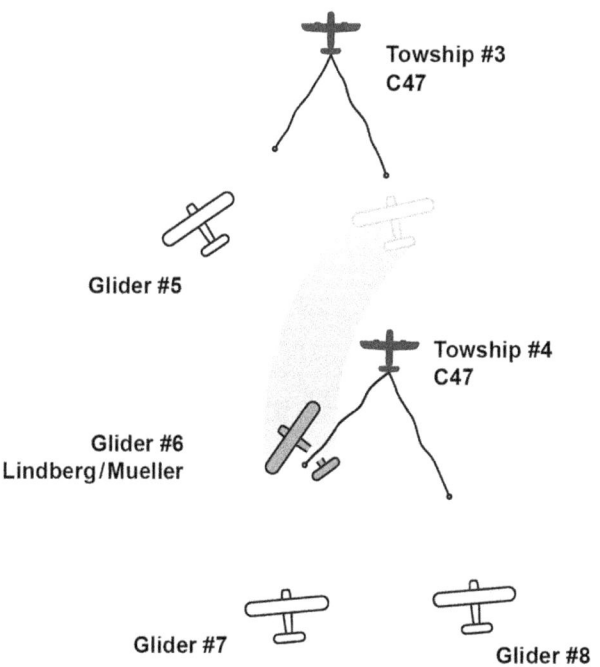

Visual Description of Glider Accident – February 22, 1945

Glider #7 and Glider #8 released from Towship #4. As Glider #6 passes under the towship, the cable swings down and shears off the tail section of Walter's Glider #6.

Glider #5 has already release and is clear and in a downward descent, following other Gliders #1, #2, #3, and #4.

Justin Britton Graphics
Salt Lake City, Utah

Glider crash at Tours, France, on February 22, 1945. Practicing double tows for the Rhine River Crossing—Operation Varsity. Walter B. Lindberg and Eldon Mueller were killed during this practice mission at A39-B airfield, Tours, France.

Over the years, I have heard different reports of my father's death. It was not until I started writing this book that I was able to obtain the official accident report from the United States Military Archives. In that report, there were several other testimonies given by the witnesses to the accident. One was Private First Class Dominic Cuozzo, who described the accident almost identical to the description of Cy Shaffer above (see Appendix). He was a member of the Ninety-First Troop Carrier Squadron and was on the ground when he saw the accident. Also included in the archives is the final accident report signed by Lieutenant Colonel Charles H. Young (see Appendix), the commanding officer of the 439th Troop Carrier Group. He is the author of the book *Into the Valley*, from which I have included references at various points in this book. The accident description is described and explained exactly in his book on page 454.

Here is the official statement given at an inquiry that same day by Virgil Neal, who was flying in the number 7 glider directly behind my father's group; he described what he saw.

> Flying #7 ship behind number three element coming over the field, I was about 600 feet from the glider that was flying right wing of the element ahead. It cut about 20 seconds early. It seemed to have trouble getting the nose down and came up level with my ship flying straight ahead. After we had passed, I could see him beginning to drop his nose in a controlled glide and starting to turn under my ship. My glider cut loose about ten seconds after his. I felt a sharp jerk as if one of the gliders hit my tow rope. Nothing more happened until the tower said a glider had crashed.

A question that has not been answered is, how is it that two veteran pilots of eight previous glider missions between them end up in a glider practicing accident that took both of their lives? What was the reason that the glider was "having a hard time getting the nose down"? The answer may be in the letter written to me by Cy Shaffer. As mentioned before, he witnessed the accident and wrote what he thought may have happened: "There seemed to be a strong gust of wind, which was carrying some of the gliders down the wrong flight course." He saw the tow rope strike my father's glider. He explained to me in his letter that the pilots did not wear parachutes typically during practice, so even if my father would have had a parachute on, there would not have been enough time to get out of the plane and open the chute, considering the glider was heading straight down at tremendous speed.

The last possibility is that many of the gliders used in practice sessions were salvaged gliders from the battlefields and refurbished for practice missions. There was always the possibility of a mechanical issue in the repaired and salvaged gliders. Perhaps the former reason of a sudden gust of wind also seems likely due to the description of my father's glider remaining on a straight upward trajectory.

The day of the accident was exactly one year and twenty-one days after my dad (Walter) wrote his goodbye and promised he would come home *somehow* to both of us. Both Lil and Walt complained that letters were far and few between, though they both told each other they were writing consistently. On February 14, 1945, Walter wrote:

> "I never receive your letters in series—so I write to you most of the time and never answer your questions because I didn't receive the letter until—until I answered some other. It doesn't make sense, but you know what I mean, there have been millions of letters lost, so I don't know just which ones you have written that I've never received and probably never will, so how can I answer you?"

That last letter was posted on February 15, 1945. I have often wondered how my life would have been different had my father come home from the war. How unfortunate it was that an accident took his life. He had been on the battlefield so many times before in horrific, dangerous situations, and yet was it a mistake, a gust of wind, or faulty equipment? "It was the only accidental death during the many glider training exercises in Europe."

Operation Varsity mission began one month later, on March 24, 1945, even though Eisenhower had begun moving troops toward the Rhine River as early as February 23. By the first of March, tens of thousands of troops had gathered on the west bank of the Rhine. On March 24, the air invasion began, which included the British Horsa gliders as well as 906 American CG-4A Wacos in double-tow behind some six-hundred-plus C-47s carrying over twenty-two thousand paratroopers. It was the largest invasion since D-Day Normandy nine months earlier. This was indeed the last mission of the gliders in WWII. The invasion of Germany brought closure to the war in Europe two and a half months later.

F/O Walter Lindberg and F/O Eldon Mueller

The fatality rate of the glider pilots in Operation Varsity was greater than 60 percent. Would my father have been one of the survivors? The fact that Walter Lindberg had survived the missions of Normandy, Southern France, Holland, and Belgium was beyond a miracle. How was Walter's life preserved on battlefields but then lost in a freak accident? As Mueller's and Walter's friend, Goldie said about his own survival under incredible circumstances, "Only God knows." Many decades later, Goldie explained in a documentary about the loss of his close friend, Eldon Mueller, who died in that ill-fated practice mission with my father.

Angels of Death

The glider pilots of WWII, who flew their silent wings into enemy territory delivering troops, battle artillery, medical personnel and supplies, are the silent heroes of that second "great war." My father is just one of many of those heroes who did not return home. The much-feared telegrams, which carried the names, dates, and places of death kept loved ones and family members constantly on edge.

Messenger boys, as young as fourteen years old, often were given the heavy and sorrowful burden to deliver those yellow envelopes with the dreaded news. The words, typed boldly within a Western Union telegram, might be about a husband, brother, father, son, or women serving as nurses or in other capacities in the war zones. The messages were always brief because a telegram's cost was determined by the number of words on the page.

The young boys delivering those telegrams were sometimes nicknamed the "angels of death." The "angels of death" came at any hour of the day or night with a knock on the door or the ring of a doorbell. The boys were the copilots, so to speak, of the specially marked Western Union telegram service vehicles, for the boys were usually underage for driving.

The driver waited in the car, watching as the boy walked cautiously to the door. Once the delivery was made, the boy hurried back to the car and the driver, who waited anxiously for his return. Neither the boy nor the driver wanted to be present when the envelope was opened. They drove together quickly to the next recipient's doorstep.

It was stressful for everyone to hear the same voice every day on the radio about defeats and retreats or about battles won or lost. Even if the news was turned off, the angels of death were ever visible as they drove by and/or delivered the realities of war to a neighbor's front door.

My father's plane crash in France happened on February 22, 1945, but the Western Union telegram did not arrive in Louisville until three weeks later, on March 14, 1945. It was delivered at 10:53 a.m. Lil saw the Western Union vehicle from the front window of her apartment building at 900 South Sixth Street. The building had many residents, so it was not clear at first who was to receive the telegram.

Chrysteen, my mother's sister who lived in the apartment house next door, was just leaving for work that morning when she saw (as Lil saw) the Western Union messenger approaching the gate of the building next to hers. She ran next door and caught the messenger before he rang the bell to enter the building. Aunt Chrys knew in her fearful heart, as she told me many years later, that the telegram was for Lil. However, a telegram did not always contain death news; it might just inform of "missing in action" or "prisoner of war" status or injured and in the hospital.

There was a glimmer of hope when Chrys saw that the telegram was not from the War Department in Washington, DC, but from Walt's mother in Los Angeles. She told the delivery boy, "I'm the sister, so I will take the telegram. My sister lives on the first floor." Chrys opened the telegram before she went inside. She faced a heart-wrenching dilemma in those next few moments.

As Chrys entered the hallway of the building, Lil opened the door to her own apartment. She knew instantly that the telegram was meant for her even though Chrys had opened it. They flew into each other's arms, both crying and wailing at the same time. There was also loud crying from inside the apartment. A baby needed attention at the exact moment, as if she somehow knew of the tragic news.

Aunt Chrys told me, "It was a horrendous moment that I have lived over and over again, even in my dreams!" Mama Chrys, as I called her sometimes, was the only one who had knowledge of that day. My mother never talked to me about it. Those memories were too painful to bring back. Later, in my young teenage years, my aunt told me, "Lillian has never gotten over the loss of your father." The following telegrams brought the news of my father's death.

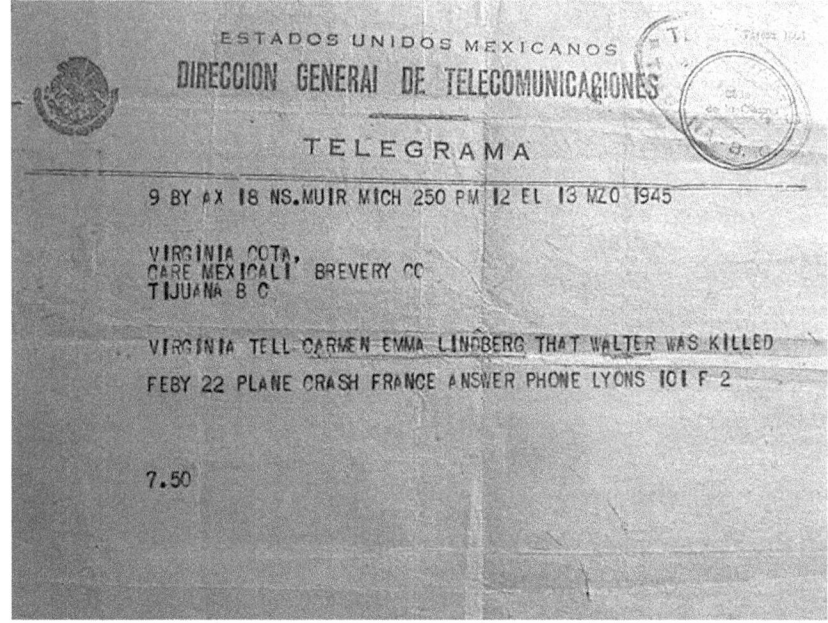

Telegram no. 1

As I have delved deeper into my father's life story, there are so many questions unanswered. One telegram, above, is from my father's wife, originating from Lyons, California, sent to Walt's aunt Virginia in Mexico. It is not even addressed to her home but to the place of her employment. My dad was very close to his aunt Virginia, as he spent much time with her in Mexico during his early childhood. Maybe that's why Virginia received the first telegram about my father's death rather than Peach.

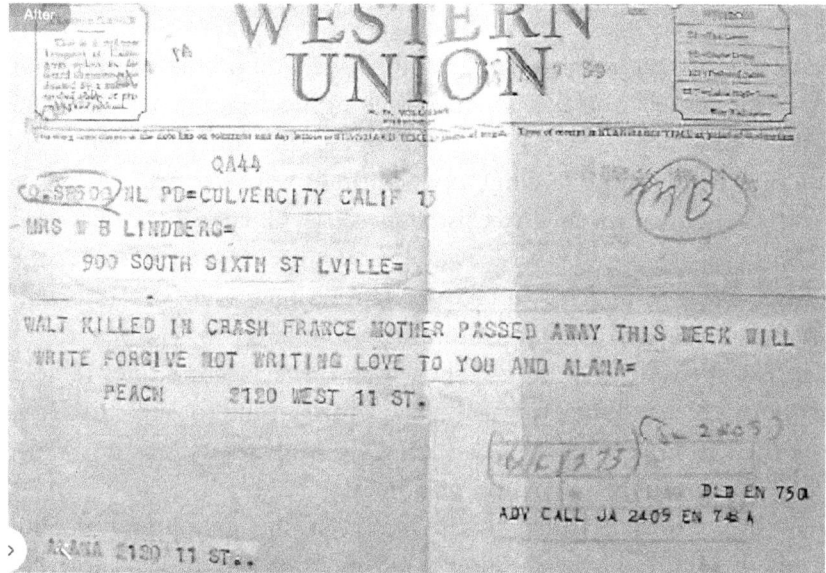

Telegram No. 2

    Telegram no. 2 is from Peach. It was sent to my mother notifying her of Walt's death. Not only did Peach bear the grief of her son's death, but she had recently buried her mother, as the telegram refers. It is the same one Chrys intercepted and opened beforehand. It is much more personal than Telegram no. 1, sent to Walt's aunt Virginia.

    Why would Walter's wife think my grandmother (Peach) would not have been the first to know of Walt's death? Her address, 2120 W. Eleventh Street in Los Angeles, California, is the address on my dad's dog tags, which I have in my possession.

    I have put the puzzle pieces in place, as I have uncovered each one, from information I have received from my mom and dad's letters to each other from what close family members have told me, from my father's close glider pilot buddies, and from government archival records. I can only try to have empathy for the emotional pain my mother and grandmother must have been going through due to the various complex personal problems, which could not be resolved when there was a world war going on and my father's participation in it.

My father's death brought into focus a whole new set of problems for my mother and new decisions she would have to make not only for herself but also for me. Making decisions emotionally in unsettling times is never a good idea, but at that time, emotions were about the only thing to cling to when times were so uncertain.

Even more problems existed because Chrysteen, Peach, and Johnny, Walt's brother, were aware of Lil's dire circumstances. None of her other siblings or immediate family knew that she and Walt were not married. Peach and Johnny wrote letters of condolence to Lil, as if she were his wife, but she was not. Peach sent money to help with my care, and she eventually set up a trust fund for me. However, the trust fund's money, which I knew nothing about, was not available to me until my eighteenth birthday.

Lil's emotions ruled in the decisions she made, and alcohol seemed to be the only calming thing for those emotions. How my mother coped is beyond my own comprehension. She was twenty-three years old and had a baby from an unwed circumstance beyond her control. Her future husband had died, and she was unemployed—truly untenable, emotional, but very real circumstances.

The angels of death on March 14, 1945, delivered more than the message of my father's death. That telegram's aftermath lingered so much longer for my mother and me than just the momentous opening. It must have been the same for every family that received that kind of telegram, and there were thousands! Mine and my mother's story is only one story of so many that have never been told. Each one is an individual portrait of a family's experience after such a loss.

The operations in the European Theater officially ended on June 8, 1945, three months after my father's death. Wars may end, but the consequences of those enormous conflicts never do, whether for those who win or for those who lose. The angels of death brought more than momentary shock and grief. The telegrams were more than announcements of a death; they brought months and years of loneliness and uncertainty to my mom and me and everyone else who received one about a loved one.

18

War Orphan's Tale

My birth at the Jewish Hospital in Louisville, Kentucky, on June 27, 1944, was twenty-one days after the beginning of the D-Day invasion known as Operation Overlord by the USAAF. Though the attack began on the beaches of Normandy in France on June 6, 1944, it lasted almost three months. So my mother gave birth during the biggest invasion battle in history. Where the French beaches had once been empty and welcoming for the beginning of summer, instead there were over 177,000 Allied vehicles and thousands of soldiers occupying the space.

As the battle continued, everyone in the United States and across the world were tuned in to radios to get the latest battlefront news. My mother was intently listening while awaiting my birth. Nursing staffs at most hospitals were working long hours with little time off because many nurses had volunteered to go to the battlefields. Many older, retired doctors as well had returned to hospitals to cover shifts due to the younger doctors being needed overseas and in military hospitals. Dr. Pearlstine, who delivered me, was one of the older doctors back on duty. As was mentioned earlier, my dad received the Air Medal on the day of my birth.

By 1946, my mother had become despondent, depressed, and overcome with grief. She told me, "You looked so much like Walt, and every day you reminded me of him. I just couldn't deal with that." When I was barely over a year old, she put me in a home-care situation with a woman who took in orphaned war children for a living. Her name was Mrs. Huffine. I lived with six or seven other "war children." My first childhood memories are of Mother Huffine and my time there. I remember meals at a long table with other children. I also remember getting burned while playing ring around the rosy around the big furnace in the basement.

My mother came to take me home, to be with her, shortly before school started in September of 1949. I cried in Mother Huffine's arms on that last day; she was the mom I knew. After leaving the Huffine home, as young as I was, I saw my "real" mother's unmanageable emotions rule her life every day.

The post-WWII economy and the fears fostered from those war-worn years affected every war child's experience. We children may not have understood or realized specific details about war recovery efforts, but adults everywhere were anxious and on edge. That anxiety was transferred to us in many ways for years after the war was over.

When I started kindergarten, there were bomb shelters at school, and we had drills, which hustled us into shelters in an organized and disciplined way. Instead of fire drills, we had air raid drills. When we heard the alarm, we knew what to do. We slid down fire escapes, which led to the shelters. This was 1949 to 1950, when still another war, the Korean conflict, was about to begin! I completed my kindergarten year in June of 1950. My home life was not as organized and structured as it had been at Mrs. Huffine's makeshift orphanage. I was five years old and had been living with my mother for less than a year when my life became endangered but not because there was a war.

My mother brought a boyfriend home to live with us. He was a photographer and he taught my mother the skills of his profession. In those days, professional cameras were big, clumsy, and awkward. Film came in big rolls, which had to be developed in several different kinds of chemicals. Flash bulbs were only good for one shot, and they made a loud popping noise when they went off. My mother was employed at the boyfriend's photography business in the daytime while working as a cocktail waitress at night. We were still living in the three-story apartment building on Sixth Street in inner-city Louisville, Kentucky.

It was a very unhappy and stressful time for me. Sometimes I had a babysitter, but most of the time I was home alone, except at night, when the boyfriend was there with me. I never liked him. My aunt Chrys told me, "Whenever he entered the room, you ran out."

If not for my dog, Rocket, I would have been more afraid. I got him when I was five years old. We became inseparable. As a puppy, he followed me everywhere. I played with him as if he were a doll, and I put him in my doll high chair. He slept on my bed with me all the time.

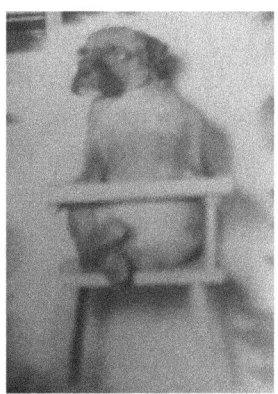

Alana at five years old and her dog Rocket

Being a boxer, he outgrew childish things sooner than I did. By the time he was a year old, he was my babysitter and my protector. If I had to be spanked or reprimanded, my mother took me in the bathroom and closed the door. Rocket bit her arm once when she tried to hit me.

I disliked the photographer so much I hid in a secret place behind the dark stairwell outside our apartment. I called my secret hiding place Wisconsin, and I have no idea why I gave it that name. At five or six years old, I'm sure I had no idea what or where Wisconsin was. Under the stairwell was a safe place for me because no one knew where my Wisconsin was, not even my mother, only Rocket.

I have read much about war being a war orphan. Stephen Ambrose, an American historian, stated this about war, "[T]he cost of victory is never fully paid, that the gods of war keep demanding further tribute…" I think this was especially true for those of us who were born during or shortly after the war. The younger we were, the less understanding we had. We did not even know that we were "war children" or "war orphans," but it was a category that we fit into.

We continually paid "tribute to the gods of war," for the loss of our fathers in so many negative, difficult, and challenging ways. Our mothers' grieving and the poverty, which many of us lived in, have been part of that "tribute" paid by each of us, though our war orphan experiences were obviously much varied, for sure.

Interesting how, in my case and others' too, my father has been a huge part of my life, though I never knew him. His picture sat on my dresser for as long as I can remember. Most adults, especially our mothers, did not speak much about our dead fathers. If adults were talking about them when we entered a room, the conversation usually ended or became whispers that they thought we couldn't hear or understand.

Walter Bert Lindberg (1914–1945)
The picture on my dresser

The culture of the day dictated that we were children that could be seen but not heard. We never dared ask about the war or why our fathers did not return home. The only thing we knew for sure was that death was permanent. However, understanding our fathers' deaths as a sacrifice for a purpose was another matter. There were no safe spaces made for us anywhere. There was no place where we could go and talk about our loss and our grief.

When I wanted to ask my mother about my father, I didn't because I knew the conversation would make her sad. Sometimes when she had too much to drink, she would tell me, "You look just like your daddy." Then she would go into a babbling mood and begin to cry. I knew I had to change the subject when that happened. Sometimes she would not cry but be mad and ask, "Why didn't he come home?" Like me, most of us war orphans probably did not even know exactly why our fathers never came home. How could my mother or anyone explain war and the necessity of it to me or any small child?

When I was seven years old, we moved from the apartment building to a house. In the apartment building, there were people I knew and were able to visit, but in the new house, I was home alone most of the time with Rocket when I wasn't in school. As a forlorn child, home alone, I often went downstairs to open the dark-green army footlocker or trunk, which belonged to my father. I took out his uniform and put his jacket on.

I remember the trunk contents smelled like mothballs. It was kept in the basement in a shed, which had previously been used for coal storage. The trunk wasn't locked, so I had easy access to it but only when my mother was not around. As silly or weird as it may seem, when I had that big jacket on, I thought my father's arms were around me. I pretended to have conversations with him. Most of the time, those conversations did not end well. I ended up sitting in that dark space on an old wooden bench beside the trunk, crying my eyes out.

I asked the same question about my father as my mother, "Why didn't you come home?" Then I would also wonder and ask myself another question, "Could my daddy still be missing in action like my friend Sandra's?" Her dad came home two years after the war was over. I hoped and fantasized that my dad might come home someday too. In my little girl's heart, I wanted him to come home so badly. I imagined all the time how different my life might be. There was a song, which I heard on the radio, and I memorized it. It was a popular song on the Hit Parade in 1952 called "Missing in Action." These are the words I remember, and I can still hear them clearly in my mind.

> The warships had landed, and I came ashore
> The fighting was over for me ever more
> For I had been wounded they left me for dead,
> A stone for my pillow and snow for my bed.
>
> The enemy found me and took me away,
> They made me a prisoner of war, so they say
> But God in his mercy was with me one day,
> The gate was left open, and I ran away.
>
> A vagabond dreamer, forever I'll roam
> For there was nobody to welcome me home
> The face of my darling no more shall I see.
> For missing in *action forever I'll be.*

My mother, as a single parent in the early 1950s, knew nothing about welfare or handouts. She worked two jobs most of the time I was growing up. Her grief led her into depression and alcoholism and other bad habits. She had suitors besides the photographer that lived with us for short periods of time and many that came in and out but never stayed long. She had tried marriage for a couple of years, but it did not work out. I barely remember her husband; he was a semitruck driver, and I liked him and his big black dog, Jigger. I don't know when they got divorced, but I do remember riding in the big cab of his truck going to The Falls after school was out in June.

My childhood was a world of mixed messages from adults. My mother carried prejudices against all kinds of people, but I never knew why. I was not allowed to play with my Black school friends in Louisville, except at school. In the country, at The Falls, where my aunt and uncle lived and where I spent summer vacations and holidays, it was not that way. At The Falls, we children were truly free!

My life in inner-city Louisville was anything but free. It was very unsettling and full of fear. I never knew when a drunken adult would show up to push me around and scold me for nothing. My aunt Mae, my mother's sister, the one I lived with at The Falls, taught me how to pray. I prayed constantly with a favorite scripture that told me I would not perish if I believed in Jesus (John 3:16). *Perish* was the key word for me. I did not want to perish, but sometimes I thought I might.

I often prayed to my father, somehow thinking he might hear me and be able to rescue me. My mother didn't go to church, though my granny told me in her Southern accent, "Why, sakes alive, chile, Liyen Earl played the piano and the organ in church and other places too." Granny also lamented to me, "When Liyen Earl went to Short Creek High School, that's when she started bein' a feisty youngun!" Granny did not often stay with us in Louisville because she and my mother could hardly be in the same room without an argument. Of course, she wouldn't have approved of our living circumstances, anyway.

I don't know if she knew about any of the stress and abuse that my mother and I suffered. She might have tried to intervene if she did. I knew my mother was not married to the men she brought into the house. She had affairs with men that were married and received gifts from them. I was never fond of any of the men she brought home. They were all mostly like her, with heavy drinking habits and abusive personalities, with bad language and other bad behaviors. I never wanted my mother to get married because in the back of my child's mind, I always had the hope that my dad would somehow come home, like the song said.

When I was in first grade at Mary D. Hill School, near where we lived, I often stood looking out the chain-link fence down the street during recess and wondered if someday my dad would come walking down that street. It was the "Missing in Action" song that gave me that hope.

Rocket was my soul mate. Sometimes I was able to avoid my mother's boyfriends by taking my dog into a room and locking the door from the inside. My mother came home from work one night and found me sleeping on the floor with my dog in the room behind the locked door. She never asked me why I was sleeping in there, or if she did, I don't remember.

After school was out in third grade, I was sent to The Falls, as usual. When I came home for fourth grade in September to start school, I was sent to live with my mother's brother, my uncle Bill, and his wife, Addie, and Addie's daughter. My mother sent me away instead of her boyfriend, the photographer, who was still around. I never did understand that, but I was glad to live at my uncle's house.

When I lived with Uncle Bill's family, I attended Rubel Avenue Elementary School, where fourth and fifth grades were combined. There were still teacher shortages because of the war. My uncle's stepdaughter was not my biological cousin, and she was two years older than me. We got along most of the time, but she had a knack for getting us into trouble.

One time, my uncle Bill took us to the drugstore and left us in his brand-new Ford to wait for him. My cousin opened the glove box and found a can of spray paint. She proceeded to spray the dashboard with the gold paint. When Uncle Bill came back to the car, he was furious! I tried to say it was not me, but that did not work. We both got clobbered with the belt and were punished severely. Another time she opened some Christmas presents hidden in the closet before Christmas, and we both were in trouble again. After such episodes, I prayed to my dad. I knew he wasn't God, but somehow it comforted me when I was upset.

When I first came to my uncle's house to live, I was grateful for the arrangement, but my mother sent the boyfriend to pick me up occasionally on the weekends. I hated being alone with him in the car. Those were hard times! I tried to avoid going with him, but my aunt and uncle insisted that I go home. They probably needed a break from us two girls, and they needed some privacy of their own.

My aunt Chrys came from Florida to visit me at my uncle's house when she was on vacation. One night, I slept with her and I told her my problems. She held me in her arms, and we both cried. However, she told me, "Alana Jean, don't you dare tell your uncle Bill because if you do, he will go to jail for murder!" That was a very scary thing to think about when I was nine years old. I loved my uncle Bill, even with his harsh disciplinary methods. I believed what Mama Chrys told me, so I never told him anything about what was going on with the photographer.

After my fourth-grade year of school, I was sent to The Falls for the summer, as always. When I came back to Louisville, in time for school to start, my mother and her boyfriend had moved again to another house. I had to enroll in a different school once more, my fourth elementary school.

The abuse by the boyfriend continued, and I could do nothing about it. My aunt Chrys had confronted him, to no avail. In those days, such distasteful matters were not on the table to talk about. My mother always told me, "He wouldn't do anything to hurt you." I was trapped in a very bad situation at such a young age where I had no power, and I had no solution to alleviate the problem.

In the second half of my fifth-grade year, we moved again into a house my mother bought. It was in a neighborhood where I made a lot of friends, again in another elementary school. My mother only worked at the photography studio a couple of days a week, but she still worked at night as a cocktail waitress. My abuser still lived with us, and my nightmare continued.

I hated going downstairs into his studio in the basement. As I got a little older, I was able to avoid the photo sessions because I could be stubborn and more forceful in denying him. When my mother was gone at night, it was still much the same. There were always the threats of harm to her if I divulged "the little secrets." Another year passed. It seemed as I grew older, he became even more emboldened. Once, when my mother was working downstairs in the darkroom, he came into my bedroom completely naked. I was terrified and I told him, "I'm going to scream for my mother!" He said, "You wouldn't dare!" He then left me trembling in my room.

Finally, when I started junior high school as a seventh grader, my best friend, Linda, lived down the street from me. Linda's mom was so kind and loving to me, and they had a big family. She was pregnant with her fifth child when I became very close with her. One day, for some reason, I decided to tell her of my problems of abuse from my mother's boyfriend. She told me she would help me—I didn't know how. I never saw her with my mother, and I never heard her talking to my mother. Maybe she called my mother on the phone. I don't know what happened.

A few days after I confided to Linda's mother, I came home from school, and the photographer boyfriend was gone. All his clothes, all his photography equipment, and his dog that I was afraid of were also gone. He just disappeared, and I never saw him again. Linda's mom never told me that she talked to my mother, but she did ask me, "Is the boyfriend still around?" When I told her, "No, he is gone," she just said. "That's good!"

It wasn't long after that that my mother had another boyfriend. At first, he showed up at times in a taxicab drunk, and my mother had to pay the taxi fare and help him into the house. That is how I met him. When he showed up in the middle of the night inebriated, he stayed overnight. He lived in Clarksville, Indiana, across the bridge from Louisville. Louisville is on the shore of the Ohio River, and there is a long bridge connecting the state of Kentucky with the state of Indiana.

After my mother got a car, a 1947 Desoto, in the spring of 1957, we often drove across the bridge to visit her new boyfriend. He lived with his mother and his two children, of whom he had sole custody. He was a veteran of WWII in the Philippines and had four fingers of one hand missing due to a machete accident. The children's mother was a prostitute and supposedly a bad person; she was in jail, so I never met her.

One night, when we were driving back from Indiana to Louisville, across the bridge, my mother started talking about my father. Perhaps because I was older, then twelve years old, she wanted to talk to me about my dad. It is the only time I remember her ever really talking to me about him. I knew it was hard for her to bring the subject up, and that night, I don't know why she did.

She told me, "Your daddy loved you, and he always thought he would come home to us. He thought, somehow, he would survive the war." She told me he had died in a plane crash in France. She said, "He was so handsome and had a lot of curly black hair. I fell in love with him almost instantly." She said he had stayed at the hotel, where she worked as a hostess, and that he swam in the pool there. She said, "He was a very good swimmer and even tried out for the Olympics." I also loved swimming and had taken lifeguard lessons. That made me think maybe I was like my dad. It was something I could relate to about him.

Eventually, the new boyfriend came to live with us. He, too, was abusive but not in the same way. He was a very nice person, except when he drank too much. After he moved in, my mother began to drink even more than before. My mother and he became drunk and abusive to each other almost every night. His two children also came to live with us, and I had to share my bedroom with them.

Since I had been an only child for so long, that was a huge adjustment for me. They weren't my siblings, and I resented them taking over my spaces. They were products of a nasty divorce, and I was told their mother had been very abusive to them. I guessed that's why she was in jail.

The Fall of 1957, I was excited to start my eighth-grade year in junior high as a "real" teenager. I had had my thirteenth birthday at The Falls. I even felt older, but my days of paying tribute to the war due to the loss of my father were not over. That September, when I returned home to Louisville from The Falls, I was terribly upset about what had happened to all my childhood memorabilia, which had been replaced by the boyfriend's children's toys while I was gone.

I was a huge fan of Elvis Presley. I cut out pictures of him and put them all over my bedroom wall. When I was in seventh grade, I was able to get Elvis's autograph after going to his concert. That small piece of paper meant more to me than gold, and losing it would have been worse than losing my arm or leg (at least I thought so at the time).

When I found my room completely torn up, I started to cry. All my movie-star paper dolls, which I had so perfectly separated into individual boxes, were destroyed! My pictures of Elvis on the wall were all gone, and I couldn't find his autograph. My favorite doll had a broken arm and a missing eye. The clothes my granny made for my baby doll were strewn on the floor of my closet, and the little suitcase, which held the clothes, was smashed to bits!

I found my dad's picture under my bed, the one that I kept on my dresser. That picture was my lifeline to my father, and I was very upset when the picture was missing. Then I couldn't find my Elvis autograph, and I screamed at my mother. I was mostly mad at her rather than the kids because I felt she should have prevented all the damage, but it seemed to me that she didn't care. The material culture of my childhood apparently was not important to my mother but was very important to me. I cried about it for several days. My mother and I never got along after that.

My eighth-grade year in 1957 began at the same school I had gone to in the previous year, Southern Junior High School. I had come home from The Falls to a lot of chaos and unexpected changes, as I mentioned, which were disturbing, and my life once again was completely turned upside down. I saw that the boyfriend's two kids had taken over my bedroom completely! It was hard to have two more people in my small room. Many times I slept in the living room on the sofa, while those kids slept in my double bed. The girl was about six years old, and the boy was three or four years old at the time. If I had had time, I probably could have adjusted to my new "siblings" and our new shared surroundings.

However, our lives took an abrupt turn less than a month later. I could never have anticipated what was happening, and I had no power or influence to intervene. We three kids piled into the boyfriend's 1957 tan-and-white Buick with few belongings. The three of us were in the back seat. The only thing I carried was a tiny clear plastic cage with my bird, Tinker, inside. It was so small his tail was bent inside. We were on our way, leaving Louisville, going across the country to Las Vegas, a city I had never heard of! I was assured that my dog, Rocket, would also be en route by train as soon as we were settled.

As I waved goodbye to my friends and neighbors out the back window of the car, I was crying. I wondered if I really would ever see my dog, Rocket, ever again.

19

The Falls

To understand my childhood completely, I must take you to The Falls that I have spoken about previously. Falls of Rough, Kentucky, was a real place. It was not a city or even a small town. It was in mid-twentieth century simply a community of people who worked hard to make a living. They were all farmers, but second jobs like managing the general store, the tiny post office, or the night watchman's shack was not unusual. There was an old flour mill there, where corn was ground for corn flour and cornmeal, which was bagged and sent to surrounding cities. My aunt Mae and my uncle Morgan worked there, in addition to farming.

"Falls of Rough" by Gary Maglinger

I knew Falls of Rough as The Falls. It was the only place where I did not have to take care of myself. I felt safe there. I lived there during the summers when school was not in session and/or during holiday breaks, like Christmas or Easter. The Falls has a history, but hardly anyone knows about it, nor did anyone talk much about it.

Though I was born in the city of Louisville, that city is not the part of Kentucky I loved or that I always yearn to see again. "My Old Kentucky Home," which Stephen Foster wrote about, was not in Louisville. That song always brings to my mind the thriving little place about a hundred miles from Louisville, which everyone who lived there called The Falls. Stephen Foster's songs were part of my elementary school music study in Louisville, and "My Old Kentucky Home" is Kentucky's state song, The tune is melancholy, and one feels nostalgia coming on when the chorus begins, "Weep no more, my lady." I'm that lady sometimes, trying not to weep, even as I write about my carefree childhood there.

The Falls I knew as a child was a post-Civil War community with a history of slavery. However, as one of the only four Commonwealth states, Kentucky always claimed to be neutral. There were people on both sides of the issues of the Civil War, and there were young men from Kentucky who fought on both the Union and Confederate sides. Other states in the north, like Illinois, also claimed soldiers on both sides.

The Falls had a population of Black families who were descendants from those previous slavery days. There was once a small tobacco plantation there owned by people who had slaves. Their descendants lived about a half mile down the road from my aunt and uncle's farm. My cousin, Charline, and other kids and I played with them. We squeezed ourselves inside old discarded, tubeless, tractor tires, and we rolled down the rooted and overgrown banks above the sandy road in the old tire carcasses. We laughed until our stomachs hurt, and we got so dizzy we thought we might be sick.

We picked and ate wild blackberries until our hands and tongues were stained dark purple! We splashed around in the water under the pump at the well. No one ever told me I couldn't play with the Black kids. I don't even think we children knew we were different colors.

If we did, it made no difference. We were just kids having fun in the rural landscape. We were truly free! Our parents and/or grandparents were too busy to check on us. We had to be in the house by dark, that's all that mattered.

Backstory—a special birthday

I have a special birthday memory that happened at The Falls. It was my sixth birthday. On the morning of June 27, 1950, my aunt Mae told me, "You have a great big surprise for your birthday!" She didn't even hint at what that surprise was going to be, no matter how I begged to know. Some of my friends knew it was my birthday, and they showed up early at the farmhouse. We all went down to the sandy road below the house to play for a while before my party.

We heard a car coming and looked up from our sand-building projects to see a shiny, goldish car approaching in the distance. As always, we ran up the tree-rooted hill as fast as we could to watch the car pass by. However, it stopped below us, and a small lady in a light brown suit with a matching hat got out of the car. None of us recognized the car because there was seldom a car on that country road. No ladies we knew dressed like that lady either.

We ran back down the hill to see who it might be. The lady's suit had long sleeves and gold buttons. She had on high heels on her tiny feet, which sank deep into the sand. That encounter on that day is so clear in my mind it is as if it happened yesterday. Who was that lady?

We children walked slowly toward her, and when we got close, she singled me out of the group and put her arms out to embrace me. She said, "I'm your Grandma Peach, you must be Alana." I was very accustomed to the Southern drawl that everyone in my life had, so I knew at once she was not one of us. Even a six-year-old knows a different accent when spoken, but I had no idea why she sounded different than all the other people I knew.

Peach was a small person, not much taller than me. She hugged me so tight I could hardly breathe. She began to say things to me, which I could not understand—and then she began to cry. I don't know why, but I started to cry too. My friends watched in the background, wondering why we were both crying—but then, all of a sudden, Peach began to laugh at the same time she was hugging me and crying. Her laugh was as infectious as her crying, so we all started laughing as well.

She wanted to know the names of all my friends, so after the introductions, we all trudged up the grassy hill to the house, and I pulled the whitewashed wooden gate open. Before we reached the front porch, Aunt Mae was opening the screen door to let us in. My friends left us but were told they could come back for homemade ice cream and cake later.

Aunt Mae welcomed Peach into the house with a simple handshake and a "Hello, we're glad ya came. We never told Alana Jean you was a comin'." Our accents must have seemed strange to Peach as much as hers sounded strange to us. English does not sound the same in Los Angeles, where she was from, as it does in rural Kentucky and much of the Southland in the United States.

We went into a special room in the house that no one was ever allowed to go into, at least not kids. The door to that room was always closed. There were rugs on the floor, not like the linoleum in the rest of the house. It had a beautiful, flowered couch that was made into a bed. The room was only used in the summer because there was no potbellied stove in there to heat it. There was a separate door to the front porch, however, to let in the cool air at night when it was hot. Aunt Mae kept that room in perfect order for those special people who were allowed in. Since it was my birthday, I must have been special for that day. Aunt Mae left us alone in the room and closed the door.

I thought my grandma Peach was so pretty with her reddish hair. She let me try on her hat, which was the same color of her skirt. She just kept on laughing and crying at the same time in between all the hugs that she gave me. She stayed overnight at the farm with me. We slept together in that special room on the special pull-out bed. It seemed she couldn't quit hugging me all that night.

Peach kept saying to me over and over, "You look just like Walt." Much of what she said to me I could not understand, but I loved hearing her voice. She was this magical person who came just to see me on my birthday. She sang to me and talked to me in the sweetest voice I had ever heard. Peach was the best surprise I ever had for any birthday!

I don't remember much about the next day, but as we hugged and said our goodbyes, I knew she was someone special in my life and not just because she was allowed in that special room. After her visit, I often received presents and short letters from her. She traveled to Europe and sent me gifts from there. She went to Jerusalem and sent me a Bible, which I still have. It has a carved wooden cover. She also sent me an embroidered red felt jacket from Spain. It was always too big for me, and I don't know what happened to it. I loved the wooden Bible, though, so I guess that's why I have kept it all these years. Now that I look back on that special time with Peach, I wonder how she found Falls of Rough. My mother did not come with her.

Peach drove all the way from Los Angeles by herself to see me. Unlike the first time, when I was eight months old, no pictures were taken. We had cameras in the city, but there were no cameras at The Falls. I have always been sad about that because I have only the memories I carry in my head and my heart. Peach's hugs, her perfume, and the sound of her voice all came to mind each time gifts or letters arrived from her when I was in Louisville. I have always wished for pictures of my sixth birthday event, but there are none.

Each birthday after my sixth, I hoped to see Peach again, but she never came. My mother never spoke of her unless I asked, but when I did ask, the responses were short. I have since learned I am her only grandchild, and my mother intentionally kept us apart. Sadly, little did I know after that day, I would never see my grandmother Peach again.

On my tenth birthday at The Falls, it was the last time I saw all my little childhood Black friends. All their families left in one large group, parents, kids, and grandparents. I cried when my playmates left. It was never the same after that. Farming was becoming less and less a livelihood, and the Black families were not the only families who left The Falls for better job opportunities in the surrounding small cities.

The mill and the general store were still functioning at The Falls in my childhood. I loved the general store because it seemed to have everything we wanted or needed. There were stacks of different colors of bolts of fabric, pickles in a barrel, and multiple-flavored suckers in a box on the counter, which were free to kids. JoAnne and Polie, who worked there, always welcomed me by name. "Alana Jean, are you back here again for all summer?" Gwen, who worked in the back room, where the only telephone in the community existed, helped me crank the black phone on the wall to get the operator so I could talk to my mother in Louisville.

The biggest house at The Falls was owned by Miss Jenny Green. I visited the colonial-style Green Mansion many times. It was a grand place situated among tall trees and surrounded by a whitewashed fence. The plush grass and cobbled walkway, which led to the house, was guarded by two dogs—a Doberman and a boxer. They barked and growled at anyone that passed by. The biggest library I had ever seen was upstairs. There were beautiful, imported carpets and furniture throughout and large paintings on the walls of historical people like George Washington. Miss Jenny showed me the silverware in the big hutch in the dining room, which she said was made from Spanish silver coins. I remember Miss Jenny's house was like Scarlet O'Hara's home in *Gone with the Wind*.

At The Falls, there were great fields of what we called Boone County corn, which shimmered in the summer heat as far as the eye could see. The smell of the cornfields and the sound of the waterfalls are a few of my cherished memories. I can close my eyes and see it so clearly that I think if I opened my eyes, I would surely be there. It wasn't Disneyland, but for me, in my childhood for thirteen years, it was the happiest place on earth.

If I were able to time-travel back to my childhood, I would be ten years old and follow my uncle to the mill, where we hung fishing poles out the third-story window. It was a sacred place to me. I had a very spiritual connection with all the people that lived there. I say spiritual because Aunt Mae, my granny, and my uncle Morgan taught me the real values of life by their examples. They were completely self-sufficient, and they worked hard every day to maintain that self-sufficiency. There was no alcohol around, not even moonshine, and I don't remember any profanity. It was a world of difference from my life in the city, which had all those things to the most extreme.

I went to church with Aunt Mae every Sunday, and the church women gathered during the week to quilt or to preserve food for the winter. I was sent to Vacation Bible School where I gained mastery of the scriptures. We went to gospel revivals or what they called tent meetings when they came to the nearby towns of Hardinsburg or Leitchfield.

At my aunt and uncle's farmhouse, there was no central heating, no inside bathroom, and no plumbing for water in the kitchen. The outhouse was about a stone's throw from the house and scary with cobwebs and spiders and a cold concrete floor. The smell was not pleasant either! There were white porcelain chamber pots in the house with red trim on the lids for nighttime personal issues. They had to be emptied in the morning, and it was often my job to do the emptying.

I did not mind helping with the chores, whether in the barn, the kitchen, the garden, or feeding the chickens. Kids were expected to do their part in daily life-sustaining activities. I never thought of it as work. The job I didn't like was collecting the eggs from the hen house. The Rhode Island red hen pecked much too hard when protecting her eggs when I had to fetch them from underneath her warm body.

I was never mistreated, even when sometimes I did not mind my elders. I didn't misbehave too badly because there was always the threat of my uncle Morgan's razor strap, though he never used it on me. It was about the size of a necktie but was made of thick leather and cracked loudly when slapped against the hand to demonstrate its punishing possibilities.

A main reason I loved The Falls is because it was all about *one*. There is one river (Rough River) one waterfall, one bridge, one post office, one general store, one telephone, one gas pump, one flour mill, one night watchman's hut, one church, and one great house in the middle—Miss Jenny's. There were a few smaller houses scattered between the cornfields and on the other side of the bridge. I knew just about everybody who lived there. I met Miss Jenny Green many times. She was old and she owned most everything at The Falls, but she was really nice to me.

Alana Jean at The Falls, 1947–1948

At Miss Jenny's house, I did not get to do the milking, so I stayed in the kitchen with the Black girl, Betty. I helped her skim the cream off the buckets of milk. She sang the Stephen Foster song—the one I learned at school. When she sang the words, "Weep no more, my lady," her voice sounded like an angel's voice. She asked me to sing, but I was too shy. Being at Miss Jenny's house with Aunt Mae and Betty was the happiest of memories.

"Weep no more, my lady."

I can hear those words in my head as clearly as Stephen Foster wrote them in 1852 and as clearly as Betty sang them a hundred years later. "My Old Kentucky Home" was an antislavery song before the Civil War written about slaves leaving Kentucky. Foster was an abolitionist who wrote songs about the South. Kentucky is considered the South but not the deep South.

I love the words, which were first brought to my third-grade ear in the music class at school in Louisville. The words and the melody are melancholy, inviting longing and yearning, a tugging at the heart. I surely cannot relate to a slave's plight, but if they were sad to leave Kentucky, I can relate to that. I was very sad to leave Kentucky and The Falls. I always add "I" and "my" to Stephen Foster's words to make them personal.

> Weep no more, my lady, oh! Weep no more today!
> [I] will sing one song for [my] old Kentucky home
> For [my] old Kentucky home far away.

The Black people I knew and loved at the Falls, like Charlie and his granddaughter, Betty, and the kids I played with, were not slaves. They were farmers, like everyone else. I knew them almost like family. They lived and worked and were self-sufficient, just like my aunt Mae and my uncle Morgan. They plowed their own fields, and they shopped at the same general store as everybody else. There is a story in the words of the song.

> The corn top's ripe and the meadows in the bloom,
> While the birds make music all the day.
>
> The day goes by like a shadow o'er the heart
> With sorrow where all was delight.

The scariest thing at The Falls was if there was a thunderstorm, which could come about unexpectedly. One minute there was sunshine, and the next minute the clouds were filled with anger. There were times when we traipsed a long distance to the storm cellar in the middle of the night. I was frightened of thunderstorms and those enormous lightning streaks flying across the dark sky. Those stormy nights were filled with crashing thunder and howling winds, and the rain poured down in big heavy sheets. Umbrellas weren't much use, and they were hard to hang on to. I did not like the storm cellar with its musty smells, damp earth, and burlap bags full of onions and carrots. I knew all about the spiders hiding under those big bags of vegetables. There were other critters too.

The kerosene lantern Uncle Morgan carried made the cellar ghostly with its dim light shining on the sagging wooden shelves filled with jars of fruit, beans, pickles, corn, and homemade ketchup. We sat on a rickety wooden bench in the middle of the dirt floor to wait out the storm. Aunt Mae's house sat upon stilts about three feet or so from the ground. They must have thought the house was going to blow away or float away. Why else did we have to go to the cellar?

The Storm Cellar
By Alana Lindberg Jolley

In the middle of a misty, eerie, summer's night
I awoke with the sounds of crashing thunder.
I suddenly leaped up in the bed, as with a fright,
Then I grabbed the covers to get way back under.

I heard something faraway, a muffled scream.
Granny left our bedside to go look up to the sky.
It was a nightmare, but it surely was not a dream.
As it happened so often, I wanted to know why.

My uncle came in carrying a big lantern aflame,
Saying, "Get flashlights and your shoes on quick."
No angry storm was he ever going to try and tame.
Terrified and so afraid, my stomach felt so sick.

Rapidly to the storm cellar we all had to traipse.
The house was shaking and the roof clattering.
The slippery stumbles caused many painful scrapes.
The shutters and the windows were loudly shattering.

Like a kind of race, we all sloshed in a straight line,
Holding the crazy umbrellas flapping and fluttering.

Clomping through the weeds, all with a shivering spine,
Rain pelting hard down on our soundless muttering.

> The cellar door was always, forever, a bit stuck.
> Dirt floor inside, smelling musty and so creepy.
> Wily legged creatures all scurrying in the muck.
> Storms always lasted long, and never was I sleepy.

> *What if there's no storm cellar?* I wanted to ask aloud.
> Would the house just sink or calmly float away?
> The roosting chickens never moved under a cloud.
> Even mooing cows in the barn were made to stay.

> That's how it always was in my childhood's plight.
> It's just a frightening memory and still vividly clear.
> If an eerie summer's storm awakens me now at night,
> The storm cellar beckons me still, yet I have no fear.

When things were calm in the evenings after dinner and the chickens were fed and gone to roost, we walked next door to Aunt Della's and Uncle Arlie's. Farmhouses are not close together, so it was not exactly next door. The adults sat in green-and-white metal chairs with arms and discussed the news and other happenings of the day. I caught glimpses of how it was "during the war" or how awful "the flood of '37" was or "what will happen when the new dam is built?"

My cousin Charline and I kept ourselves busy catching lightning bugs. We confined them to glass jars to watch their twinkling lights. The bugs are little flying beetles, easy to catch, and they don't bite. However, a sniff in the jar was not a good idea. When a whole bunch of the bugs were in one jar, flapping their wings, they seemed to blink all at the same time. Though lightning bugs don't bite, red chigger babies do. Our bare feet and legs attracted them, and they made us itch like crazy! Before bedtime, we had to wash them away with warm saltwater to get rid of the itching welts so we could go to sleep.

Daytimes at The Falls in the summer were sweltering hot, so gardening was done early in the morning or in the late afternoon. Granny had painful arthritis, so she did not do any gardening. She sat outside in the shade with a quilt and quilting frame. She made beautiful quilts called The Wedding Ring, which were sold for $12 each. She taught me how to sew, sewing quilt pieces together on her treadle Singer sewing machine. Even with arthritis, she could peddle that sewing machine at high speed. I had to go slower not to make mistakes—I hated unpicking my mistakes.

Each summer, I kept walking past that special room, and I would remember how Peach and I slept in there. I wanted to go back in there and relive the time I spent with her. I wished she could have stayed longer. I knew I wasn't supposed to, but one time I went into that room, anyway, and closed the door. I sat on the flowered couch and looked around, thinking, and then I began to cry. Aunt Mae must have heard me because she barged in, ready to scold me. When she saw I was crying, she backed out of the room and closed the door. I wished for a hug from Peach.

As each summer waned and the nights began to cool, school was about to start in the city. Aunt Mae always took me to the general store, where the one telephone in the community was in the back room. I called my mother to see when I was to come home. My mother, on the other end, asked, "When do you want to come home?" I said, "I don't," but I knew my uncle Bill would come to pick me up to take me back to Louisville.

As always, when Uncle Bill arrived to get me, I took off running. I knew I was in trouble, but I did not care. Eventually, I had to emerge from my hiding place. Unlike my uncle Morgan, my uncle Bill gave me a few swats with the belt for misbehaving, and I went bawling and running down the hill to the car, waving goodbye to everyone. Uncle Bill never even gave me time for hugs.

20

Life in Las Vegas

At the end of my seventh-grade year in 1957, I was twelve years old and finished my first year at Southern Junior High School. I did not know it was going to be the last time I went to The Falls as I always did for all those years since I was a child. I liked school, but at the end of each year, I looked forward to seeing my cousin Charline, my aunt Mae and uncle Morgan, Granny, and all the people I missed that lived there. I still loved going to church at the Lone Star Church, and Vacation Bible School was always so much fun.

That summer was somehow different—it seemed to go by much too fast. When I first arrived there, everyone kept telling me how grown-up I looked. "Alana Jean, you ain't never gonna stop growin', are ya?" The saddest thing for me was that Charlie was no longer there even though the green bench, and the spit barrel was still outside the general store. Then JoAnn behind the counter whispered to me, "Alana Jean, ya know all your friends are gone. They just up and went, ever last one of 'em to Hardinsburg or Leitchfield, I reckon."

Aunt Mae did all the washing because Betty was gone. I was sad, and my birthday was not much fun either. I turned thirteen, but no one hardly knew it. What was supposed to be a celebration for being a teenager ended up being not a very fun birthday. My cousin Virginia had moved to Hardinsburg, and she was recovering from having a baby. She didn't bake me a chocolate cake as usual. Every day just seemed to be filled with work.

Whereas before, the chores I helped with were just chores—not work. I went with Aunt Mae to the flour mill and helped sack the corn flour. That was another job that never seemed like work. Uncle Morgan didn't want to hang out the fishing pole from the window anymore. All he talked about was how much lives were going to change because of the "damn dam" being built farther up the river.

There wasn't much playing that summer because there was no one to play with, or maybe I really was growing up. My granny was not herself, as she seemed always out of sorts, and Aunt Mae had had a recent cancer scare with a mastectomy. Uncle Bill picked me up from The Falls right before Labor Day, as always. School was about to start, but I had no idea my childhood days were over.

When I came home, my mom was still with the same boyfriend with the two kids, only he was no longer living in Indiana. He and both of his children had taken up permanent residence at my house. This was a big change for me, a child without siblings. I no longer had my own bedroom or my own anything. Most of my personal belongings were stuffed into the closet, and there was an extra twin bed in my room. The kids bugged Rocket; he wasn't too excited about all the new boarders either.

My mother was home most of the time because she quit both of her jobs. I could feel in the air that something was different, though I started school as usual. The new boarder-boyfriend left for a couple of weeks, but he kept calling all the time to see how everything was going. I began to listen in on those long-distance conversations. There was talk of selling our house and moving. I wondered what they were talking about. Moving, moving where? Why?

When the kids' father returned from his trip to Las Vegas, things began to get hectic. I came home from school one day to find the kitchen cupboards void of dishes and bare of food. The kids told me excitedly, "We are going to move far away, aren't you glad?" I had no idea what moving meant until the sad day we all piled into the car, along with my bird, Tinker.

The back seat was a bit crowded in the 1957 Buick, what with Tinker's cage and other play objects of the kids. We waved goodbye out the back window to several neighbors, who bid us farewell. I could not hold back the tears. My friend Linda and her family were also moving away. Linda and I had a sleepover the night before and kept hugging each other all night.

The drive to Las Vegas, Nevada, was nonstop. We got out of the car only to eat and go to the bathroom.

My dog, Rocket, my constant companion and protector for eight years, was left behind. Before we left, I pouted and cried and declared, "I'm not going! Let me go to The Falls!" My mom promised, "We'll ship Rocket to Vegas by train as soon as we find a place to live."

I didn't know I would be leaving Kentucky and that The Falls would never be part of my life ever again. I didn't know I would never see my granny or my aunt and uncle ever again. I did not know it was the last time I would see Uncle Bill or that I had said goodbye to all of them for the last time or that I would not be back for twenty-six years.

We didn't even stop driving to stay overnight anywhere. Tinker, my blue parakeet, was stuffed into his tiny clear plastic cage. He could talk but he was so cramped in his tiny enclosure that he mostly just squawked. He had a very long, beautiful tail, which became curled at the end because it didn't fit in the cage. His crooked tail lasted for weeks after we arrived in Las Vegas. When we talked about our trip across the country, it was always, "You mean the crooked tail trip?"

In October 1957, our "blended" family settled into a studio apartment near the elementary school where we all were enrolled. I was back in elementary school in eighth grade instead of a junior high school. The kids' dad began working as a Keno dealer at the Fremont Hotel in Downtown Las Vegas. My mother was a waitress at the Silver Slipper Hotel on the Las Vegas Strip. We three kids walked to and from school together, and I watched the kids every day after school.

Life was much the same as it had been in Louisville, except we learned some new vocabulary words: *crap* and *gambling*. Our "parents" drank a lot of Scotch, and arguments about gambling were constant. Every paycheck of the boyfriend was lost on the crap tables. We were barely settled into the studio apartment when we moved again—this time into a duplex right before Christmas. Our

Christmas was a complete disaster and one not to remember but extremely hard to forget.

We had a Christmas tree but no ornaments and no presents under the tree. It was the worst holiday possible for us kids. On Christmas morning, the children awoke to find their father passed out on the couch in the front room. There was not one present under the tree because Santa Claus never came. I was so mad, sad, and upset but not for myself. My mother was at work. The adults we called parents just didn't seem to care about anything except their bad habits. Did Santa forget about the kids? It was unexplainable. They were not my siblings, but my heart was broken for those two children.

When I took them outside to play, the other kids on the block had new bicycles and new toys they were playing with. I didn't care whether I had any presents, but I felt so bad for them. At their tender ages of five and seven years, they had no understanding—except they saw their dad on the couch inebriated. All three of us understood that! It was a lesson learned, for me, that alcohol is nothing more than a liquid drug, which causes the destruction of families. Due to those early experiences, I have never had even one drink my entire life.

Another jolt for me happened shortly after Christmas. All three of us kids shared the one single bedroom, and our parents slept on the pullout couch in the living room. Tinker shared our space in the bedroom, and he only was put in the plastic cage at night. We had to be very careful going in and out of our room so that Tinker could stay confined since he didn't have a cage.

One Saturday, I was across the street with a new friend I had met. I never invited friends to my place for only reasons I knew. On that day, however, I decided to bring Carol over to see my bird. She didn't believe he could talk. When we came into the house, my bird was about to be flushed down the toilet! Tinker was dead! My little bird had been slammed in the door while trying to fly out of the bedroom. There was laughing; the boyfriend thought it was funny! His two kids stared in horror. One of them had caused that predicament, but it didn't matter. I hated that man at that moment! I started to scream at him as I grabbed my dead bird from his hand that had all the fingers.

Carol left abruptly, and there I was holding the still-warm feathered relic of my childhood, completely lifeless. I had had Tinker almost as long as Rocket. I wanted to go back to Kentucky. I wanted to go back to The Falls. I wanted to see Aunt Mae and my granny and ride my bike in my old neighborhood. I wanted to go to Linda's house and talk to her mother. I spent the rest of the day walking around the neighborhood and crying my eyes out.

It didn't seem possible that things could go downhill from that moment, but they did! After I graduated from eighth grade, we moved again to a shabby house, where there was only desert sand in both the front yard and backyard. The house was furnished, but none of the furniture was ours, except the TV. My mother continued to work two jobs: as a waitress at the Silver Slipper on the Las Vegas Strip during the day and as a photographer at the Tropicana Hotel at night. She took pictures of guests at the shows and developed the film and presented the framed pictures to them afterward.

We lived next door to a family that I began to babysit regularly for. They had a little girl, who was two years old, and the mom was pregnant. I became very close to them. They came to the knowledge that things were not so good at my house. They heard a lot of yelling and profanity and saw drunken adults come home. In today's world, someone might have called Social Services to investigate, but no one came to our house.

I was lucky to have a lock on my bedroom door. When I heard loud arguments, I locked my bedroom door and crawled out the window to hide behind the cinder block wall until it was calm inside. I was afraid for my mom and the kids, but I was more afraid for myself, so I had to get out of the house. Things continued much the same way month after month, until I graduated from ninth grade. My elementary school had changed into a junior high school, so I had two graduations in two years' time. Soon after graduation, we moved again about a block from where we had previously lived.

My mother had a terrible nerve disfigurement that made the side of her face draw up to one side. She could barely talk or eat.

Her doctor attributed it to some kind of "unimaginable stress." Well, that stress was the product of the several years we had been living in a nightmare. Both my mom and her sleep-mate did "unimaginable" things. It was months before her face was normal again.

There was another lady who lived on the corner in the same neighborhood that I sometimes babysat for. Both she and her husband had high-profile jobs. They traveled a lot and they seemed to be workaholics. I was barely fifteen years old when they invited me to come live with them so that I could take care of their four children in their absence. I guess my mom thought that was okay; she gave permission and didn't oppose me after I told her what my new circumstances would be—and I was still close by, not far up the street.

In my new home, I had a room of my own. The only chores I had were to entertain and watch the children after school, and I helped them with their homework. Room and board were my only compensation from them. They gave me money to take their kids to the movies or downtown on the bus. I was happy with my new family, but unfortunately, living with them did not last long. They gave me a weekend off, and I decided to stay at my mom's house with the kids. That decision turned out to be another catastrophe, which led to a further upheaval in both my life and my mother's and those poor children as well.

That weekend, I stayed overnight with my pseudo siblings. We had a lot of fun playing Monopoly, playing cards, and watching TV. Neither of our parents were home. My mother came home from her night job, but she had to get up at six o'clock the next morning to go to her waitress job at the Silver Slipper. I stayed there with the kids after she left.

Soon after my mom's friend Penny picked her up for work, the dad came home. The sordid details were once again "unimaginable" and not easy to write about. It was a Saturday morning, and I was in the kitchen at the sink; the window overlooked the carport attached to the house. The kids' father drove into the carport, and I could see a woman in the passenger side, and it was not my mother.

I hurried to the kids' bedroom and told them not to come out. I went back to the kitchen, which was near the front door. The couple came inside; they were both drunk and laughing and stumbling around. The two ended up on the living room couch wrapped in each other's arms. I was not sure what I should do next, but I was really upset and mad at the situation.

I went into the living room and screamed at them, "Don't think I'm not telling my mother!" I just did not know what else to say or do in the state of mind I was in. There was violence after that. I grabbed the kids from their room and hustled them outside the back door, out of danger.

Long story short, I called my mother at work from a friend's house. She came home, and there was more violence. I had to leave my child-care job, and Mother and I moved seven more times before I graduated from high school. Sometimes we were with the boyfriend and the kids, sometimes it was just the two of us. Seven times in about two years was enough for me.

At every turning point in my life, I moved my father's picture from one place to another. When I took his picture from my dresser, it made me ask, "Daddy, why did you have to die? Why didn't you come home?" I felt that my life would have been so much different if he had come home to us, like he promised in my baby book. I told my mom many times, "You know Daddy would not like the way we are living!" She never had a reply.

Alana Lindberg at thirteen years old, an eighth grader at John C. Fremont Elementary School

In Las Vegas, there were still reminders of war, which made life even more anxious. As unbelievable as it seems, there was a nuclear test site sixty-five miles from Las Vegas. Nuclear bombs were tested aboveground, and the great mushroom cloud from such a test was seen for miles. In the early dawn, people could be seen on their rooftops watching the flash of light and the fireball curling in the air. There were advertisements put out to alert people where the best vantage points were to watch these tests. Everyone who watched were advised to wear sunglasses and not look directly at the flash, as it could damage eyesight.

Las Vegas was known as the Entertainment Capital of the world for many reasons, including the bomb-watching. There were billboards everywhere along the Strip and Downtown, along Fremont Street, showing who the great entertainers were and where they were performing. Famous hotels hosted such talents as Frank Sinatra, Judy Garland, Shirley MacLaine, Ella Fitzgerald, Louis Armstrong, Dean Martin, Liberace, and Bing Crosby. They performed in showrooms, where drinks and food were plentiful, and the cost was minimal. Minors were not allowed in the casinos, but the showrooms with entertainment, dinner, and pictures were exciting places for our teenage dates, especially proms.

Life continued to be unstable and unpredictable over the next few years, but being in high school made matters a little better. I was older and familiar with bus transportation, and I had money from my babysitting jobs. I also began working for Holiday Models and modeled for some of the dress shops on TV, which made my life more interesting and fun. Being in high school also presented me with some new excitement, like dating options. Soon my life would be changed forever because of those dating options.

Alana/Lee–Las Vegas High School

Once upon a time, I was late for study hall at Las Vegas High School when a cupid struck my heart. It wasn't a dream, but it might have been. I was on my way to the library when a handsome guy, whom I had seen before but did not know, crossed my path.

Instead, it was Wednesday, November 11, 1959, that I was introduced to him. He was on the junior varsity basketball team and the varsity football and baseball teams as well. He was so handsome with his flat top, sparkling blue eyes, and perfect smile. We had seen each other the previous day and taken second looks. We had passed each other as I was on my way up the stairs to the library, which was my study hall period. I knew of him from the sports rivalry between our junior high schools, but he did not know me. I had no idea he might be interested in me until I turned around for another look at him and discovered he was also turning around for another look at me! His name was Lee Jolley. I had seen him a year ago playing basketball at a junior high game, but I did not meet him.

It was Homecoming week at Las Vegas High School (LVHS) in 1959. Alumni and others came back to school to celebrate. Every year there was a bonfire held at night, a great rivalry football game between Las Vegas High School and Rancho High School, and a Homecoming dance. Homecoming coincided with November 11, Veteran's Day, so there was always great excitement and anticipation for the Homecoming festivities.

My best friend, Sally, and I rode the bus to school every day. Sally was going steady with John Vass, Lee's friend on the baseball team. After the "library" incident the day before, at Lee's request, the two of them got together to make sure we could be properly introduced during the lunch hour. I was a little shy about meeting someone of his high profile. He was well known at school. I basically had only one good friend, Sally, because I wasn't involved in any extracurricular activities at school. My home life was still unstable, so I never invited friends to my house, not even Sally.

At this hastily planned meeting, John and Sally, Lee and Alana stood awkwardly, trying to make sense of the introductions.

Lee started the conversation. "My name's Lee Jolley." I said, "I already know your name." Lee said, "Really?" I said, "Yeah, but it is a long story." About that time, the school bell rang, letting us know lunch was over and classes were about to begin. We all quickly decided to meet up at the Homecoming dance on Saturday night after the football game.

Sally and I had been best friends since eighth grade at John C. Fremont Junior High School, but the rigors of high school had caused our friendship to wane. We weren't in the same classes, and we didn't have the same schedules. Sally's boyfriend, John, also took up most of her free time. We still walked to the bus stop together before and after school and met at Sally's house to do homework in the evening, since she lived only a block from me.

On that same day, after the awkward introductions, Sally and I walked to the bus stop, and I told her, "I'm going to marry Lee Jolley." Teenagers' plans are known to go awry, and so it was that Lee did not show up at the Homecoming dance after all. I ended up dancing with my ex-boyfriend from junior high the entire night! I still liked Mike, but my heartstrings were being pulled toward someone else I had recently met.

In Las Vegas, I lived near one of the most unique hotels at the time, the Showboat Hotel, located on what was then Boulder Highway. It was a few blocks from my house and had two stories and boasted a hundred rooms. It was designed like an old-time river steamboat and had great forty-nine-cent breakfasts on the weekends.

School buses did not run for high school students, so my schoolmates and I caught the city bus near the Showboat Hotel each morning to get to Vegas High. I still had to walk several blocks from the bus stop Downtown to reach the high school. When I arrived on the school grounds on the Monday after Homecoming, I went straight to the lockers downstairs. Lee was there to meet me with apologies for not being at the dance. His mom was sick, and he had had to stay home to care for his younger brother and sister. At those sophomore lockers downstairs was the place our romance began. I ended up sharing the locker with Lee and his other locker mate too; three people in those skinny lockers was very crowded.

Lee and I were both extremely busy, so there wasn't much time to be together. I worked after school at a local dress shop Downtown, and Lee had either basketball or baseball practice after school. We did not have any classes together, so we met for lunch at the Lunch-a-teria, at school each day. The Lunch-a-teria is what our lunch place outside was called. It was a covered area with picnic tables and benches, but it wasn't enclosed because Las Vegas wasn't that cold in the wintertime. We had to go up to server windows to order our lunch and bring it back to the table.

A trivia thing which helped in bonding us together was our exchanges of lunch. Lee's mom packed him a brown-bag lunch every day with such great sandwiches. My mother gave me a silver dollar every day to buy my lunch. (Silver dollars were common in Las Vegas at the time.) I did not particularly like the menus at the Lunch-a-teria, so I gave Lee my silver dollar. He bought his lunch, and I ate his packed-lunch sandwiches. Lee's mom was known for her famous sandwiches on homemade bread with real butter. They were amazing sandwiches to a girl like me that had never had a homemade lunch in a bag.

Lee and I were only fifteen years old, so it was hard to date when the only transportation available was parental pickups and drop-offs and/or buses. Lee started walking with me to the bus stop Downtown if he had time before going to basketball practice. Our talks at lunch and our talks while waiting at the bus stop gave us the time to get to know each other. We conversed easily, and it seemed like we had known each other forever.

Later in the year, my mixed-up family finally moved into a house where I felt comfortable inviting friends. Of course, I had to be very careful of when would be a safe time to have friends come in. I never knew when there might be some kind of violent eruption involving alcohol and a lot of profanity or something worse in our household.

The first date Lee and I had was the GR or Girl's Reverse dance, to which I had invited him to accompany me. After my invite to him, there were no finances for me to be able to buy a formal dress to wear to the dance. He said he didn't care about the dance; he wanted to be with me.

He came to my house in a brand-new suit and tie so his parents would think he was going to the dance, but we did not go. Instead, my mother fixed us dinner, and we watched a movie on TV. We also put on some 45 records (small records with a hole in the middle played on a specific kind of record player) and danced to some slow dances because Lee did not like to dance fast. Once again, teenagers' plans changed in the middle of the stream.

Christmas came, and Lee and I exchanged gifts, and I met his parents and his two younger siblings. Lee spent his first eight years of childhood in Los Angeles, where his father played with the big bands of Hollywood fame. Lee Senior was a trumpet player and spent a lot of time on the road too. That's why the family moved from LA to Las Vegas, so his father would not have to travel so much.

Lee Senior was the lead trumpet player at the Sands Hotel on the Las Vegas Strip, playing two shows nightly. Lee eventually told me that his dad had played the trumpet in Antonio Morelli's band when Bobby Darin had performed at the Sands. Lee's father also gave trumpet lessons in the daytime to local high school kids who played in their school marching bands.

I liked Lee's mom, Gail, right away. Her smile seemed to light up the room. She had the cutest laugh and a sneeze that made you wonder where it came from. She was tall, very pretty, blond with brown eyes. She was a stay-at-home mom and was claimed by all to be the greatest cook. I was invited to dinner with their family occasionally, and Gail's dinners were even better than her packed lunches.

Lee's parents weren't keen on him having a steady girlfriend. They wanted him to focus on sports and homework. Since his father worked at night, playing at the Sands Hotel's dinner shows and second shows each night, Lee was required to be home at night to help his mother with the younger kids. Nights were never a time we could arrange to meet or be together.

In addition, Lee had a job bagging groceries at Safeway, so there wasn't a great deal of time for dating, anyway. I also had a job modeling with Holiday Models on TV, as well as working at the dress shop. Holiday Models did special events all around town, which I was also involved with. Everyone I knew had jobs, in addition to school—that's just how it was. Parents did not dole out money to kids; most of us were expected to earn our own spending money.

The weeks seemed to fly by with pretty much the same daily routines. Lee and I saw each other at lunch after school and talked on the phone. Soon it was February and time for the Sweetheart Ball. Lee and I were named the Sweetheart Couple, and our picture was on the front page of the school newspaper, *The Desert Breeze*.

"Alana Lindberg gives Lee Jolley an aloof look as Cupid prepares to shoot an arrow into Lee's heart" (LVHS Newspaper, *The Desert Breeze*, 1960).

At the close of the basketball season, Lee did not have a car, but we were able to meet at LVHS for the last basketball game. He played in the first game, which was the junior varsity game, and then he went to the PE locker room to shower. When he came back, we watched the varsity game together, sitting on the wooden bleachers in the high school gymnasium.

At this game, during halftime, we decided to go out into the dark football stadium. We walked across the track and up the concrete steps to the concrete benches and sat down. It was completely dark with only the stars watching over us. Las Vegas High School is located inside a family neighborhood, where there is little traffic, so it was not only dark but also silent except for an occasional car passing by. It was a welcome respite from the noisy, crowded, and smelly gymnasium.

That was the first time we talked about serious things, to learn more about each other and what the future might bring for us. We both believed we were in love for the long haul, but many young teenage romances probably assume the same thing. This is how our conversation played out:

> LEE. So how long have you been in Las Vegas?
> ALANA. About two years. I was born in Louisville, Kentucky, and lived there in the city during school.
> LEE. Oh, did you live somewhere else in the summer?
> ALANA. Yeah, I lived in the country with my aunt Mae, my mom's sister, my uncle Morgan, and my granny.
> LEE. Granny? Ha ha, that's what you called your grandma?
> ALANA. Oh, I guess that's what I've always called her. She was never Grandma.
> LEE. Is your granny still there in Kentucky?

ALANA. Yeah. I haven't been back there since we left. I miss her. Where does *your* grandma live?

LEE. She lives in Los Angeles. My mom's mom, that is, lives in LA.

ALANA. Where does your other granny live? Your dad's mom?

LEE: She used to live in LA, too, but lives in St. George, Utah now. In fact, we all used to live in LA because my dad plays the trumpet. He used to travel a lot and was never home, playing with the big bands all over the country.

ALANA. Your dad's a trumpet player?

LEE. He is, he's really good, too! He teaches lessons to me and other kids. What does *your* dad do?

ALANA. Uh, I don't have a dad. I mean he died in WWII.

LEE. Oh, I'm sorry. I didn't know. Is your mom married again?

ALANA. It's okay, I never knew him. He was a glider pilot and died in France—and no, my mom didn't marry anyone else, but… well, I have a stepfather, sort of…"

LEE. Do you have any brothers and sisters?

ALANA. Uh, no, well, yes…sort of. My life is complicated—I mean two little kids live with us, but they are not my brother and sister. They are the kids of my mother's boyfriend—Mom and their dad, he's kind of my stepdad, it truly is complicated. How many brothers and sisters do *you* have?

LEE. There are four of us kids—my older sister, Bonnie, who lives in Texas, my younger sister, Cheri, and my little brother, Paul. He's almost four. Then there's me, I'm the second oldest."

ALANA. So you play basketball and what else? I mean what other sports do you like?

LEE. Yeah, I'm on the football team and the baseball team. The track coach wants me to run, but I can't do both—track *and* baseball—so I do baseball. I love baseball. I have been on teams since I was eight years old, you know, playing Little League, and I also play American Legion Baseball.

ALANA. What guys do you hang out with? Mostly your friends on the basketball or baseball teams?

LEE. Not really. Most of those guys party and drink, and I don't do that, so I don't hang with them except at school and practices.

ALANA. You don't drink? Wow, that's amazing, that's cool! Me neither, I don't like it at all. Too many bad things happen when people drink and get drunk.

LEE. Well, there are a few reasons I don't drink. One, I don't want to be out of control of myself. Guys look and act stupid when they are wasted. And two, my religion prohibits drinking, but not only that, I don't drink coffee or smoke either. And three, I like to be in shape when I'm playing sports. Drinking keeps you from being the best you can be. I'm Mormon. My parents don't drink or smoke either. Do you go to church?

ALANA. I was baptized into the Baptist church, but I haven't gone to church since we left Kentucky. I don't know anyone who is Baptist. I don't have anyone to go with.

LEE. Would you go to my church with me sometime? Hey, I hear the whistles blowing in the gym, halftime is over. We better hustle. Can I take you home after the game? My friend Bruce has a car.

Of course, I had no idea at that time how that nighttime conversation in the football stadium would impact either of our future lives. One thing I did know at that time was, I would never marry any man who drank. I had written this statement in my little white Bible when I was eight years old, "I will never marry anyone who drinks." The conversation with Lee was a major event for me; even at my young age, I felt it was a major event.

I had already had enough experience with alcohol and the destruction of lives associated with it. I was bearing the brunt of abusive adults at the time, which I did not reveal to Lee. He did not know that my mind was already made up about drinking long before we had that conversation under the stars, and my nondrinking had nothing to do with religion. However, I had read somewhere that "people who pray together stay together." I wanted my own future life to stay together.

Like most high school romances, we had our ups and downs, including a few breakups and dating other people. We rarely saw each other on weekends unless Lee came over to my house after a football road trip before he went home. I lived near the railroad tracks, and one of those nights, when he came to my house, he risked his life. He barely made it across the railroad tracks, rolling down the embankment into a hobo camp as the train rushed by. The engineer yelled, "Get off the tracks!" Teenagers are often reckless, but actions in the name of love are okay, even when life-threatening. Lee had to take the risk because he had to be home by curfew.

Shortly before graduation from high school, my mom was beginning to get her act together, and she left boyfriends behind. She bought a house, and we began to have a somewhat normal life. My aunt Chrys came to live with us, which made a big difference in my mom's behavior. I suppose being the older sibling, she had some influence, which was good. She brought her dog with her, reminding me of the sad time I had when I had to leave my own dog, Rocket, behind.

My eighteenth birthday on June 27, 1962, provided me with another life-altering event. I received a letter from the Veteran's Administration saying that I had money for college. What? How? I flew to the Veteran's Administration in Reno, Nevada, to have an interview and collect the money. Peach had set up a trust fund for me that became available when I was eighteen years old. Peach? I had not heard from Peach since we moved to Las Vegas. The letter was more than a surprise! It opened the door for me to further my education, to go to college.

The letter and the money caused a lot of tension between my mother and me. She felt she was entitled to the money. I felt sure Peach intended the money for me, not her. Things had abruptly changed! I remembered Peach as that "magical person" who came to my sixth birthday at The Falls. At age eighteen, I realized just how magical she truly was!

Lee was working every day and playing baseball several times a week at night with the American Legion. His dream of being in the Major Leagues seemed to be getting closer. Scouts from the Dodgers, the Giants, and others came to watch the games. A coach from Brigham Young University came to ask him personally to go to BYU, so it was settled. We did not want to be apart, so we ended up at the same university in September of 1962. I truly thought I had gone to heaven! I had recently been baptized into the Mormon church, and at BYU, there was no alcohol, smoking, or profanity. And there was also no violence—it was a whole new world for me!

The summer after our freshman year at BYU brought another surprise and a big decision as we began thinking seriously about our future. As soon as we returned to Las Vegas from school, Lee received an opportunity to do what he always dreamed. A major league scout approached him about signing for a New York Yankee farm team, but there was another opportunity, which became more pressing. Lee was surprised to receive a call to serve a mission for his church. It meant postponing signing for professional baseball. Instead, it looked like we would be apart for the next two years while he was gone. At that point, we did not know exactly where he would be going. We didn't know if it would be stateside or foreign, which could make a difference of six months more.

Lee left for New Zealand in September 1963. I left him at the airport in Salt Lake City. Both of us cried as we hugged and said goodbye. I drove back to Provo and BYU by myself. On my drive, I began to think of my life as a university student and how grateful I was to have the opportunities that were before me. I was sure the next two years would be hard without Lee by my side. I registered for school and checked into my dorm with my new roommates for the coming semesters.

My new roommate was a girl from Salt Lake City, who spoke Spanish and was majoring in International Studies. Since I had taken two years of Spanish in high school, we began to speak Spanish to each other. She was much better than me, as she had spent the past summer in Mexico. As we became more acquainted, I told her about my grandmother, Peach, who spoke Spanish, and my sixth birthday and that I had not seen or heard from her in years. I told Nancy that it was Peach who had made it possible for me to be at BYU because of the trust fund she had provided for me. One thing led to another, and Nancy said I should contact Peach and that she would do the speaking for me in Spanish.

I knew my dad's brother, my uncle Johnny, lived in Los Angeles. I found him easily in the greater LA phone book and made the call. When a woman answered, I asked, "Is Emma Carmen Lindberg there?" I thought surely my uncle would know where my grandmother [his mother] was—and maybe she would even be there living with him. I wanted to thank her for all she had done for me with all the gifts and the money in the trust fund. My uncle came to the phone and asked, "Who is this?" I replied, "It is Alana. Is my grandmother there?" The phone call was short. My uncle said, "Your grandmother passed away in August." I was in shock and didn't know what to say. I said, "How come I didn't know about it?" The answer I received was, "She didn't—we didn't know where you were." There was another long silence. My uncle asked me, "Why are you calling her?"

I couldn't talk anymore, so I just said, "Okay, bye." I called my mother to tell her the sad news, but she already knew. My sadness was overcome by the fact that my mother had not told me—it made me mad and upset!

College life continued, and my mom and I were not exactly friends. I went home to Las Vegas for the summer and worked at the Stardust Hotel in the purchasing department. My aunt Chrys was still at my house, so the environment wasn't too strained.

The following year at BYU, while Lee was in New Zealand, I lived off campus and became very close friends with a girl from San Leandro, California, from the Bay Area. Her name was Jane, and we made plans to live together at her home in California after school was out.

I went to live and work there for the summer of 1965. It helped to be somewhere else than Las Vegas as I was excitedly waiting for Lee to return from New Zealand in September.

22

Uncle Johnny, My Father's Brother

The summer of 1965, shortly before my twenty-first birthday, my girlfriend Jane and I took a trip to Los Angeles from the Bay Area to go to a wedding of a mutual friend. While in Los Angeles, we stayed at Jane's uncle's house. He was a makeup artist at one of the major motion-picture studios. The view from his window across the valley was of the "HOLLYWOOD" hills sign. We were right in the middle of Los Angeles. Jane had activities to go to with regard to her being a bridesmaid in the wedding. I had nothing to do, so I milled around her uncle's house, looking at all his displayed awards, alongside pictures of dozens of famous movie stars.

I was staring rather blankly at the pictures when I remembered Jane's mother's words, "You must contact your father's brother while you are in Los Angeles, if you can." My mom once told me that Johnny had a flower shop in LA, so I called Information and got the number of the Lindberg Flower Shop. As the phone rang, I became a little apprehensive, since our last phone call had not gone well. I wasn't even sure why I was trying to call my uncle, except that Mrs. Hansen had insisted that I do so. A lady answered the phone, "Lindberg Flower Shop, how can I help you?"

I told her, "I'm looking for my uncle, John Lindberg. Is this his flower shop?" "Yes, it is," she said, "but he is with a customer, do you want to hold?" I told her I would. She came back to the phone and wanted to know my name. "I'm Alana, his brother's daughter." After a long pause, Johnny came to the phone. He was rather shocked to learn that his long-lost niece had found him once again! "Where are you, Alana? Are you in Los Angeles?"

I told my uncle, "I will be in Los Angeles for a few days. Could we get together somewhere?" At first, we planned to meet for lunch. He couldn't think of a place, but he called me back within an hour and said it would be better if we met at his home that evening. I had never been to Los Angeles, but somehow, I found my way to his house. I was trying to navigate the freeways to his address on Westmoreland Avenue while at the same time I was thinking of the many questions I wanted to ask my uncle about my dad. I hoped the meeting would not go as badly as the phone call two years before. It was June and hot in Los Angeles, and I did not have air-conditioning in my 1962 Corvair. I was sweating from both the heat and the anticipation of meeting my uncle for the first time. I knew he had written to my mom from France after my father's death,

It was twenty years after WWII ended, twenty years after my birth, and twenty years since my mother had received that letter from my uncle, where he had told her, "I will stop by to see you and Alana on my way home from France. I want to hold her in my arms, as I feel I have some stake in my brother's only daughter. Tell Alana I love her very much."

I still have the letter, dated September 1945. My mother told me she had no communication from Johnny after that letter. He did not visit her like he promised, nor did he ever call to see how she and I were getting along. My mom was a little mad when she talked about Johnny but a little bit sad too. I knew it had been upsetting to her that there had been no more communication from him over those twenty years.

When I arrived at my uncle's house that evening, I parked in front and walked slowly up the steps. I had no idea what the reaction of our meeting would be like. I rang the doorbell. I was stunned when he abruptly stepped out of the door onto the porch and grabbed me into his arms! He held me so tight while at the same time whispering in my ear, "I love you very much no matter what happens. Remember, I love you." Just as abruptly as he had stepped outside, he stepped back inside and welcomed me as if what he had just done had never happened.

That event on the doorstep made me even more apprehensive than I already was. Just as suddenly as he grabbed me into his arms, the questions I had wanted to ask him vanished into thin air. I was a little dazed, and it made it uncomfortable for me to be there. I have relived that moment many times, but I was not able to explain it or grasp the meaning of his actions until many years later.

I expected my uncle to look much like my dad, but he did not. He was not much taller than me. His dark brown eyes were set within a round face with puffy cheeks and thin lips. His dark complexion was ruddy-looking under his salt-and-pepper curly hair. He wasn't exactly fat, but I would describe him as perhaps a bit overweight. He wore a plaid shirt and khaki pants, and he wore flip-flops for shoes.

He offered me a seat on the couch next to him. His wife, Addie, came into the front room, and she brought a chill in the air with her. She sat across from me in an overstuffed chair, smoking a cigarette and blowing smoke rings into the air. I did not feel welcome or comfortable at all. I felt confined and tongue-tied. The conversation was cold and seemed almost scripted. Addie did not even say hello or introduce herself to me when she came into the room. Her piercing blue eyes were as cold as our conversations.

Our time together seemed empty and nothing like what I had expected. It was nothing like Peach's warm embraces on my sixth birthday. My uncle was interested only in what I was doing in Los Angeles and what classes I was taking at Brigham Young University. I thought he was glad I came to see him after his actions outside, but we didn't discuss anything relevant. I was too "gun-shy" to ask the questions I had been thinking about. I wanted to know about my father's time in France because he had sent me a baby ring with my initial on it. I wanted to ask about how my father died, but I was afraid to start a dialogue about my dad. I felt it was not the right time or the right place; the atmosphere was stifling in a way that is hard to explain. Maybe I should try it at another time after we know each other better, I thought. Saying that to myself made me feel better.

My uncle kept saying, "Walt would be so proud of you. Walt would be so proud of you," over and over. He kept telling me, "You look so much like him," as tears came to his eyes. I asked him about how my grandmother (Peach) had died, and I asked him, "Do you remember that I called you soon after she died?" He did remember and then proceeded to tell me that there were no family members left alive. He said, "Everyone is dead, except me. I'm the last one of the Lindbergs, and all of my mother's family is gone too."

There were so many questions I could have asked my uncle, if only I had been informed enough and comfortable enough to know what to ask. Addie was the one who asked me the superficial questions. "What are you doing in Los Angeles? Where are you staying? How long will you be here?"

My father died during the liberation of France in 1945, and he was buried in France. Peach forwarded a letter to my mom from my uncle Johnny seven months after the death of my dad. He wrote to Peach:

September 19, 1945

Dear Mom,

>Today I went to visit Walt's grave in Saint-André-de-l'Eure. It is located about 48 miles west of Paris and about 103 miles from where I am stationed in Le Mans, France. The complete address is St. André Cemetery, Saint-André-de-l'Eure, France, Plot C, Row 10, Grave #189.

Peach brought my father's body back in 1949 to the States, where he was repatriated from Saint-André-de-l'Eure Cemetery into the Inglewood Park Cemetery, in Inglewood, California. I did not know that at the time of my visit with my uncle. Neither Johnny nor Addie told me my father's grave was only a few miles away or that I should visit there. Many years later, when I found out about my dad's remains being brought from France to Los Angeles, it was upsetting to me that my uncle had not told me. I could have visited my dad's grave while I was there. That fact is another question, "Why didn't he tell me?" One would think he would have told me, or even wanted to accompany me to my dad's gravesite.

That knowledge of my father's grave being nearby would have been earthshaking for me at that time. I was there visiting an aunt and uncle I had never met before, but they did not feel like family to me. It felt strange, as if they did not want me there. We were all in the same room, but we were miles apart. It was not like visiting my other aunts and uncles on my mother's side either.

My visit lasted a little over an hour, but at the time, it seemed much longer due to the strained and cold ambiance in the room. Conversations were not forthcoming as they should have been between family members that barely knew each other. I thought my uncle should have been as anxious to see and meet me as I was excited to have found him. As I was about to leave, Uncle Johnny looked at Addie and asked her, "Should I give it to her?" I had no idea what he wanted to give to me. I thought maybe it might be some memento or picture of my dad.

My uncle left the room and came back with a large brown paper bag, which he opened to pull out a triangular transparent plastic package, which appeared to have an American flag folded in triangular perfection within it. I recognized it to be in a military covering. "I think Walt would want you to have this. It is the flag from his casket before he was buried." He handed it over to me, and I did not know what to say or what to do. I had little reaction at that moment, except to say, "Thank you."

As I was driving back to meet Jane, I kept looking at the plastic-covered American flag that lay on the bucket seat beside me. I had something representing my father riding with me in my car. I was as near to my father as was possible. It was symbolic of what had happened to my father, why he never came home from the war. The thought of my dad riding beside me pierced my heart, and I began to weep, barely seeing the traffic ahead of me.

So it was after twenty years my uncle Johnny was able to hold me in his arms and tell me himself that he loved me. Twenty years ago, he had expressed that same thing in his letter to my mom. The hug, along with the whispered endearments, was shocking on that brief visit, but unfortunately, I did not feel the love so quickly said but not exactly conveyed. The next day, I told Jane about my visit, and she thought it was strange how my aunt and uncle both reacted to my visit.

I contemplated telling my mother right away about my visit to my uncle Johnny, but I waited for several weeks. Jane and I went back to the Bay Area, where we both were working full-time for a temp agency. Lee was still in New Zealand and would be home in September.

We were sure we were going to be married soon after he returned home, so I was busy designing and making my wedding dress. Jane's mother took me to San Francisco, where she coached me on what materials would be suitable for my wedding dress. Mrs. Hansen was a widow and sewed for other people. If not for her help, my wedding dress would still be on the cutting board.

Finally, I decided to call my mother and tell her about my visit to my uncle's home. She was surprised I had the courage to look him up. She wasn't surprised that I found him at the Lindberg Flower Shop because she told me he and my dad were planning to open a flower shop together after the war was over. My mother asked me, "Why did you do that? What in the world made you call him?" I did not answer that question because I didn't want to tell her that someone besides her had encouraged me to find him. My mother wasn't happy at all about my visit to them. In fact, she showed disappointment in me for doing what I felt I needed to do. I did not learn the reason for my mom's bitterness until the last letter she wrote to me before her death.

Another point is, when I told my mom about meeting my uncle, she did not ask me if I visited my dad's grave while I was there. I now understand and realize with sadness that my mother was not aware that my dad's grave, which she could have visited, was within a four-hour drive from Las Vegas.

This is the grave marker in the Inglewood Park Cemetery.
(www.findagrave.com)

On the phone, Mother asked me, "Did you meet Addie?" (Addie is Johnny's wife.) I told her how Addie had sat in the chair blowing smoke rings into the air while I was there. My mother had nothing good to say about her. She said, "Addie was jealous because she had no children, and I was pregnant." My mom had met Addie when they were all in North Carolina together before my dad and Johnny left for the European Theater. She said, "Addie treated me coldly, just like she treated you, Alana. Walt didn't like her either, but she was the wife of his brother."

I have never been able to analyze that visit to my uncle as either good or bad. I keep asking myself, "Why was he not truthful?" I don't want to say that he lied to me, but he did. Why did he not tell me about our family (my family) in Mexico? Why did he say he was the only living family member left? Which family was he talking about? If it were the Lindbergs, it was certainly not true because I was a Lindberg sitting right there in front of him! I was not dead! He implied there were no other family members on his mother's (Peach) side either. Why did he not tell me of my father's grave just a few miles away? So many questions, so few answers.

I had to wait until my uncle's death six years later, before I was able to get answers to all these questions and many others as well.

23

Life and Letters

Lee returned home from New Zealand to Las Vegas in September of 1965. We left for BYU two days later. We were excited to continue our university studies together after two long years of being apart. No time was wasted, and we became engaged, planning our wedding to be after school was out in the summer. Soon after we arrived in Provo, Lee received a phone call from his sister, informing him his mother was diagnosed with terminal cancer. It was a shock since he had been home from his mission in New Zealand only a few weeks.

Our wedding plans were moved to semester break in January of 1966. We had a reception and a one-night honeymoon given to us by a friend who was the vice president of the Dunes Hotel in Las Vegas. The next day, we went back to Provo and our jobs: Lee worked in the wee hours of every morning for a janitorial service, and I was working as secretary to the president of Walker Bank in Downtown Provo.

Soon, it was spring baseball practices and BYU games for Lee. He played centerfield and was still hoping to get the chance to play Major League Baseball, as he had been offered before his two years in New Zealand as a missionary. We went to Las Vegas for the summer because we were fortunate to be offered a chance to "house sit" for family friends who left for their summer home in Wyoming. It was a big house, and we had a lot of fun entertaining our friends and listening to great music on their big console in the living room.

The Vietnam War was in full swing, and all young men over the age of eighteen were eligible for the draft. Lee was twenty-one and had been on a ministerial deferment while on his church mission.

After returning home, he was deferred because he was a full-time university student. Deferments kept changing, and young men were anxious, and parents were afraid. The next deferment was a full-time student and married. We met that one.

The last and final deferment was the married with dependent children. I found out I was pregnant on the day Lee received his induction notice to serve in the military. Whew! During the months Lee had been home, it was like playing Russian roulette; we never knew what might be in our mailbox. Had Vietnam been a world war rather than a conflict, all young men would have entered the service. There would have been no deferments, except for ill health.

Lee's mother's health continued to decline, and we didn't know how long she could hold on. Lee was offered a chance to play with the Dodgers' summer baseball league in Minnesota. He decided not to take the opportunity because of his mother's illness and not knowing how much longer she would live. It was another huge decision and a great disappointment for Lee, but he felt we should stay in Las Vegas, especially since he still had young siblings at home. Lee remained working at the Shell gas station while I worked for the assistant district attorney, Addeliar D. Guy, in the Nevada District Attorney's Office in Las Vegas.

The summer of 1966 ended; the dependent deferment was granted, and we went back to Provo. Lee continued with school but started working for an architectural firm. I worked full-time for an insurance agency. We lived in an old home, which had a basement for tenants. The two students who lived in the basement helped pay our rent. We had no refrigerator, but we had a couch for the living room and a double bed for our bedroom. We bought a used crib for $25 and awaited the birth of our daughter.

It was in February, two weeks before our daughter was born on March 4, 1967, that I received the sordid news from the Social Security Administration denying my benefits for college. Lee's mom was in and out of the hospital, Lee was working two jobs while taking classes for school, and life was on edge as we struggled in our new parenting roles.

Another summer was upon us; Lee's mom died on July 24, 1967. No matter the setbacks, our lives moved forward. Lee was trying to finish his engineering degree when we bought a small traditional brick home in Provo, Utah, a block from BYU. We made a small down payment, and my parents cosigned for the loan. What made it possible for us to own a home was the full basement, which allowed for four university students to pay us rent. Their rents each month paid almost our entire house payment!

We were a young family in an old neighborhood—rather, an anomaly. The neighborhood was much like one big family. Everyone knew everyone else. We all went to the same church, shopped at the same market, and we all loved BYU sports. There were many teenagers who seemed to think we were good role models, and a few of them hung out on our doorstep, which we loved. Even with students renting our basement, Lee working, and me working part-time, money was scarce.

Another turning point for us, which upset our little apple cart once again, was the remarriage of Lee's dad just a year after his mom died. We had no idea the consequences it would have for us. Lee's younger brother and sister were still at home. A girl in high school with a twelve-year-old brother, the new wife, and Lee's dad working two jobs, their household became "the wicked stepmother syndrome" house. It was a very bad situation for the kids. It was the stepmother's third marriage, and her children were all grown. She found herself once again in the throes of raising young children—and she was not happy about it!

Lee's sister came to live with us as soon as she graduated from high school, leaving her little brother behind. Her first semester at BYU, she met her future husband, and after a year, they were married, and she went off to dental school with him. Soon, another crisis arose.

Lee's younger brother and the stepmother became hostile to each other; she was extremely abusive to him. Their life in Las Vegas had so much turmoil and stress that we intervened and brought Lee's brother to live with us permanently. It was a conflicted situation, and we were told by his dad and his wife, "If you take him, don't expect any money from us." Lee's younger brother was thirteen, and we had two daughters under three years old. Lee continued working two jobs and going to school.

Our house was crowded. We had only two small bedrooms upstairs, so my young brother-in-law slept in the living room on the couch, which made into a bed. We kept his clothes in our closet in our bedroom. He was a sad youngster, having lost his mother at a young age. Lucky for him, our neighborhood was a haven of boys his age. He soon had many friends, which made it easier for him to deal with the loss of his mom. The move-in with us turned out to be a good thing for him and for us. We had so many laughs, but there were also a lot of tears, which were shed for the loss of his mother. He was such a good boy that we believed raising a teenager was easy.

I had my hands full being a young mom when a friendly neighbor lady, Arlene, introduced me to the world of genealogy. It was hard not to listen when she was so passionate about her hobby. It seemed interesting delving into the past to find long-lost ancestors. At age twenty-seven, I had been married for five years with two children, with another one on the way, besides raising a teenage boy.

I wasn't sure I had time for researching or if it was the right time. My dad's request to learn about the family tree came back to my mind. He must have thought it was important to make those words a postscript to a goodbye. I told her I needed to find my father first before anyone else. Arlene assured me she could help me find my way.

After she heard my story, she told me, "You need to find your father's family." Those few words confirmed to me that it was the right time, and it was the right place to start to find not only my father but also the rest of his family. I knew my dad died in France in an airplane crash, but I did not know much of anything else.

My six-year-old's memory of my dad's mother, Peach, was still vivid, and the memory of how she spoke and how she showed her love toward me, even today, is very lucid. Starting research with my grandma Peach seemed the most natural place to start because I already had a name, a place, and a death date, along with my childhood memories of her. I thought it was going to be harder than Arlene told me since according to my uncle Johnny, everyone was dead.

With information about Peach and a little faith in the documents in my possession, Arlene helped me to formulate a plan to investigate further my own beginnings. I took my father's picture out of the drawer, where I had placed it after the event at the Social Security Administration. I put it back on my dresser where I could see my dad every day. That was a good beginning; I had missed him.

Peach was no longer alive, and my uncle had told me when I visited him, there were no relatives alive to contact. That never sounded right to me. There must have been relatives somewhere, I thought. If I could find some family members by chance, I might be able to find out how I became the daughter of a man who "had no children." That was my end goal. The "by chance" came to me after a phone call Arlene had insisted I make.

I told Arlene about when I had felt the urge to call Peach in 1963, and I called my father's brother to see if I could talk to Peach. I shared my great disappointment with her about that phone call. I told her, "My uncle told me his mother had died a few weeks before, in August 1963." I shared with a few tears, "I mourned my grandmother's death for several weeks after that phone call." I told Arlene how my memories of Peach kept haunting me. Arlene kept coaxing me to find out more, and she promised me, "Your genealogy research will help you know what questions to ask, and it will help you to find the answers to those questions." I hoped she was right.

I needed to know, who was Walter Bert Lindberg? Where did he come from? Who were his parents (my grandparents)? What were the circumstances of his death? Where was he buried? Where is his family? I wanted to know, did I have aunts, uncles, or cousins? Why didn't my mother and I ever meet any of his relatives? Where did he grow up? Was he rich or poor? How did he end up in Louisville, Kentucky, to meet my mother? Once again, Arlene promised me it was possible to answer all those questions through diligent research. She reiterated, "Your first step is going to be to call your father's brother once again." Why I did not call him soon after I received the information from the Social Security office, I do not know. I think it was because I was mad and so sad.

I finally had the courage to call my uncle in Los Angeles for the third time in 1971. His wife, Addie, answered the phone. She was not happy to hear from me. She was as cold on the phone as she had been on that evening when I visited them six years before. She gave me more sad news, "Johnny passed away on Valentine's Day three weeks ago." I told her, "I'm so sorry to hear of his passing." There was silence on the phone.

My promptings seemed to always come too late. I thought I had reached another dead end until Addie told me she was in the process of moving, and she said, "I'm selling everything and moving to New York. I have been busy going through Johnny's things. I have something that was Walt's that you might want."

She told me, "I found a box of letters written to Walter while he was overseas. Do you want the letters? I certainly don't want them. I can mail them to you before I leave for New York." I gave her my address in Provo. "Yes, please send them to me." At that time, I did not know how such letters written to my dad so long ago could still exist. Who were the letters from? and what did they say to a soldier overseas? What, if anything, would I learn from those letters?

The box arrived at my home several weeks after I talked to Addie. There were ten or twelve crumpled letters inside, all in airmail blue envelopes of the 1940s era in which they were written. The thirty-year-old return addresses were from California and Mexico. I wanted to know who wrote those letters to my father. I thought they must be relatives, yet I did not recognize any of the names on the envelopes or in the letters. Since I did not know who any of the letter-writers were, it became a "draw straws" kind of a decision. Which of them was I going to write to? And I didn't know, maybe they were all dead, as my uncle had told me, but I felt I had to take a chance.

I wondered if the letters I wrote would get to any recipients after thirty years had passed. I chose three names from three different envelopes: Virginia Cota in Chula Vista, California; Beatriz Contreras in Chula Vista, California; and Tonia Marin in Ensenada, Baja California Norte, Mexico. I included my phone number, hoping I would be lucky enough to reach someone who might want to connect with me. I wasn't sure if any of the women at those addresses, if they were still alive or still lived at the same address, even knew of my existence. After all, the soldier they wrote to in Europe had no children!

It wasn't long before I received a phone call from Beatriz Contreras, known by the family as Tichy. She was quite emotional as she spoke to me. "Alana, we have wondered all these years where you were. This is the best news the Cota family could have received at this time." I thought to myself, my grandmother's name was Emma Carmen Lindberg, who was the Cota family that Tichy was referring to? I had never heard the Cota surname or anything about a Cota family. Why did they wonder about me or care about me? Why was it the "best news" for their family?

A week later, I received another phone call from my great-aunt Virginia Natalia Cota. She was the favorite aunt Virginia that my father was so fond of. She said, "I am your grandmother's sister." She spoke with a strong Spanish accent, and she sounded just like my sixth birthday memories of Peach. I began to cry when she said, "You have so many aunts and cousins that want to meet you, Alana!" I replied, "But my uncle said all the family had passed away." Aunt Virginia did not know that I had ever communicated with Johnny. She wanted to know, "When were you in California? When did you see Johnny?"

According to my uncle, the people I wrote letters to, and those I talked to on the telephone were all dead, but they weren't dead! Why did my uncle tell me that? How was that possible? Why did he not want me to meet them or know any of my family? When I sat in his living room that day, five of Peach's siblings were still alive! Three of them lived in Southern California, and the other two lived in Tijuana, Mexico. Maybe I could have met them when I was in LA. Wasn't Aunt Virginia my dad's favorite aunt? Why did Johnny not want me to meet her when he knew she was still alive?

Aunt Virginia told me about the five sisters still living, which included Tonia, who was ill with cancer. She told me they were so excited to meet and see me and wanted me to come to meet them as soon as possible. She hardly let me get a word in edgewise on the phone as she kept speaking so fast. "You are family! We are *your* family. We want to see you. Tichy will call you, and she will tell you what to do."

I soon learned my uncle Johnny had not told any of them about my visit to him. They were all surprised that I had been to Los Angeles to visit him at his home. They, too, wondered why he did not tell them about meeting me. Aunt Virginia told me, "What Johnny did would not have made Walter happy. Walt loved family." It was almost three years before Lee and I, with our four little girls, set off to California to see my dad's (and my) many aunts, uncles, cousins, and other extended family members.

We arrived in Chula Vista, California, in June of 1975 and checked into a hotel. I called my great-aunt Virginia right away. She was very upset that we were in a hotel. She said in her sweetest accent, "Alana, you are family, it is not the Mexican way! You should not stay in a hotel when you have family here." I did not know what to say. She kept talking. "You will stay with Tichy and her family. They have made all the arrangements for you. Check out of the hotel and come to my house trailer." Virginia and another sister, Beatriz—called Biti—lived together in a trailer in a nearby trailer park.

Aunt Virginia sent a handsome young man, who was a cousin I did not know, Bernardo Cota, known as Nando by the family, to the hotel to get us and lead us to the trailer park. When I first saw him in the parking lot, I was very surprised. I'm not sure what I expected him to look like, but he was so striking with his black curly hair and bright blue eyes. He was the first one I met of my lost family. He was my dad's cousin and the son of Peach's brother, Bernardo Cota. Nando was Bernardo the second. His relationship to our aunt Virginia was much the same as my dad's relationship had been. Aunt Virginia was more than an aunt to Nando. He had spent much time with her growing up.

I was living a real dream at that moment when Nando showed up at our hotel. He was so kind and loving; I loved him immediately. From that moment on, he became like the brother I never had. He said his wife and children were at the trailer waiting to meet me. It was a dream I hoped I would never wake up from.

24

Familia–Mexico/Aunt Virginia's Book

Aunt Virginia and Auntie Biti had prepared a special dinner for all of us. We met Nando's wife, Georgia, and their four children who stayed for dinner. My two great-aunts were in their eighties, but they had the energy of teenagers as they greeted us and took our girls into their arms with all their sweet nothings in Spanish. There are really no words to accurately describe the overwhelming feelings I had when meeting each family member. Our meal with the two elderly sisters and Nando's family at the trailer was the first of many meetings over the next week.

Being an only child with a single parent and very few close family relationships on my maternal side, it was overwhelming that I suddenly had paternal relatives that seemed to care about me. I began to learn precisely why the Cota family considered finding me as the "best news" their family had received.

They explained to me that the two sisters, Tonia and Peach, were very close, and even though Tonia was very ill at the time, she was very excited that I had contacted the family. She knew Peach had been very unhappy not knowing where I was all those years. Tichy told me, "It gave us all something to hope for in the future, that we would get to meet you, because we all thought of Walter so fondly and loved him so much. He was the cousin that everyone looked up to. He was our hero."

Tichy, Nando, and Biti weren't the only ones with two names. Almost everyone I eventually met had two names—a birth name and a "family name"—which is the Mexican tradition in close-knit families. I thought that was why my grandmother had a different name until I learned the real reason everyone called her Peach, though she was also called Camelina.

Meeting the paternal side of my family was the first time I had the opportunity to learn about my dad's life from those who knew him personally before his military service. While I was growing up, my mother could not fill in the gaps because she did not know anything about my father's upbringing or the family he was part of. She knew he had a brother, a favorite aunt Virginia, and a mother he called Peach.

I uncovered my dad's complicated personal life when I learned from our aunt Virginia about his hasty and failed marriage due to prejudices and his wife's objections to having a "Mexican baby." His wife did not like his beloved mother, Peach, and she would not attend family weddings, christenings, or confirmations with Walter. Aunt Virginia told me, "She was somewhat of an alcoholic, and Walter was embarrassed to bring her around the family from the very beginning. She was not nice to any of us."

I thought back to my visit with my uncle Johnny. It was nothing like the warm welcome I received in Chula Vista. My conversation with my uncle did not reveal his and my dad's sibling rivalry or their closeness as friends, not just as brothers. The only evidence that I was family to my uncle was his abrupt, untimely, and awkward hug on his front doorstep.

The older members of the family who remembered my father had pictures and many stories. They were eager to tell me about him. Walter, they said, "was always a favorite." They believed him to be a true hero. Aunt Lucia told me, "He was a kind and generous boy with a big heart." Armando, his cousin, told me, "Alfonso [Peach's brother] and I received your papa's casket when it came from France to Los Angeles. We took it to the cemetery in Inglewood for the funeral." What? I knew nothing about what I had just been told. My dad's body came from France to Los Angeles? Was there a funeral?

My mom never went to any funeral! Did she know about it? I asked them, "When was the funeral?"

I realized right then there was still much more to learn, as my friend Arlene had promised. I had to do more research and ask more questions to the elders to "get the lowdown on the family tree," as my dad told my mom when they were in North Carolina. The more I intermingled with my newfound family and listened to them talk to each other about Walter and show and tell their feelings about him, the more I was completely mystified that I belonged to a family from a different culture and country and who spoke a different language!

Not only that, but like my father, I was the oldest in my generation, making my place in the family even more special! Not only am I the oldest in my generation, but I am also the only grandchild of Peach, the oldest of all the children. I couldn't help thinking to myself, *My father had no children, but here I am!* My heart had never been so full, and I firmly believe copious blessings from heaven were poured down upon me all during those first close encounters.

Peach's four sisters with Alana in the middle

As you can see by the photo of me with my four great-aunts—and they really were *great* aunts—they were not all dead, as my uncle

Johnny had told me. This picture was taken in 1975 in the front of Tichy's house in Chula Vista, California.

Tichy and her family did not know us or what kind of people we were, but they all said, "You are family!" They turned the entire upstairs of their home over to us for the time we were in California.

Aunt Virginia was the first person to tell me my father was not only part Mexican but that "he was also part Swedish." I had a Swedish grandfather? That information was unexpected. She offered even more, "Oh, the marriage of your grandparents was not made in heaven. Camelina [Peach] and Bert married against both parents' wishes." She continued, "Walter, your father, grew up in two or three worlds. He lived in Los Angeles and spent time with Bert's, his father's family there, but he spent a lot of time in Mexico with our family. He was very good at learning languages."

Virginia told me, "Walter spoke a little Swedish, but he spoke the sweetest Spanish because he spent a lot of time with me and my mother, your great-grandmother. Of course, he spoke English because he grew up in the United States!" Aunt Virginia's voice was high-pitched and excited as she wanted to tell me everything all at once.

So much joy came from meeting my dad's family because I was able to capture the memories of him, which still lived within the hearts of those that knew him personally. Aunt Virginia said, "I raised Walter much of the time. He was like a son to me." Through my great-aunts' and many others' voices, I found a father who lived and breathed, who went to school, who loved to fly kites on the beach, who painted rocks and drew cartoons, and who loved to fish and swim in the ocean, as well as a son who loved his mother dearly. And—the people I learned all this from were not dead!

I think we met at least a hundred family members during that week's visit. One cousin I met was the very beautiful Olga Alicia Cota, who came all the way from Mexico City to see me. She and Tichy were the same age, and like all the cousins in the Cota family, they were close. Another relative who came to Tichy's house was 104 years old. She was in a wheelchair while observing all the activities of the children and adults. Her name was Elvira Cota, and she was the matriarch of the family and very revered. I learned Mexican families did not take their elderly family members to nursing homes for caregiving. Tichy said, "It is disgraceful for a family to do such a thing."

Michaelin, Rachael, Rhonda, and Diedre with Clarissa and Melissa Diaz, their newfound twin cousins, taken in 1975

I have always thought cousins were special because they were best friends that you didn't see very often. Being related made cousins different than other friends. My girls became instant friends with their cousins, who were the granddaughters of Josepha, Peach's youngest sister. The English/Spanish language barrier made no difference to them.

My daughter, Rachael, the one in the yellow dress, was greeted by her great-aunts with, "Oh! Camelina, Camelina, you look just like Camelina!" Of course, they were referring to Peach. Some pictures of Peach in her childhood do look very much like Rachael. My aunts expressed to me, "Alana, you are just like our mama because you have so many children." Their mama was the mother of fourteen children!

I learned from Aunt Virginia firsthand the story about Peach's red hair. She told me, "Camelina never wanted to be a Mexican girl. When she was a teenager, she dyed her hair red and tried hard to speak English without a Spanish accent." I do remember my grandmother's "reddish hair" when she visited me at The Falls when I was six years old. Virginia said, "When she dyed her hair, it didn't turn out very good, and that's why she is still called Peach!" Each of her sisters told me the same story.

My aunts could not talk enough about my father or Peach. They wanted me to know every small detail. Virginia said, "Walter loved to come to Ensenada to be with his cousins, so he stayed with me, *y su bisabuela, nuestra madre*, when he wasn't in school." Virginia very often hurriedly kept going in Spanish but then changed back to English. I took Spanish in high school and college, so I understood some of what she was talking about my great-grandmother, her own mother.

The first night at Tichy's was getting to know many other family members. While we were getting acquainted, Tichy's phone kept ringing. "Yes, she is here, they are all here. Yes, Walt's daughter and his grandchildren." We were interrupted by phone call after phone call until it was time to go upstairs to bed. After the last phone call, Tichy told me, "We have a surprise for you tomorrow, more of the family wants to meet you."

The surprise for me was an extended family reunion not only for me but also to honor my dad. I was experiencing a degree of happiness I never thought possible. The relatives arrived one by one and two by two and sometimes in large groups. Tichy's house was a large two-story home with a big backyard. The party lasted all day and into the evening. Each person or group brought trays, plates, and pots and pans filled with every kind of delicious Mexican food they had prepared. None of us had ever eaten so many beans or so much rice, homemade tortillas, or tamales.

My girls, even the baby, could not stray from the extraordinary flan that one of my cousins brought. There were also little yellow peppers stuffed with cheese and chicken. Lee ate a little too much and went to bed with his stomach on fire! My cousin Armando kept telling us, "That sauce is nothing but fruit salad!" It was to us quite a bit hotter than fruit salad!

Many family members came across the border from Baja California. I learned for the first time how extremely important family is in Mexican culture. I was a total stranger to them, but no matter where I came from, I was Walter's daughter and I was family. It didn't matter that my parents weren't married or that my existence had been shrouded. They loved Walter and they loved me unconditionally. It was a profoundly strange and wonderful experience for me!

Peach's family was big, so the extended family was also big. I lost count of all who came that day to greet me and to pay respects to my father. He was a heroic family member in their eyes. I was met with so many hugs and so many tears. Since my grandmother was the oldest in her generation and my father was the oldest in his generation, the family now had the oldest grandchild among them after thirty years of absence. The family happily inserted me into my rightful place as the "oldest" in my generation. My cousin Ignacio had previously held that position, but he was very happy to relinquish the title of "the oldest" to me.

Peach and her mother were both named Carmen, so the name Camelina separated her in family conversations from her mother. Camelina was the oldest of those fourteen children, born in Ensenada, Baja California Norte, Mexico. The Cota family cherishes their heritage as mostly Spanish, not Mexican, because they are descendants of historically famous Spanish soldiers who explored and settled in early California in the late 1700s and early 1800s.

I wanted to learn everything and explore everywhere my dad had been and where he spent time with his family. Tichy drove us across the border to the family home where Carmen Fernandez [Peach's mother] raised her ten living children after her husband, Fermin Cota, died of pneumonia. The family home in Ensenada, Baja California, was a treasure to behold.

Upon opening the front door, the first piece of furniture was a grand piano sitting in the living room. It had been Peach's piano. There was a picture of my dad sitting on top of it. Peach had placed the picture there after my father died, and she gave strict instructions that the picture should never be removed from its resting place on her piano. It was the same picture I have had on my dresser my entire life, and it had been sitting on that piano since 1945—thirty years.

Seeing my dad's picture in his grandmother's home, where he had played with cousins and had been surrounded by the same people I was meeting, brought so many emotions to the surface. I cried with tears of happiness. Tichy said, "That picture of your dad has been there ever since Camelina put it there. Peach told us never to move it, so we didn't dare!"

The Cota family home on Gastelum Street,
Ensenada, Baja California, Mexico

All the people in the picture are either my kids or my new relatives. The home is located on Gastelum Street in Ensenada, Baja California Norte, Mexico. As the oldest in the family, Peach had inherited the home from her mother but passed it on to her younger sister, Lucia, who in turn gave it to her daughter, Tichy (Beatriz Contreras). There is so much family history attached to that home.

It is a small house with an overhanging roof over the front porch. The siding on the house is constructed with wooden slats. It is painted yellow and has white wooden frames around each of the windows. Tichy told me, "Your grandfather, Bert Lindberg, built the porch on the front of the house." I asked myself, "How in the world did ten children grow up in this little house?"

I went out the back door to the fenced backyard, where Walter played as a child. An amazing thing happened. There were a few small rocks in a pile in a corner. The rocks were different sizes, and each one had patches of faded paint. The colors could only be seen by looking closely at the rocks. I picked up one about the size of the palm of my hand, and I was told, "Walter painted those rocks, which his grandmother—your great-grandmother—saved. Walter was an artist at a very young age." We all laughed at that statement.

There was an old chair in the backyard, which I sat down on. Tichy, Lucia, and Biti took the children in the house and left me alone in the backyard. My heart was so full as I tried to envision my dad as a little boy running around in the yard and grabbing rocks to paint. I got up and walked around, back and forth, and thought to myself, "I am walking probably in my dad's footsteps." It was a strange feeling. I honestly felt like he was there with me, and somehow, someway we connected.

Culture is passed down through generations and binds peoples and communities together through language, traditions, and family ties. I was amid a family that I barely knew, and I was in a country completely unfamiliar to me. I had people all around me speaking a language I could only slightly understand. How was it that my life then became sealed to them with few, if any, cultural ties joining us together? I had not known any of them for over thirty years, but they all knew about me. I was suddenly, and permanently, bonded to my father's family. As Virginia said, "Walt loved family." I knew if my dad knew where I was—with his painted rocks—he would have been happy and glad that I had finally found "the family tree."

This Cota family picture is indeed a family heirloom for more than just the people in the picture. The story around this picture, as was told before, is known by all, and it has been told over and over and each time with a little more detail added to enhance both the picture and the story. It is shown here to identify the location, which was in the back of the family home. The previous picture, is in the front of the home on Gastelum Street.

Take a closer look at the photograph, taken in 1918. My great-grandmother, Carmen (sitting in a chair on the left), wanted the family picture with only herself with her ten living children. My grandmother (Peach) is on the right, sitting beside her. The picture, along with the beloved story, shows Walter's persistence to get what he wanted one way or another.

The picture also portrays four of the sisters, Josefa (sitting on the ground), Lucia (standing to the left of her mother wearing a white dress), Virginia (standing directly behind her mother), and Beatriz (standing behind her sister, Peach)—all of whom I met in the twilight of their years. They were not dead in 1965 or in 1975 when I first met them!

MY FATHER HAD NO CHILDREN

Fast-forward

After several more years and several more visits with many of my newfound relatives, I decided I needed to delve more deeply into the past, which my friend Arlene in my neighborhood had been prodding me to do. It was in the summer of 1980 when I took my eleven-year-old daughter with me to Chula Vista for a special visit to see Aunt Virginia.

She had expressed to me several times that she wanted the family to know her story. She said, "I always wanted to write a book, but I was always too busy taking care of my mother and my nieces and nephews. I also helped my brothers and sisters with their lives and their children. I was very busy." Rachael and I took a flight to San Diego, and Nando picked us up at the airport. He drove us for the second time to the trailer where my great-aunts lived.

Aunt Virginia welcomed us, but she didn't have room for both me and my daughter to stay with her in the trailer. In our past visits to Chula Vista, Rachael became more acquainted with her twin cousins. She wanted to stay with them in Tijuana while I stayed in Chula Vista with my two aunts in their trailer. So off she went with Nando to Tijuana to be with Clarissa and Melissa. Aunt Virginia and I had the next few days uninterrupted, and we worked hours at a time to get the timeless recordings of her personal story.

My visit with Virginia was primarily to focus on her personal history and to write the book she was too busy to write. During the recording sessions, she did not always stick to the subject at hand and drifted off into another time and place in her life. Within her story, she talked about Walter and Johnny when they were children and how they often were in competition against each other. She said, "Walter was much more outgoing, and he loved to speak Spanish. Johnny was shy and only wanted to speak English."

I did not interrupt her when she did this, but it was hard transcribing it later to get it in the correct chronological order. Tichy agreed to help me with the book. We worked together over the phone and in letters to tie Virginia's fragmented conversations so they would make sense to the family members who would be reading the book.

I sent Tichy a few transcribed pages at a time. Our aunt's memory was too flexible when it came to exact dates, but she was not flexible when it came to exact details, like when she received the telegram about my father's death. She became very emotional when that event came flooding back into her memory.

I interviewed Virginia for four days in a row, recording her personal stories about her family and the memories of other family members. There are six cassette tapes with an hour of discussion on each side. I wrote her book for her—over 125 pages. It includes family group sheets, stories about her mother and father's romance, the births of her siblings, copies of marriage documents, pictures of her and her sisters as the beauty queens of Ensenada, the tragedy of her father's death, and much more. Many family members contributed to the stories in Virginia's book. She told me, "God did not want me to have children." All of us, younger than she, became her children in one way or another. Her story contributed greatly to my dad's story, which helped me to know him.

Virginia Natalia Cota (Peach's sister)

Virginia became the editor-in-chief for her book. As Tichy received the pages from me and she read them, she gave them to

Virginia to review and make changes, if needed. We wanted her book to be as accurate as possible. The last stages of writing, editing, and making changes became more urgent when Virginia came down with pneumonia. Lee finished the artwork on the cover, and we gave it to the publisher. It was six years in the making!

The day all our efforts came back as a completed book on May 30, 1997, I received a call from my cousin Nando. Our beloved aunt Virginia had passed away. She never saw her finished book. What should we do? Nando and I talked about what Virginia would want us to do, and we decided we would still celebrate her birthday with a family reunion at his house in Chula Vista, which we did. It was a glorious party! So many branches of Walter's "family tree" were once again altogether. He would have loved being there to cherish his aunt.

I remember the first time I heard Aunt Virginia's voice. She called me after she received the first letter that I wrote to her. In today's world, handwritten letters are few and far between, but it was those thirty-year-old letters, written in ink and hand-scripted, which led me to my lost family.

Peach's sisters, Nando, Tichy, and many others are all gone. I am eternally grateful and thankful that I was united with my dad's family. I am glad that during my busy life raising seven children, I took the time to explore more, as my friend Arlene prodded me to do. In 1990, more handwritten letters came to me from another unexpected source, not from family members but from those who trained and flew in combat with my dad. Letters from those who were with Walter in his last days provided me with a better understanding of him that not even family members could have told me.

25

The Glider Gang
More Letters

While I was busy writing my great-aunt's personal history, my husband's electrical engineering company had obtained several government jobs in Southern California. We moved our family from Salt Lake City to California in 1987, soon after we celebrated Virginia's birthday and gave copies of her book out to family members. Our family moved first to Port Hueneme and then to Camarillo.

By the spring of 1989, three of our children had left home and were off to college. We had two children in high school and two in grade school that were still with us. Lee's office space was in Ventura, California, about ten miles from our house, so when Lee needed to go through paperwork from the office, it was easier to go over to the local library rather than make a trip back to his office ten miles away. We thought it would be good to take our two elementary school children to the library in the evening to make a sort of family night of it. We did this at least one night a week. Lee worked on business paperwork, the kids did their homework, and I was free to roam the bookshelves, which has always been my thing. I love libraries.

We wanted it to be a good experience for the kids to start learning to study using the library's resources. (Those were the days before iPhones, iPads, or Internet services at home.) Everything needed to complete their homework was at their fingertips at the library. Plus, there were no distractions like phone calls or trips to the refrigerator.

Those nights at the Camarillo Public Library turned out to be fun memories for the four of us for many reasons.

Ever since my own high school experiences, spending time at any library has always been enjoyable for me. I love libraries because I love books, and I love books because I love to read. I wanted to instill in my children the same love for books. Whenever there were dancing or piano lessons for their other siblings, I took the other kids to the library for story time or browsing while we waited for the lessons to be over.

One of those library nights, while the kids were quietly studying and Lee was busy, I slid my chair back from the table and went browsing the book aisles. The discovery I made was entrancing and spellbinding; it was a finding that was a pivotal moment in my life. It was a moment which opened a whole new world for me concerning my father. I'm sure I'm not the first person to have an "aha" moment in a library, but my personal discovery that night absolutely changed everything. It turned out to be a discovery of part of my dad's life that even his immediate family had only a vague knowledge of.

That night, for some unexplained reason, I was suddenly curious to see what might be on the bookshelves about gliders or glider pilots who participated in WWII. To my surprise, I found a book called *The Glider Gang* by Milton Dank. After inspecting the book, I realized it was written by a former glider pilot of WWII! I took it back to the table and started thumbing through the pages. There were many interesting photos of glider pilots, their planes, and their crash landings.

The photos in the book helped me become more familiar with WWII glider missions, which I previously knew nothing about. My curiosity led me to check the book out and take it home to read and study. Since the author of the book was a glider pilot, I thought I might learn more about what my father did in the war from a credible source, someone who had been there and done that.

When one mentions glider pilots of WWII in a conversation, most people draw a blank. I have found the public in general is completely unaware of the glider pilots' essential role in WWII. I was no exception, except I wanted to know more because my dad was a glider pilot. I thought it would take me a week or two to finish reading the book, but I became so engrossed in the content I read it in a couple of days. When I got to the end of the book, I flipped through the footnotes. I discovered Milton Dank's military service information. His service record matched my dad's! I was shocked! The first thought that came to mind was—and I said it out loud—"I wonder if Milton Dank knew my dad… What if he did?"

Dank was in the Army Air Corps and served with the Eighty-Second Airborne, 439th Troop Carrier Squadron (TCS), which was exactly the unit my father was assigned to in the European Theater of Operations (ETO). I remember thinking, *What an incredible coincidence, I have to call him!*

Reading *The Glider Gang* changed everything for me and brought me closer to my dad than I ever dreamed possible. I knew I could not rest until I located Mr. Dank. The flap of the book noted that he lived in Pennsylvania. I called directory assistance, which I could still do in the late 1980s. It was easy to get his phone number and address.

For the second time in my life while inquiring about my father, just like when I went to see my uncle Johnny in LA, I was extremely nervous as the phone began to ring at Milton Dank's residence. I wasn't sure how to start the conversation when he answered the telephone. I heard a man's voice and I briefly told him my name and that my father had been a glider pilot in WWII. I told him, "I just finished reading your book, Mr. Dank, about glider pilots." I blurted out, "My father was a glider pilot too. His name was Walter Lindberg. Did you know my father?" There was quite a pause before he answered, and my heart was racing. As it turned out, it wasn't as easy as all that. His answer came in a "good news, bad news" scenario.

The bad news came first: "No, I don't think so, but I have a roster of some of the glider pilots in the 439th TCS. I can send you the roster of names. I will look and see if there are any notes on anyone that might have known your father. I did a lot of research for my book. I knew many glider pilots but not all of them. There will certainly be some pilots on the roster that would have known him."

When the conversation ended, he asked for my phone number and address and said, "I will call you if I find anything."

Sure enough, a few days later, a letter arrived, along with a roster of the names of surviving glider pilots with phone numbers and addresses where they lived. Dank put a star beside twenty-five of the glider pilots' names on the roster who were still living. He wrote, "The stars I penned beside the names indicate the pilots who almost for sure would have known your dad!" Two days later, Milton Dank called me on the phone with more news, "Yes, I did know your dad. We were together for thirteen days crossing the Atlantic!" It was twelve years since he wrote the book, and he said, "My memory is sometimes not that good, but your dad and I traveled on the SS *George Washington* for thirteen days across the Atlantic to England."

Over the next few weeks, I wrote twenty-five letters to glider pilots. I mailed them with self-addressed stamped envelopes inside for a possible reply. I was very anxious to see if any would come back. With my heart pounding every time I made a trip to the mailbox over the next few months, one by one, letters from the glider pilots started to trickle into my mailbox. Of the twenty-five letters I sent, twenty-three responses came back. I was once again overwhelmed with emotions each time I read, "Yes, I knew your dad."

As I took each letter out of the mailbox, I knew in my heart the letter would not have come back if this person had not known my father. It is impossible to describe the feelings which came over me as I read each line of each letter. Some of the letters included photographs of my father, which they had kept all those years. The pictures were ones I had never seen before. One picture of my dad was in his dress military uniform. Another picture was of my dad in full flight gear, with hat and sunglasses! Written on the side of the picture from glider pilot Robert L. Pound is "F/O Lindberg, killed in Tours, France, 1945." With a five-o'clock shadow and a slight grin, he looked somewhat different than the picture I have always had on my dresser; the widow's peak on his forehead and the cleft in the chin is undeniable.

ALANA LINDBERG JOLLEY

WWII glider pilot Walter Bert Lindberg Glider in
full flight gear, taken in England, 1944

As I read each letter over and over, I began to form a different picture of my father in my mind. I began to grasp the kind of person he really was. My experience reading those accounts, as each pilot wrote what he remembered about my father, was truly thrilling. Some of the letters were humorous, but most of them made me cry. Nevertheless, with my father being absent from my life for over fifty years, I felt like I was getting to know him. It was no less than a miracle I picked up Milton Dank's book that night at the library, especially when I think of the circumstances that existed when I found it. The timing was at precisely the moment when I had been reunited with my father's family. I now was able to share with his family the details of his service and eyewitness accounts of how he did die in the service of our country. My dad's own words were fulfilled; he came back to me "somehow" as he had written to me so long ago that he would.

I learned that my dad "could walk on his hands for a block." He was very athletic and well built and had a calm and steady personality. Some of the letters described him as an artist, as well as a poet. More than one letter told of his athleticism.

Later, those letters inspired me to research my father's past as a young man. I found a picture of him in his high school yearbook and discovered he was a star gymnast at Long Beach Polytechnic High School. That explained how my father was able to "walk on his hands for a block" (see picture in chapter 5 for reference). My mother had mentioned to me that my dad tried out for the Olympics in Los Angeles. For some reason, I always thought it was swimming he tried out for, so again I learned something new about my dad.

There were a few letters which described how they were bunkmates of my father's. They told about conversations, which included their feelings about the most important question of all: "What happens if we die?" Their conversations progressed into discussions of religion and ultimately family. From many of those pilots' letters, I learned that my father talked about his new baby daughter back in Kentucky. It was reassuring to know that my dad talked about me often with his GP friends, especially from someone who supposedly "had no children." One of his best friends, Pershing Carlson, wrote to me, "I'm sure his last thoughts were of you. I'm sorry you had to live your life not knowing your father."

Sadly, there were some glider pilots who witnessed the crash of my father's CG-4A glider on that fateful day of February 22, 1945. Those letters included memories of his glider diving headfirst and plunging into the earth. It was not hard to imagine in my mind that event as they described while watching in disbelief! Each account by each pilot was consistent, and they concluded my father died instantly. One pilot said, "We all hoped, if we had to die, it would be quick," which they wrote "was somewhat reassuring."

The best and most descriptive account of my father's accident was given by Flight Officer Cy Shaffer in a letter from December 1990.

Dear Alana,

Your December 1st letter touched my heart! My wife and I welcomed your inquiry, and we are deeply appreciative of your remarks concerning the role of glider pilots in WWII.

I flew from England to Châteaudun, France, to join the 439th TCG on a cold blustery night in early January 1945. I was assigned to quarter in a bombed-out French military academy. Walter Lindberg and Eldon Muller were quartered in a nearby room. Both were very solid and experienced pilots for they had participated in previous combat missions. We newcomers pumped them for combat information and advice. They were never reticent to talk.

We put in time by walking the countryside, talking a great deal, reading, and flying practice missions. Our practice field was in Tours, France, about 40 miles south. It was in one of these practice missions that your father and Eldon Muller were killed in an accident.

We were practicing for the Rhine River crossing, later to become known as Operation Varsity, on March 24, 1945. On February 22, 1945, as you indicate, we were briefed to practice 360-degree landings, releasing and coming out of a formation of two C-47s in echelon to the right, which put our four gliders behind them in close proximity.

The wind was brisk from the left as the formation approached the field. I was standing near the runway, having just completed a flight, watching your father's formation above as the gliders peeled off four at a time. Perhaps the wind increased in strength at the time, I do not really know, but the gliders turning left out of the formation were being carried down the flight to the oncoming formation.

> My worst fears were realized when I observed a tow rope just released from a glider and swinging downward to strike a glider and tearing the tail completely off. I did not want to walk to the wreckage a couple hundred yards away, but it was reported that Lindberg and Mueller were killed instantly. I can only say that most of us hoped that if we had to go, it would be merciful and quick. I can assure you it happened that way in this case.

Another glider pilot, Virgil Neal, was flying in formation directly behind my father, and he witnessed the event from behind. He, too, was one of my father's roommates. He told me that he and Grady Wright, another of my father's friends, took my father's remains to the small town of Saint-André-de-l'Eure, France, and acted as pallbearers at his funeral. Walter Lindberg was buried alongside other fallen Americans, including Flight Officer Eldon Mueller, who was the pilot of their glider on that tragic day. One of the glider pilots' letters included a photo of Eldon Mueller who was acting as the pilot on the day their glider plunged to earth, killing them both.

My father remained buried in France until May of 1949. My grandmother, Peach, did not want my father's remains to be in a distant country, far from his home and family. Peach decided to bring her son back from France to the United States. Walter's casket arrived at the LAX where my dad's cousins, as mentioned previously, received his remains. Peach and the family had him repatriated in the Inglewood Park Cemetery, Inglewood, California, on May 5, 1949. My mother did not attend that belated funeral. I don't know if she even knew about it because she had never mentioned that fact to me. If she did know, one would have thought she would have asked me about it—if I had been to the grave when I was in Los Angeles visiting my uncle.

Over the years, I have read those letters again and again. I never fail to realize how fortunate it was to receive each one of them. They are primary sources, which have helped me get to know my father in a deeply personal way. They were with him and they knew him best during the last year of his life. The glider pilots who wrote the letters were the last persons who talked with him and shared in an important part of his life amid a war, which held so many uncertain circumstances.

What was at first a seemingly insignificant night spent at a library with my two youngest children became one of the most important events of my entire life. Those letters changed my focus, and they gave me inspiration for a lifelong quest to locate family. They helped me to uncover my dad's story and the truth about how he died. Before I received those letters, all I had heard from the family, including my mother, was, "Your dad was shot down in France," or "He died in an airplane crash." Neither turned out to be correct. It was also assumed that he had died in a combat situation. Instead, he died in a tragic training accident preparing to cross the Rhine River (Operation Varsity), which was to be the last glider mission of WWII.

The union with my dad's family and the letters from those glider pilots who knew my father have brought a peaceful closure to my life as a war orphan. I learned from family members about my father's childhood and his life before the war. I was able to see another side of my father from the letters I received from the glider pilots. The glider pilots who shared tent accommodations in freezing weather, scraped ice from the wings of their aircraft, and crash-landed with Walter in combat missions tell a story of courage, bravery, comradeship, and sacrifice in the most difficult of times. The letters confirmed what my uncle said about his brother: "[A]bove all, defeatism was not in Walt's vocabulary."

26

Lost in the Victory

The histories of war usually include the battles that were won or lost and the important players in those battles. History tells of the cities ruined and the statistics of those who died on the battlefronts. How many historians write about the children's lives lost in those victories or defeats? Untold thousands of children, like me, faced uncertainties for their futures because they lost fathers and/or loved ones during the upheavals of war. My story, I am sure, is only one of millions that have never been told.

The countries of Europe were freed from years of German occupation when the Paris Peace Treaties were finally signed in February of 1947. There were over four hundred thousand American military deaths during the years of WWII. Those deaths were sacrificed to liberate other countries, not directly the United States. Of all the military deaths in that extraordinary victory, how many were fathers of children left behind? It was a great victory for "the greatest generation," but we children lost in that victory are seldom mentioned. We never knew our fathers were part of the Greatest Generation before Tom Brokaw's book came out. Fortunately, I was left behind in the United States, not in the war-torn places of Europe, Japan, or the Philippines, where the ruins and devastations were in plain sight.

Lost in the Victory by Susan Johnson Hadler and Ann Bennett Mix was written fifty-one years after WWII. It contains personal stories of many war children like me. My experience as a "war orphan" of WWII is much the same as many of the recollections in their book with some variations and/or twists and turns in our own individual stories. The children who were lost in the victory of WWII were victims of circumstances, which were completely beyond their control. All of us war orphans throughout our lives have had to make concessions because of the loss of a parent or parents during that war.

The children left behind in the rubble of their homelands were less fortunate than those of us left behind in America. I do recognize that reality. Many children left behind had more problems than just being labeled orphans. There were thousands of German and Japanese children fathered by Allied soldiers. Those children went to orphanages with no hope of ever being adopted. Why? They were categorized as "children of the enemy." There were Black and Brown children fathered by African Americans and by Latino soldiers all over Europe. They weren't children of the enemy, but their skin-color heritage, nevertheless, made them unadoptable in that era.

Few children lost and left behind ever knew who their fathers were. Even if the names of their dead fathers were known, they might have been told, like me, that their fathers had no children.

Other topics deserve mentioning, which were and are critical losses to a child's early identity. Such critical losses rarely have been explored and examined within the context of family structures, including extended families. To be a war child and not know who your parent or parents are or were is problematic for any child. After reading *Lost in the Victory*, the authors, some of whom are also war children, I can accept, though unwillingly, the truth of those painful words spoken to me so long ago in the Social Security office. "These things happened during the war, you know, it's not unusual." In that moment of shock, when I heard those words, I was not capable of realizing what the word *unusual* meant.

The children of Japan and Germany were particularly scorned because they were "offspring of the enemy." They became unwanted outcasts in their own societies. Children always seem to bear the biggest brunt of society's bad choices. I don't know how unusual my own circumstances were after my father's death.

I spent nearly five years in a boarding house with other war children. I lived with a woman who took care of other war children. There were probably eight or ten of us who boarded there. Sometimes one or two of the children went home on the weekends. I did not go home on the weekends because my mother worked nights. I was boarded there until I was old enough to start kindergarten. I remember clinging to Mother Huffine, as we children called her, standing on her front lawn. I cried, not wanting to leave her safe little home. It was a sad day for me because it was like leaving my own siblings behind. I had lived with those other war children both day and night for several years. I went home with a mother I barely knew. Children are said to be resilient, but it was a big upheaval for a five-year-old.

War children born in the United States were born mostly to single women, but the servicemen, unfortunately, were not always single. Those women, like my mom in the 1940s, were better positioned socially if their soldier died in the war. Single motherhood, which my mother faced, was a taboo if the unwedded affair or secret became known. In my mother's case, none of her immediate family knew she was not married. My aunt Chrys, though, surely knew because she shared an apartment with my mom during the time my parents met and fell in love in Louisville. Later, when Walt and Lil lived together, Chrys lived next door to them, still in the same apartment she and her sister had shared before the war began.

For us war children, the war was never over. My father's death has been like wearing a scarlet letter because it is usually the first thing everyone learns about me. Today, children of veterans killed in action belong to Gold Star Families. I have never been designated as a Gold Star daughter. I'm sure my mom knew nothing about Gold Stars. When I started kindergarten, I learned physically and mentally about war. There were air raid drills at my school, though WWII was over.

War was never talked about with any regard to how we war children were functioning in our world of loss, poverty, and grief. The war was never about us right here in front of everybody; the war was always something far away that happened in the past. No one ever thought the war affected us—only the adults knew anything about the war. It only affected them. I guess we didn't understand war, but we knew what it was like living with the consequences of our dads being gone. We all knew there was something different about us. There was always the "pity" factor surrounding us when older adults talked about our missing fathers.

How was it that war children didn't count? It always seemed that way to me because I felt I was a burden to my mother and other family members too. My mom told me many times, "I provide a roof over your head, food in your mouth, and clothes on your back." That's what she said to me whenever we had a conflict. I was never supposed to forget that fact. It hung over my head that she took care of me, and I wasn't nearly appreciative enough. It seemed like I could never be good enough for all her sacrifices for me. I'm sure that's why my mom wanted my trust fund money! As children, we don't understand what sacrifices are. Our experiences after becoming adults are what enable any of us to understand the word *sacrifice*.

Every war orphan has had vastly different experiences, but one thing we all shared in common was wanting to understand who our fathers were and what happened to them. It certainly was not unusual for us to have many questions, but there were few answers given to us. I remember seeing my mom sitting at the kitchen table one day with a bunch of letters tied with a string. I asked her, "Who are all those letters from?" I could tell she had been crying. She just shook her head and said, "These are from your dad." I never saw those letters out in the open anymore after that. I think she put them in the trunk with all my dad's other belongings. I have only a few of those letters in my possession that my dad wrote.

There was also shame in being a war child and the association of not having a father. I can't exactly explain it, but the shame was real. There was something about me that was unlike the other kids. I remember hearing some girls talk in the bathroom at school when I was in second grade, "Yeah, she doesn't have a dad," telling each other that's why she does this or that. They said cruel things about me that made me go off and cry alone. I felt like it was shameful not coming from a "normal" home.

All of us war children grew up feeling cheated that we lost our fathers. We all knew they died for a cause, but that cause was not understood. I knew my dad fought for whatever that *cause* was, but I didn't feel like anyone was fighting for me. There was no one to fill the emptiness I felt when I was alone and thinking about my dad.

The void was always there for us war children, but rarely was it ever exposed or recognized. I'm sure my mother clung to the love she shared with my father for as long as she could. As I look back on her loss and what must have been profound grief for her, at age twenty-three, I believe, just like me, she never really got over it. It was a burden hanging over her head, and she mourned, but I didn't know exactly why she mourned in the way that she did.

A few of my losses in the victory have been explained, as well as how my life was impacted by each. Every child who is lost in those victories and those defeats suffers cultural losses as well as the loss of a parent. Cultural losses are rarely explored and almost never spoken about, or even acknowledged. My mother kept me from my dad's family for reasons only she knew. Being that my dad's heritage was both Mexican and Swedish and he was raised in the throes of both cultures and languages, my cultural losses were many and different from others' losses.

As my childhood progressed, it seemed to end on my thirteenth birthday—the last happy birthday I spent with my granny, my aunt Mae and uncle Morgan, and my close cousins at The Falls. When I left Falls of Rough, Kentucky, a couple months after my thirteenth birthday, it was the sunset of my childhood, but I didn't know it. Most of us war children, at least the ones I knew, became independent early in life because we had to.

Four months after my thirteenth birthday, in October of 1957, which I have written about already, my mom and I, her boyfriend, and his two children left Kentucky. If not for the immaturity of the two adults parenting us three children, I might have remained in my childhood a few more years, but that was not the case. I learned quickly that I was the grown-up in the family, and my responsibilities for the two young children, who were not my siblings, were especially heavy.

I left behind in Kentucky a nice home, my eight-year-old dog, the boxer I had gotten for my fifth birthday, all my new junior high school friends, my granny, and all my aunts, uncles, and cousins, who had all been a part of my childhood. The only thing not lost were my memories, which promised me a hope that never materialized.

My mom never sat us children down to explain where we were going or why we were leaving. She made all the arrangements like selling the house and taking Rocket to a ranch while I was gone for the summer to The Falls. All my beloved childhood toys, including my favorite doll and doll clothes, had been taken to the Salvation Army. Everything that made my room my room was gone. The last time I was at The Falls became the line or boundary which separated me from my childhood and the rest of my life to come.

Isn't it true that we are all the sum of all the ages (in birthdays) that we have all lived through? During times of stress and sadness, I remembered when Peach came to The Falls when I was six. I remember when I was seven and wrapped myself in my dad's uniform in the basement. I still revisit often the summers at Falls of Rough, when I was eight, nine, and ten. Sometimes I wished I could be ten or twelve again. It was hard to be an adult, but I had to be. My frustration with my mother and her men associates was a never-ending battle for me, even after I was forced to become an adult.

I can plainly see today how the loss of my father made me feel helpless. I was very vulnerable because of my feelings of sadness for that loss. Rather than time being a healing process, as I grew up, the loss compounded and became more real. Even today, in my older years, the long-held grief is still there and remains undiminished because the years have brought more details about who my father, Walter Lindberg, was as a real person, not just someone I was related to who died in a war.

Two people who harbored hidden truths from me in my first twenty years of life kept me from knowing and having relationships with my dad's "family tree." First, my mother withheld secrets from me, which I learned at the Social Security Administration. Second was my uncle Johnny, who also kept truths from me regarding the family—my family. Those hidden truths led to losses for me, which cannot even be calculated. For some unexplained reason, neither my mother nor my uncle Johnny wanted me to discover that there was family on my paternal side. The question I must ask is, why?

In the case of my mother, she probably had two reasons. First and foremost, she did not want me to learn that she and my dad were not married. Maybe she feared Peach would tell me. Second, which is an underlying reason, my mother was steeped in prejudices, as many rural Southerners were. I'm sure my mom loved my dad, but when she met Peach, she suddenly discovered or realized that Walter was somehow different than who she thought he was.

When we moved to Las Vegas, my mom knew I was only 250 miles away from Peach. I could have taken the train to Los Angeles to see my grandmother; it was Peach's great loss as well as mine. In a letter from Peach's sister, my great-aunt Virginia, in 1972, she wrote:

> I have so many things to talk about that I want you to know. Your grandmother loved you forever and felt very bad when she didn't know where you were. It's a mystery, her and I talked about it many times. Your mother moved to

another place and never wrote to her. She cried so much and never got over it. You were all her love, her only grandchild.

As far as my uncle Johnny goes, his reasons were more sinister. As the oldest in my generation and the only grandchild of Peach, I stood to inherit what she most likely would have left to me. There was a home, a ranch, and other assets and belongings, which, at the very least, probably would have been shared between Johnny and me. It also explains the reason Addie, Johnny's wife, was so frigid during my visit. She must have felt threatened that I had suddenly appeared on their doorstep, and she probably thought her inheritance as well would also be diminished.

Material things, as well as cultural things, were lost, which would have been passed down to me, according to tradition, as part of my Mexican heritage. In today's world, where there is such confusion in self-identities, we see how each loss contributes negatively to a child's growth along the path to adulthood.

Back story

It was, in 1983, after twenty-six years that my heart yearned to go back to The Falls. Lee said, "I think we might be able to get along without you for a little while." So I took two of my daughters, a twelve-year-old and a one-year-old, back to Kentucky. It was a nostalgic trip, and it was filled with undeniable emotional trauma.

The two children I took with me are the only ones I have shared The Falls experience with. My youngest daughter celebrated her first birthday and began to walk while there, but of course, she does not remember. The twelve-year-old has very vivid and fond memories of her great-aunt Mae and her distant cousins, Virginia and Charline.

My cousin Virginia's son, Mark, picked the three of us up at the airport in Louisville and drove us the rest of the way to The Falls. My first encounters were such a great disappointment because after twenty-six years, things had changed. Most of the people I knew were no longer alive, except for my aunt Mae, who was eighty years old. My uncle Morgan had passed away four years before, and my granny died my first year of college, in 1962.

Instead of Mark taking us to my aunt's farmhouse that I remembered, we arrived at what I might consider a suburb of The Falls. Aunt Mae no longer lived by Miss Jenny's house or the general store or the old mill. The bridge over the Rough River falls was still there, but Aunt Mae lived a few miles away from all those familiar places. I wanted to see what I remembered, and I wanted to see the people I had never stopped thinking about since my thirteenth birthday.

Mark took us the next day to the familiar old farmhouse, where Aunt Mae and Uncle Morgan had lived, which was in disrepair and uninhabited. The sandy road was still sandy, but nothing else was the same. Aunt Della and Uncle Arlie had long passed away. The red water pump was still on the hill near where their house had once stood. The general store was there, but Polie and his daughter, JoAnn, were long gone. No one tended the store, and the windows were covered with particle board. The bench Charlie sat on was still there, but it wasn't green. There was no wooden barrel there for anyone to spit tobacco juice in. I wanted the store to be open so I could go in, but it looked like it had been closed for a long time.

The old mill stood like a gravestone in the community. The doors were chained, and Mark said it had been abandoned years before. The bridge over the falls was modernized with concrete and steel rather than being made of wood. The night watchman's hut was there, too, but no signs of anyone living in the area. The Methodist Church where my granny and I often walked across the bridge to Sunday services looked like the only building still in use. My grandparents and my great-grandparents were all laid to rest in that church cemetery behind the chapel. Aunt Mae and I walked among the weeds around the gravestones as she reminded me and pointed to names that I had not heard or thought about for many years.

The cemetery was overgrown with weeds covering some of the gravestones. It looked nothing like the well-kept burial ground that I remembered. My granny never missed a church meeting in that chapel no matter how bad her arthritis was. Uncle Morgan drove

Aunt Mae and me to a church farther away, but I always wondered why he never drove Granny across the bridge to her church.

Unlike my vivid memories, The Falls I knew had faded into the distant past, just like the little girl I once was. My eyes filled with tears as I realized the fabled place of my childhood happiness was no longer the same. I stared at the road, where I first saw Peach's car approaching on my sixth birthday. The road was still unpaved and full of sand; it had not changed, but everything else had. I picked up a handful of the sand and put it in my pocket. I still have a little plastic bag full of that sand.

At Aunt Mae's house in the evenings during my visit, there were long talks with my cousins Virginia and her daughter Charline about my dad. I told them all that I had learned at the Social Security Administration. I told them about meeting my dad's family in California and Mexico. Aunt Mae and Virginia remembered when Peach came for my birthday. I learned that Aunt Mae and other relatives knew nothing of what I revealed concerning my parents. Charline said, "Granny didn't know either? I reckon…she would have been shocked!"

The Falls was my childhood refuge and the place where I felt safe. The people I loved the most took care of me, taught me core values, and protected me. It was a place where I was immensely happy. Leaving The Falls and Kentucky was such a traumatic event in my childhood that I have a great sense of nostalgia as I reminisce. Falls of Rough was the only place during my childhood where I did not feel "lost in the victory."

When my aunt Chrys learned I was at The Falls, she drove from Cincinnati, Ohio, to Kentucky to see me. The questions I had for her she did not want to answer. All she said was, "You need to talk to Lil about those things, she's your mother." When I returned from my visit to The Falls, I decided to talk to my mom to get more information that she might be withholding from me. It was not an easy task. She was still holding on to more hidden truths that I would learn later.

What If? Walter's Legacy

It was a hard decision to approach my mother about the past that she had hidden from me for so long. I remembered Mr. Bowcutt had informed me that he had been in contact with her, so she probably already knew that I knew. Yet it would have been difficult for me to talk directly with her, so I wrote her a letter telling her what had happened at the Social Security Administration. My mother was not happy that I had uncovered her secret. In fact, she was furious! She said they had no right to tell me, yet I was an adult, married, and expecting her first grandchild.

There are many times in life that we ask ourselves, "What if?" And I have asked myself many times over the years, "What if I had not gone to the Social Security Administration that day?" I would never have been able to meet my paternal family. "What if Peach had not set up the trust fund for me?" I would not have pursued university studies. My great-aunt Virginia told me, "Camelina [Peach] was misunderstood by your mother. Your mother hurt her very badly, not letting her see you or know where you were for all those years. She cried all the time over you. It was a very sad thing. Camelina wanted to take care of you, but she didn't know how to find you."

While I was writing Aunt Virginia's history in 1985, I told my mother what Aunt Virginia had told me about Peach being distraught over not knowing where I was. My mother asked me in a very condescending voice, "How did I hurt Peach?" As a mother myself and a grandmother, too, I understand the sadness Peach must have felt. What I do not understand is how my mother did not perceive that an only grandchild in the family would be missed. She obviously did not know that my father was so well remembered and loved by all his family. Of course, she did not know that my dad's picture was on the piano in the home in Ensenada for thirty years! I am so glad my mother did not take her secret to her grave when she passed away suddenly in November 1986.

What if Lee and I had never moved into the neighborhood in Provo, where I met Arlene, who mentored me and prodded me to search for my father? What if I had not called my uncle for the third time, as Arlene had insisted? What if Addie had not sent me those letters? What if I had put the letters in a drawer and forgot about them? What if Peach's siblings had been dead, as my uncle told me? What if I had not found my dad's family, those who were still living that held memories in their hearts of him? What if I had not found the library book that led me to twenty-three glider pilots that knew my father in his last days and hours?

I have wondered, am I like my dad? We think personality traits are not inherited, but if we dig deeper into heritable traits, we know we do inherit some genes that seem to be unidentified. Those genes contain information, which has been passed down. Biological processes can form such genetic information into many combinations, which can affect our behaviors.

According to recent research, paternal genes have been found to be more dominant than maternal ones. That might be the reason that daughters tend to look more like their fathers than their mothers. Those who knew Walter as a child and as a grown-up confessed to me in sweet Spanish phrases, "Yes, you are just like him." They said, "Your eyes are his." Each relative told me, "We love you, Alana." "Si, eres como el, tus ojos son los suyos, te amamos, Alana."

When each relative saw me, there were other loud and exciting exclamations like, "Oh, Alana, you look just like Walter," or "You are just like *mi madre!*" What was it my grandmother's sisters observed in me, which made them say I was like their mother—my great-grandmother? How did they see in my daughter their sister, Camelina (Peach)?

In hindsight, I believe whatever imprints my four great-aunts and others saw in me or in my children, who resembled their siblings and/or their mother or others in the family, was very real to them. They even called our third daughter Johnny because she reminded them so much of him when he was a small child. Karma, then, is all about the cycle of birth and rebirth and the influences of that cycle. It seems rather obvious in my father's family—my family—something was there that helped us connect in unexplainable ways. I loved them immediately and I knew they loved me.

Ancestral karma is said to run deep in indigenous cultures. For instance, in ancient Iroquois philosophy there is the belief that patterns of behavior are influenced by seven generations before us and that we ourselves will influence seven generations in the future. From my father to me, to my children and my grandchildren are already four generations. How much karma has already been passed down?

My father, to my grandmother, Peach, to her father, to his father is another four generations before me. It seems probable that memory both ways may play an important part in the concept of what may be called karma.

Blood relations are not the only ones who can observe or "feel" a kind of karma. Friends and other associates can also be observers but are unlikely to realize what it is. Sometimes simple communications with others, even without actual observation, can be a bonding experience.

Alana's seven children—Walter Lindberg's seven grandchildren

Such was the case with the letters I received from my father's comrades in arms, those glider pilots he bunked with, ate with, trained with, and flew gliders into battle with in WWII. They observed in my dad some of that karma, and they wrote about it. As soon as I contacted them, there was an immediate connection. When I talked to Milton Dank and another glider pilot who lived in Ogden, Utah, who shared a tent with my dad, there was something that connected between them and me. They had known my dad in his last hours, and they knew about me from conversations with my dad. One glider pilot wrote, "We spent hours talking about our little girls, Walt wrote a poem titled 'My Little Girl,' which he gave me, but I don't have it anymore."

My father is descended from a long line of soldiers who fought for and explored for the king of Spain in the 1700s, fought in the Civil War in the United States and in World War I and World War II. Perhaps the karma of courage and bravery were passed down to my dad through those generations. One of my dad's glider pilot friends told me, "Walt volunteered for everything, every mission, every task that was to be encountered. He never complained or made excuses as to why he could not participate."

Whatever it was, karma or something else, Walter Lindberg left his mark on his family on the town where he lived, worked, and went to school on the glider pilots he led as a flight officer and eventually on the world. He wasn't rich in money or possessions, yet he had an impact on people and places. That impact did not make him famous, nor are there books or movies made about his life.

How do I, as Walter's daughter, and my children and grandchildren, as his descendants, want my dad to be remembered? Like so many others who have died for a cause, my father left the world a better place because he was here during a time when history needed him. What my dad accomplished throughout his short lifespan of thirty years says much more than the words I am writing down on paper to preserve his legacy.

First, there was his loyalty to his mother and her Hispanic heritage. Every aunt, uncle, and cousin attested to Walt's uniqueness and genuine character as one who cared for others. His postscript on the goodbye note states, "Get the lowdown on the family tree from my mother," and that I have referred to so many times. Second, Walter's brother, John, wrote to my mother, "In Walt flowed the blood of one of the finest human beings who ever lived."

Walter was a born leader, as his gymnastics coach and teammates agreed that he was the star athlete. Then there was the loyalty to his country. His mother had worked hard over many years to become an American citizen. She made sure her sons had a chance to live the American dream, but after the Pearl Harbor attack, they both dropped out of college and enlisted in the United States Army.

Walter had worked in nurseries and took courses in horticulture, hoping to start his own business after the war as a florist in Los Angeles. One of his glider pilot friends noted in a letter, "Walt knew a lot about flowers and plants." Walter's childhood and adolescence were lived within three different cultures, and he was comfortable in all. He and Peach traveled often to Ensenada, where Carmen Fernandez, his grandmother, and her other nine children, welcomed her grandson with open arms. Walter loved going to the Cota family ranch in Rosarito, where he gained a love of horses and the art of riding. He sent pictures to my mom from England, where he and a good friend went horseback riding on their leave.

There were also the cultural influences from his Swedish father and his Swedish grandmother, Mary Johnson. He was her favorite grandchild, whom she doted over and loved teaching and speaking Swedish with.

Peach and Walter visiting his Swedish grandmother in Los Angeles after his graduation from flight training at Victorville Flight School in 1943

Walter was a quick learner of languages, speaking Spanish and English fluently and elementary Swedish as well. One of the glider pilot letters said, "Lindberg got along very well in Paris, and the language didn't seem to be a problem for him." Before leaving California and after graduating from flight training, the last family member Walter said goodbye to was his father's mother, his Swedish grandmother, shown in the picture above.

Family, on all sides, was very important to my dad. His grandparents obviously had an enduring influence on Walter's early life. Their diversity of cultural beliefs, family values, and love surely impacted the way Walter treated others and the reason his glider pilot buddies said he got along very well in Paris with the language.

Another glider pilot letter explained, "Lindy loved to entertain us with his art. He was a character artist and kept us laughing." This must have been a great diversion from the stark reality of the war with its inconvenience of living in tents on frozen ground in a foreign country, where military leaves were few and far between.

My father set a positive example for others through his actions, words, and deeds. He often gave up his leaves to earn extra money cleaning other officers' uniforms, which was money he sent home to both his mother and my mother. Walter's kindness, generosity, and ability to grasp the uncommon responsibilities of war positively impacted his fellow glider pilots.

Last but far from the least was the bravery and heroism he exhibited as an officer and veteran glider pilot of four combat missions. My father's legacy of selflessness and courage cannot be measured. He received medals for his bravery; the first one was on my birthday. A PS on the bottom of a letter postmarked August 3, 1944, from France, Walter wrote, "Tell Alana her daddy got the Air Medal on June 27, 1944. "He received that medal for his participation on D+1, June 7, 1944, in the invasion of Normandy. Following is the medal for European, African, Middle Eastern campaigns in the frame.

MY FATHER HAD NO CHILDREN

The Air Medal on the right of the picture is awarded for single acts of heroism while participating in aerial flight or actual combat in support of operations, and it is equivalent to the Bronze Star. Walter also received the Bronze Star for his meritorious service in a combat zone, which was his glider mission to Holland, better known as Operation Market Garden. He received other medals as well but did not live to claim them. His heroism impacted many of his glider pilot buddies, helping them to be stronger and more committed in their own duties. Every glider pilot letter had praise for my dad.

All good deeds by good people leave a mark on the world, even if not recognized in their own time. I want my dad's bravery and heroism to be recognized by his descendants and to be passed down. The more understanding I have gained about my dad's life, the more strongly I have felt the need to transmit the information in writing for his posterity and for him to have a legacy.

As the years have gone by, and I have researched and studied so much about my father's life, I now realize what a heavy burden he carried with him when he said goodbye to my mother in North Carolina. At the time of my meeting at the Social Security Administration, I did not have enough knowledge and/or experience to understand the real meaning of what I was told.

With the truth exposed on every front and life's dilemmas of my own, I understand better the impact of impossible situations in life. However, I did not walk in my parents' shoes. I have no idea the anxieties they must have felt living during a world war, like WWII. What if my dad had survived the war? Why he had no children in his marriage was not known until my aunt Virginia shed her light on the situation, "Walter loved children, but his wife was German. She did not want any Mexican babies. That is the truth!" Virginia also said, "His wife did not want Walter to be around the family in Mexico because it made her uncomfortable." Virginia said my dad had tried to get a divorce, but the war closed in too quickly.

There was not enough time for my father to pursue divorce proceedings. My uncle Johnny's wife, Addie, wrote to me, "She [Walt's wife] would never let him loose no matter what!" The day after Thanksgiving in 1943, my dad wrote a very long letter to my mother. Peach had visited him in North Carolina for Thanksgiving. Here are his thoughts:

Dearest Lil,

> Mother finally came to visit me here in NC yesterday. She was only here for one day, but I was really glad to see her. I told her about you and me and about the (?) and I also let her know just how much we mean to each other. She is going to write to you and try to see you before she goes home about the fifth. She wants you and I to always keep on loving each other and stay together for always.
> Darling, I hope she can make you understand me a little better after you talk to her—I just know you'll love her, she's so sweet and understanding and honest. Lil, she's not like other mothers at all, so please answer her letters, and I'm sure, honey, that what she tells you will make you a lot happier because then you'll understand the situation a little more clearly. I think she can help us both—because honey I'm going to marry you and have you for my very own just as soon as I can get a divorce. No use talking about it anymore. I want you and the baby...above every-

thing in the world, darling, I love you so much. I certainly don't want to lose you because if I did, I wouldn't want to live anymore. That's all, and I can't go on feeling that I might lose you because I don't keep my mind on my flying or anything – just muddles me up inside so I can't do anything right – and you can't keep on flying when you feel like that."

While stationed in North Carolina, my dad went to Michigan, where his wife was staying with her family. My father wrote to my mother afterward, "She refused to talk about divorce." My cousin Tichy told me, "I believe she didn't want the divorce because of the death benefit she would receive if Walt died in the war." One of my dad's older male cousins suggested, "She didn't like Walt going off to fight the Germans."

The conversation with Mr. Bowcutt at the Social Security Administration seemed to shed a negative light on my father, but the truth revealed something different. In Bowcott's position, he could not dig any deeper because rules were rules. As he told me about his own investigation, "Nothing can change the facts."

My father wanted children, and he loved my mother and wanted me and loved me as his daughter. He confirmed it over again in every letter, not just this one. He closed the letter to my mom, saying,

"Well, sweetheart, I'll sign with love and kisses to my perfect [most perfect] wife, and I hope this letter makes you a little happier because I am trying to do the right thing, and I do love you very much." Walter

My dearest father gave me life, and in return, I gave him descendants who will carry on his legacy in their own hearts and in their own lives. Everything a person does in life works together to create the whole picture of his/her legacy. The whole picture of Walter Bert Lindberg (Army ID #T1179) is much bigger than the few words spoken to me at the Social Security Administration long ago. The impact of my father's life on my own and on my children's lives has been positive. My grandchildren have also shared in the positive legacy, which their grandfather left behind.

The loss of any parent is a great void in a child's life, and mourning for that parent is the greatest example of love a child can give. Even though I did not know my father, I have mourned his loss my whole life.

My father, as a glider pilot and soldier on the battlefields of Europe, was lost in the Allied victory of WWII. I was also lost in that victory because he did not return home. Within this book is his story, and within his story is mine. He did come back to me, and I have carried the torch that he could not carry, which promises that his legacy is not lost.

Closure

On October 11, 2019, I attended the Forty-Ninth WWII Glider Pilot Reunion at Fort Bragg, North Carolina, where my parents said their goodbyes. I had the opportunity to honor my father and to pay tribute to all the glider pilots who served in WWII by presenting a PowerPoint presentation about my dad. It has been said, "Without the glider pilots, the war may not have been won." Having researched all the glider pilot history and the combat missions they flew, I believe that statement to be true.

They flew aircrafts without engines behind enemy lines, crash-landed in unpaved fields, and unloaded supplies, troops, medics, and/or vehicles while under fire. After landing, they became embedded in combat activities upon leaving their aircraft. They had to find their own way back to the Allied airfields to get ready for their next glider mission.

My father did all those things and more. Glider pilots were also trained in how to construct the aircrafts they were about to fly. Previous chapters have noted the courage and bravery of glider pilots in all aspects of their service. According to Colonel Charles H. Young, commander of the 439th TCG, the mortality rate was more than 80 percent. Out of the thousands of glider pilots who served, only a few hundred returned from the war. Some of those survivors I have had the privilege of communicating with in a personal way. I am forever grateful for their service and for their wonderful memories of my father, which they conveyed to me both in letters and phone calls.

The presentation I gave was about forty-five minutes long, and it was a dramatic closure for me. The standing ovation I received brought tears to my eyes. I met descendants of those warriors I paid tribute to. One older gentleman came up to me and said, "I think I knew your mother at the Seelbach Hotel."

After my presentation, one woman, a young Air Force glider pilot trainee at Fort Bragg, came up to me and asked, "What happened to your mom?" I told her, "My mom finally got married a year before I did, but before that, she had a very hard time." I did not mention much about my mother in my presentation because it was about my dad.

However, in 1967, it was several days before I confronted my mother with the disturbing information I had received from the Social Security Administration. She was angry and upset and she didn't want to discuss any of the details. She was bitter that the government had let the cat out of the bag. It was many years later when she finally was able to open up to me about those painful events in her young life. She didn't want to talk face-to-face or on the phone, but she wrote me a very long letter. This is the last letter I had from my mom prior to her passing in 1986.

The following are parts of the content of that ten-page letter. She described Walter as she remembered him.

> He was very athletic and in very good shape. He didn't have all the ugly muscles that Mr. America has and all the bodybuilders, but he did not have an ounce of fat on him. He had very broad shoulders, a slim waist, and hips, which when you were born you were shaped just like him.

She wanted me to know the circumstances of how they met, which is not exactly how she told me many years before, but these are her memories:

> I remember when I first met him. He had been swimming in the hotel pool. His black curly hair was all wet, he always had a curl hanging in the middle of his forehead when it was wet.
> One night at the hotel, he came over and asked me to dance, so we did until 1:00 a.m. I got in a cab and went home alone and he back to Bowman Field. This was on a Wednesday night. I never expected to see him again. But come Saturday, a corsage of white and red carnations was delivered to my desk (I was cashier) with a note saying, "Could we dance until 2:00 a.m.?" because on Saturday nights, all the places were open until 2:00 a.m.

As mentioned previously, Walter knew much about flowers, according to his glider pilot buddies and his mother. So what my mother wrote next is not surprising.

> Every Saturday a box of red and white carnations arrived at my desk with some little note

of humor and love. I'd go out, and there he was, so handsome. No wonder I fell in love with him.

After writing about how they met and how their relationship continued to progress, she abruptly began to write about "Peach's visit."

> Walter was killed February 22, 1945. Peach was attending her mother's funeral in Mexico… So her family kept the telegram—which I think you have—from her and did not tell her until she was back home at her apartment in LA. Her family was there, so she knew something was wrong. They told her, and the next day, she called me. I think it was sometime about the fifth of March. She told me she would come soon. From then, my mind was sort of blank. I don't remember when she arrived or how. I know Chris took me to work that night.
>
> After that, things are sort of vague. I know she was there because I have pictures and I know we went to Bowman Field to see Walter's commanding officer, and the two of them set the wheels in motion, and I remember her telling me she would make provisions for you because that is the way Walter would want it.

The part my mother wrote about her and Peach going to Bowman Field was the first I had ever heard of that. That visit must have been the reason I was able to receive the Veteran's benefits for college but not the Social Security benefits. The letter continues,

> That you were a part of him, he loved you more than anything in the world—but he always said, "Bad pennies come back," and he was so sure he would. I don't have much memory how

> long Peach stayed and I cannot remember if she went to NY to see Addie [Johnny's wife] or not. Everything was sort of foggy after that. I was somewhat numb and in a daze. While she was there—it was sort of discussed that she would like for me to come to California, and she would like to set me up in a little cocktail lounge.

Again, my mother never mentioned to me that my grandmother had offered such a thing to her if she would go to California. The subject of the letter changed, and she wrote about my dad's brother, Johnny.

> Johnny was still overseas. I had a letter from him later on, which I sent to you, telling me of his visit to Walter's grave, and when he returned to the US, he would come through Louisville and see me—which he never did—but I'm getting ahead of my story. After Peach was there sometime in March 1945, I started getting things together to take a leave of absence from work and go to California, which to me was a big decision.

My mother never revealed to me that she had started packing and was about to go to California. This letter was full of so many surprises and dynamics of relationships. My mother harbored resentments for so many years without airing them to anyone, as we can grasp in her writing. She continues:

> About the time I had it worked out—I thought—a letter arrived from Peach saying, "Maybe it would be best if you didn't come to California just yet, as there are a few problems," and she did not feel like she should hurt Addie. Johnny was not yet home, and Addie was upset.

Addie was Johnny's wife, and she was also a good friend of Walter's wife. After I read the next part of my mother's letter, I was shocked to learn more details. I also understood my visit to my uncle a little bit better than before.

> At this time, she [Peach] casually wrote—and to my knowledge, it was the only time it was ever mentioned. She [Peach] had known of situations like this that the baby would be given up for adoption to the wife of the father. Well, you know me—Chrys [Lil's sister] and I both hit the ceiling, and I fired her [Peach] off a letter immediately, and I told her in no uncertain terms we had gone to bat. I had been appointed as your legal guardian through the courts with the approval of the US Army Air Force as Walter being your legal father, you had all the benefits as approved by the government and that's not easy.
> So if there were any thoughts in their minds of doing so, <u>I would see them in hell, or it would be over my dead body, or something similar</u>, and no, I would not dare to hurt Addie. I told Peach maybe she should just forget about us. So she did.

According to family members, Peach did not forget about me, as my mother said in her letter. I know she didn't forget about me because I received presents from her while we lived in Louisville. She sent me the gifts I have mentioned before: a beautiful rabbit coat, a hand-embroidered poncho from Spain, and a Bible with a hand-carved wooden cover from Jerusalem. I also received birthday cards and Christmas cards from Peach but not after we moved to Las Vegas because she did not know where I was.

It is painful for me to think about that because Los Angeles is only a little more than two hundred miles from Las Vegas. A short flight is less than an hour. I would have been overjoyed to visit my grandmother, and I know Peach would have been overjoyed to see me again, her only grandchild! Further explanation of my mother's anguish over the situation was on page 7 of her letter.

> Johnny was being processed to come home, and one of my letters [to him] reached Addie. She wrote me, if I wanted any more information on Walter's death, I could get it from Peach. "Do not write John anymore"—I didn't. That was my last contact <u>ever</u> with him. The letters from Peach got shorter and further between.

I was thirteen years old when my mom and I, her boyfriend, and two children left Kentucky. The next part of my mother's letter reads:

> When we went to Vegas, she did know we were there because I wrote and told her. As I said, letters were shorter and further between. When we lived on Chicago [street], I wrote and asked maybe if she would like for you to spend a weekend with her during the Xmas holidays.

When we lived on Chicago Street, I was sixteen years old, so my mother waited for three years before she wrote to tell Peach where we were. I collected the mail when I came home from school, while my mom was at work. There were no letters from Peach. I'm not sure I believe that Peach knew where we lived. Aunt Virginia's statement that "Camelina [Peach] wanted to take care of you, but she did not know where you were" was a contradiction to what my mother's letter says.

> She [Peach] wrote me her husband—I think his name was Jim, I'm not sure…he was not too well—he was betting the racehorses very heavily and was drinking and spending everything she [Peach] had. And the way she said it he had about

> broke her. And she was going to Mexico to get away from it all. You see, Alana, I never told you all these things. But that was the last I ever heard from her.

My dad wrote to my mom when he was in North Carolina that his mother [Peach] was going to be married. That was in 1943. However, Peach did not get married to James Inghram until 1947, and he died in 1962, which would have been shortly after my mother said she wrote to Peach. I can see that my grandmother may not have wanted me to come visit in the circumstances she was dealing with.

After I met my father's family in Chula Vista, California, years after their letter-writing and years after Peach died, I told my mother about my visit. I did not tell her previously that I had found them and was planning a visit. After I returned to Utah from the visit with the Cota family, who were all my aunts, uncles, and cousins, my mother was astounded that I did that! She asked me, "Why did you want to do that? What were you thinking?"

I told her about the letters that Addie sent me that were my dad's. I told my mom about how I had written to the family and about the letters I had received back. She was upset that I had gone to California to meet them. I told her what Aunt Virginia told me about Peach not knowing where I was. When I told her they were all Mexicans, she was taken aback by that revelation. Apparently, my father had not told her of his Mexican heritage, though he had told her he had family that lived in Mexico. Maybe that's why the postscript from my dad in my baby book said, "Get the lowdown on the family tree." My mother responded in her letter to what Aunt Virginia told me.

> I also don't know what Aunt Virginia has told you. But in my heart, the way things seem to be falling into place was like a jigsaw puzzle, and I think she has the inside track. The statement your Aunt Virginia made, "that I hurt Peach very much,' and that she needed to talk to me...I'd love to—I'd go with you.

She said that she would go with me, but she never wanted to, or it was never a convenient time. I wanted her to go with me to Aunt Virginia's when I did her story, but my mom said she couldn't take off work, so it never happened. My mom did not understand that Peach was hurt by her actions of keeping me from the family. She wrote:

> I cannot imagine how I could have hurt Peach. Since Walter was already separated from his wife, and he is the one that called from North Carolina when she [Peach] was visiting him for me to talk to her—I never interfered. Now if I hurt her over the suggestion on her part that she had known of situations where the baby was adopted to the legal wife—I have no regrets. Because I would never have given you up…but that still bothers me. What did I do? Could you find out?

It is obvious what my mother did to hurt Peach. She denied her any communication or association with me, the one and only grandchild Peach had. Maybe my mom was afraid somehow that Peach and/or the family might get guardianship over me. My mother reminded me over and over how she took care of me with no help from anyone else. I realize now how hard it must have been for her and how grieved she was over all those years. I wish she and Peach had made up and cleared the air, but they didn't. I also have learned when things go wrong at such a young age, it is hard to pick up the pieces and move on. Mom's letter continues:

> But you see, I never at any time ever asked for anything from any of them—for you. Only the government and that you were entitled to, your father died for his country. I don't know if they thought I would try and make trouble or what? But you and they all can see after all these years I loved Walter very much. All I ever wanted out of

it for us was that he come home safe. And I really and truly believed with all my heart had he come back, everything would have been ok. After all, he was in divorce proceedings before he ever met me. As I said, I'll never ever know what the outcome would have been, but no one will ever make me believe that Walter could have been that <u>deceitful</u>.

Now that I understand my parents' complicated situation, my heart is filled with empathy, the kind of empathy I could not feel for so many years. I don't know why she wanted to take all her hurt, her heartbreak, and the truth with her to her grave. I wish so much we could have had a face-to-face, honest conversation about all the things she wrote in that letter. Here are her final thoughts:

> There is only one thing I have regrets about now and would do differently. I would have let him [Walter] make his insurance ($10,000) to you, not me or Peach, and he wanted to. Other than that, I'm not sorry for anything. For I loved him with all my heart. I could love you and hold you and look at you and almost feel like he was there with his arms around us both. Even with my being so saddened over his death and looking to a future <u>alone</u> with a little baby, not knowing exactly what to expect and what life held in store for me, I never felt any regrets. I was never sorry. All I felt was a great relief of having you—and a great consolation of having a part of him no one could ever take away from me.
>
> And whether I ever showed it or not, you were a great consolation to me through all the years… So that's my story—so Be it. I love you very much.
>
> Mother

As for me, over my long journey, the bad feelings I once had toward my mother for so many reasons and the disappointment and misunderstanding I had of my father have led me to a state of complete forgiveness. I always loved my mother no matter the circumstances we lived in, and I love my father even more as I know him now.

Forgiveness is an easy word to say but not as easy to implement into action. Forgiveness has lifted the burdens I once carried. I have come full circle and I can now express genuine love for both of my parents in a deeper way than just a biological child-parent love. I hope with all my heart that I can see them together someday.

In 1988, we took our seven children to the Inglewood Park Cemetery to visit my dad's and their grandfather's grave plot. It was the first time I had been there, and as I think back, I realize when my mom died two years prior, she may have thought my father was still buried in the tiny village of St. Saint-André-de-l'Eure, France.

Fast-forward

In 2016, I sat down with Armando Cota, my father's cousin, at his house in Ensenada, Baja California, Mexico. He told me the story of the invasion of Italy and how he participated in the liberation of Rome. As he told of the event, he wanted to show me a few souvenirs. He went to the safe located in his bedroom, and he brought into the living room many pieces of Nazi paraphernalia, including medals and patches that he had removed from a Nazi uniform.

Armando survived the fighting in his campaign in Italy of WWII. Some seventy years later, I sat with Armando as he told of the stories of how the US military had gradually fought its way up Italy for the liberation of Rome. He showed me captured paraphernalia, including what he called *the prize*.

The prize he was so proud of was contained in a small cigar box. As he held up the box and opened it, he took out something I had never seen except in pictures. I saw distinct red and black colors. He then removed and carefully unfolded the dreaded Nazi flag. He proceeded to tell me how he saw the flag mounted high up on a building in Rome and how he took aim with his rifle at the flag's fastenings and shot it down off the building as hundreds of Italians cheered him on.

Armando Cota, 21, a Mexican WWII veteran in the Liberation of Rome

The Nazi soldier patch

Armando at age ninety-two in WWII Fifth Army of the United States uniform. It still fits well.

Epilogue

My Father Came Back

To be ignorant of what occurred before you were born is to remain always a child. For what is the worth of human life unless it is woven into the life of our ancestors by the records of history?
—Cicero (63 BC)

The postscript in my baby book, which I have referred to many times, left by my dad in the farewell message to me and my mother, "Write to Mother and get the lowdown on the family tree," brings to my mind a Cicero quote I have used often in my research efforts in genealogy. I have often wondered why my father, going off to war and not knowing if he would return, wrote that postscript. He surely felt in his heart that his family history was important.

He had dark brown eyes, lots of black curly hair, and an olive complexion. Perhaps that is why he identified more with his maternal (Mexican) side of his family than his paternal (Swedish) side, though he was comfortable with both. If my father felt it was important to seek out "the family tree," then I was obligated to carry out his wishes. By the time I reached a point in my life to feel it was important to do so, Peach could not give me the "lowdown" because she had passed away. Also, as a typical teenager and then a young mother, I had other interests that seemed more important than chasing down my roots. Even if I had had the willpower and/or the time, I would not have known where to begin. Had I not gone to the Social

Security Administration that day, my personal journey to find my father would have been entirely different, I'm sure.

My dad has become known to me through pictures, letters, cartoons he drew, family members' memories and stories, and more memories from his personal friends, genealogy research, war records, and historical records. In his own words, he told me, "I will come back to you, somehow." He didn't know what that "somehow" would be. Over the decades of my life, my father has come back, little by little, as I have shown in the previous chapters.

As I uncovered my father's remarkable story, his life, my own life, and my children's lives are now "woven into the life of our ancestors." This book is not merely a story; it is a historical record. I have not remained a child because I am no longer ignorant of "what occurred before" I was born. In fact, I know what happened many centuries before I was born.

Though my father urged us to discover his family tree, I'm not sure how much he himself was aware of his family's history before he was born. Many in his family tree were soldiers, like him. They were explorers and colonizers of great American cities in California. The Cota surname (Peach's maiden name) is associated with Spanish soldiers, foreign cities, scribes, and financial advisors to monarchs. There are well-known ancestors who became famous both in the New World and the Old World.

The Lindbergs were Swedish immigrants who sought a better life in America. They were part of the mass immigration of Swedes to Minnesota between 1850 and 1930. According to census records, there are Swedish Americans found throughout the United States but primarily in Minnesota and California. I have family ties to both places.

The United States has always been a melting pot of many kinds of diversities: race, ethnicity, religion, mixed ancestry, cultural differences, artistic abilities, occupations, and numerous other things. My father was a product of that melting pot. He had both New World and Old World, ancestral lineages flowing in his blood, just as I do and my children do.

The National Genealogical Society has a mantra, "I am who I am because they were who they were." That should be the mantra of every human being. We are all products of our heritage whether we admit it, embrace it, or shun it. Many people have gone before us to pave our way. We should be aware of their successes and their sacrifices.

Walter, as part of three different cultures, was enculturated in a way that gave him great insight as a competitor, a leader, and a family member. Aunt Virginia said, "He was never shy but wanted to be in on everything." His family circumstances gave him flexibility in meeting others and solving problems. Whether in the United States, Mexico, Africa, England, or France, Walter's cultural capital gave him an advantage in every situation.

My dad carried some heavy personal burdens with him while at the same time he was showing bravery and courage. Those kinds of details have made him a real person in my eyes, not just a father I never knew. His life was far from perfect, just like all of us, and I love him for that.

We inherit ancient traditions not genetically but culturally, and we also internalize our own historical memories. Such were the opportunities for Walter and Johnny to learn about their Spanish/Mexican heritage when they visited their grandmother in Mexico. In Los Angeles, the boys had their dad and their paternal Swedish grandmother and other relatives to learn about their Swedish roots.

I wrote this book to honor my father, Walter Bert Lindberg—flight officer, glider pilot, soldier, and hero of World War II. His life and legacy are both personal and heroic. The worth of a human life is now included and written into the lives of his descendants as well as his ancestors in "the records of history."

To My Father

My dearest and remembered father,
Whose greatest joy was to fly
In those remarkable silent wings
Towed by others to the sky.

Many pilots were dauntless and brave,
But you were of a special breed.
You followed orders—of course,
But lived by your own creed.

On the SS *George Washington*,
You went off to war one day,
Heading for your base in England
And a battlefield far away.

For thirteen nervous days, you traveled
In a convoy of ships across the sea
To meet other silent wingers
At a place called Normandy.

In the ninety-fourth Troop Carrier Squadron,
Your bravery and expertise quickly grew.
You flew single tow into Southern France
And into the dangers of Holland too.

ALANA LINDBERG JOLLEY

The CG4-A glider was the favorite girl
That you all flirted with the most.
She was so much better than the Horsa,
You GPs would always boast.

Did you ever think of another girl,
When you were all alone up there?
Did you ever wonder about little me,
Or what was the color of my hair?

Did you ever think about coming home
Or wanting to tuck me into bed?
Did you ever think of holding me
Or patting my little head?

I know you had my baby picture
And my little baby shoe, too,
But did you even know or wonder
If my eyes were brown or blue?

They told me it was a windy day
Over the airfield in France, at Tours,
And how a towline snapped off the tail
Of a Waco glider, it was yours.

Many of your flying comrades
Saw the accident, they said,
But couldn't go to the wreckage
Because they knew you were dead.

All deaths in a war are tragic,
But yours, especially so,
You weren't even doing battle,
Just practicing a double tow.

MY FATHER HAD NO CHILDREN

My beloved father, you gave me life,
And in my life, you still live.
What greater gifts to each other
Could we possibly give?

My childhood, without you, Dad,
Was a difficult one to get through,
But you must be my guardian angel
Because he has silent wings too.

Your loving daughter,
Alana

(In memory of Walter Bert Lindberg, F/O Glider Pilot, WWII, 439th Troop Carrier Group, 94th Troop Carrier Squadron. Killed on February 22, 1945, Tours, France.)

Appendix

Excerpts from GP Letters

I remember him as a very able, good-looking, dark-haired, athletic, pleasant young man, perhaps ten years younger that I was. He also was a caricature artist, entertaining us at times…he was powerfully built. I have seen him walk on his hands for a block. I never heard him speak anything but excellent English.

—Henry Benefiel
Casa Grande, Arizona

Your dad was one of my best friends. As you may know, our squadron suffered extremely high casualties during the war, losing 87 percent of our original cadre. Your father was a kind and generous person. He was a good pilot and good officer. He frequently expressed his concern as to what would happen to you and your mother should he not survive the war. I am sure his last thoughts were of you. I am really sorry that you had to grow up without him… I was a POW when he was killed.

—Pershing Carlson
Bismarck, North Dakota

We traveled together for thirteen nervous days in convoy on the SS *George Washington* across the Atlantic Ocean... With best wishes for your search and God bless you for keeping the memory of your father alive.

—Milton Dank
Philadelphia, Pennsylvania

Yes, I remember him. He presented himself well. He was the first to fall in for every formation and was first to volunteer for every job we got in the squadron. He had a smile for everybody and had a host of friends. I was a prisoner of war at the time... Those gliders had a habit of rising several feet after they cut off from their tow, so I think the glider behind him was blameless.

—George T. Hall
Glenview, Illinois

It was a very mixed emotion when I read the article in *Silent Wings* on Walter Lindberg. I was very sad to hear he had got killed in Europe but very glad to hear about one of the old gangs I served with... Walter had just enlisted, and it was his first stop [Fort Morgan, Colorado]. We were thrown together due to the proximity of our last names, I guess, and got to be very good friends.

—W. F. Koehl
Lake Charles, Louisiana

- Walter was in the Olympics for gymnastics.
- Solid as a rock, very muscular and athletic.
- To this day, I don't know if I was the one who was supposed to be in that plane.
- I was his buddy. Sent his clothes home, visited John and Peach after the war was over in LA.
- Walt was artistic, wrote poems, and drew cartoons. He was a florist.

—Clifford L. Mueller
Boulder City, Nevada

I'm sorry Virg did not get to read your letter. He spoke of your father often and was so fond of him. He said he was so handsome—full of fun and energy and that he was a bright young man. Virg saw the accident that killed him...the tow rope from the plane flew loose and cut into your father's glider. Virg took your father's remains to Paris.

—Virgil S. Neal (deceased, his wife responded)
Palm Desert, California

Lindy, as we called him, and I were very close, we had something in common (Daddy's little girls)... When most of our buddies were out on leave, we would sit and talk about our little girls. Lindy wrote a poem, "Daddy's Little Girl," which he gave to me... I saw the accident.

—Verne Ogden
Yakima, Washington

Walter Lindberg was in my squadron, I remember him...but over the years, my memory has sort of faded... I'm sending you this picture of your father. (A photo of my father in full flight gear)

—Robert L. Pound
Severn, Maryland

I knew your dad. We were in the same group but different squadron. I was in the Ninety-First. I stayed at the same hotel in England... He was a real nice person, and we ran around together. I was flying in the same formation the day he was killed.

—Harold J. Rhodehamel
Greenville, Ohio

I could find no picture identifying your father. I did see most of the accident as his glider was heading for the ground. It was a very sad day for all of us.

—T. Bleeker Ripson
Allentown, Pennsylvania

[W]e put in time by walking the countryside, talking a great deal, reading, performing small duties...and flying practice missions. These were generally flying in formation, and they were difficult. Our practice field was at Tours, France... It was one of these missions that your father and Eldon Mueller were killed in an accident... I could not go to the wreckage, as I knew they were dead. (This was a single-spaced, typed letter detailing exactly what happened in the accident from his perspective on the ground watching.)

—M. L. "Cy" Shaffer
Butler, Pennsylvania

Did not know Walt that well, but we lived together by the alphabet. He was very good-looking, dark, and had a lot of black hair. When he was in uniform—a very handsome man.

—LeRoy Theuer
Logan, Utah

In answer to your letter about Walter B. Lindberg, we were in the same squadron, and we went overseas together... We were good friends... I was flying in the airplane behind him...saw the rope hanging down wrapped around his glider, and it cut it in two. He and a man named Mueller were killed. I was a pallbearer at his funeral.

—Grady R. Wright
Melissa, Texas

Glossary

DZ. Drop zone; an area designated for drop of paratroopers and supplies.

LZ. Landing zone; and area designated for landing of gliders.

Serial. Formation composed of several flights, often in multiples of nine airplanes. Serials are comprised of V-shaped formations. Troop carrier configuration of Vs with Vs in trail. This can include powered airplanes as well as gliders.

TC. Troop carrier

TCG. Troop Carrier Group such as the 439th TCG

TCS. Troop Carrier Squadron; a subgroup of a TCG. More than one TCS makes up a TCG.

Towship. Troop carrier, powered aircraft used for towing gliders—in most cases in WWII, the C47 built by Douglas Aircraft.

Annotated Bibliography

Bagley, Mark B., and Mariane Stephens. *The G Stands for Guts: A Glider Pilot Remembers WWII*. Ashland, Oregon: Hellgate Press.

Bowman Feld History. Louisville Muhammad Ali International Airport. www.flylouisville.com/corporate/bowman-field-history.

Dank, Milton. *The Glider Gang: An Eyewitness History of WWII Glider Combat*. London: Cassell Ltd., 1977.

Devlin, Gerard M. *Silent Wings: The Saga of the US Army and Marine Combat Glider Pilots During WWII*. New York, New York: St. Martin's Press, 1985.

Goldman, Curtis. *Silent Warrior: A Photo Journal Account of WWII Combat Glider Pilot*. Springfield, Missouri: 21st Century Press, 2008.

Goldsworthy, A. K. *Caesar: Life of a Colossus*. New Haven, Connecticut: Yale University Press, 2006.

Hadler, Susan Johnson, and Ann Bennett Mix. *Lost in the Victory: Reflections of American War Orphans of WWII*. Denton, Texas: University of North Texas Press, 1998.

    https://ww2gp.org (website of the World War II Glider Pilots Association, where history of glider missions, personnel, and documented reports, and photos are found).

    https://www.archives.gov (receipt of flight logs, official crash report, etc.).

National Archives, United States Government.

"Normandy, 70th Anniversary D-Day." www.ruudleeuw.com/normandy-2014-70anni.htm.

Photo of gym club and information about 1932 Olympics, held in Los Angeles, California. Long Beach Polytechnic High School yearbook. 1931.

"Searching for Augusta: The Forgotten Angel of Bastogne," DVD at www.shop.pbs.org/WC2092.html

Schipske, Gerrie. *Images of Aviation: Early Aviation in Long Beach*. Charleston, South Carolina: Arcadia Publishing, 2009.

Tubb, Ernest. ""Missing in Action." 1952. www.songlyrics.com/ernest-tubb/missing-in-action-1952-lyrics.

Young, Colonel Charles H. *Into the Valley: The Untold Story of USAAF Troop Carrier in World War II, from North Africa through Europe*. Dallas, Texas: PrintComm, Inc., 1995.

About the Author

    The author's inspiration for this book came from her father's own words and heroic deeds, although she never knew him. It was first written as a major newspaper story years ago.

    Alana is a mother of seven and has published two children's books. She has written for historical magazines and journals. She has been a museum director and professor of Cultural Anthropology. She lives in Southern California with her husband who was her high school sweetheart.

Printed in the USA
CPSIA information can be obtained
at www.ICGtesting.com
CBHW071354180824
13311CB00047B/597